W9-BZM-594

Between
Philosophy
&
Psychoanalysis

WITHDRAWN

613328177

Between Philosophy & Psychoanalysis

Lacan's Reconstruction of Freud

Robert Samuels

ROUTLEDGE   New York and London

Published in 1993 by

Routledge
29 West 35 Street
New York, NY 10001

Published in Great Britain by

Routledge
11 New Fetter Lane
London EC4P 4EE

Copyright © 1993 by Routledge, Inc.

Printed in the United States of America on acid free paper.

All rights reserved. No part of this book may be reprinted or reproduced or utilized in any form or by any electronic, mechanical or other means, now known or hereafter invented, including photocopying and recording, or in any information storage or retrieval system, without permission in writing from the publishers.

Library of Congress Cataloging-in-Publication Data.

Samuels, Robert, 1961–
    Between philosophy and psychoanalysis : Lacan's reconstruction of
Freud / by Robert Samuels.
      p. cm.
    Includes bibliographical references and index.
    ISBN 0-415-90675-X. — ISBN 0-415-90676-8 (pbk.)
    1. Psychoanalysis and philosophy. 2. Freud, Sigmund, 1856–1939.
3. Lacan, Jacques, 1901– . I. Title.
BF175.4.P45S26 1993
150.19′52—dc20   92-42806
                                            CIP

British Library Cataloguing-in-Publication Data also available.

Dedicated to the memory of
Ira Samuels
and
Robert Slobodien

Contents

Acknowledgments

This book has been developed out of my doctoral thesis from the University of Paris VIII. I would like to first of all thank the Department of Psychoanalysis and the Ecole de la Cause freudienne in Paris. This work was in part inspired by the seminars of Jacques-Alain Miller and other members of the Freudian Field. I would also like to thank my family and friends for their support and encouragement.

Robert Samuels
New York, 1992

Introduction: From Freud's Project To Lacan's Logic

The initial task of this book is to articulate the inner logic of Freud's thought as it relates to psychoanalytic practice and theory. I believe that this inner logic is often ignored, making the field of psychoanalysis seem like a jumble of unrelated concepts. In order to help structure this field, I will turn to the work of the French psychoanalyst, Jacques Lacan, who argues that his conception of the three fields of the Real, the Imaginary, and the Symbolic serves to bring together the entirety of Freud's theory and practice.

One of Lacan's central, underlying arguments is the division of the psychoanalytic movement into three periods. The first is the initial discovery of psychoanalysis by Freud, the second is that Lacan describes as the forgetting (or repression) of Freud by the school of "ego psychology," and the third is Lacan's own "return to Freud." This return is an attempt to read Freud in a structured and logical way that makes manifest certain latent patterns of Freud's thought.

In order to flesh out some of Freud's main ideas, Lacan turns to the field of philosophy. The effect of this is to introduce a number of philosophers to the field of psychoanalysis, and a number of psychoanalysts to the field of philosophy. It can be argued that psychoanalysis can be seen, in many ways, as a response to some of the questions and paradoxes that modern philosophy has generated. In particular, the focus will be on how three dimensions of the Real, the Imaginary, and the Symbolic relate to three fundamental areas of human experience which, in philosophy, are conceived as the existential, the phenomenological, and the structural.

Existentialism, Phenomenology, and Structuralism in Analysis

Existentialism refers to the sensual existence of the isolated subject who is born into the world without any relation to any Other, without language, and without the ability to communicate. On this level of existential experience, it can be said that the subject is dominated by the un-Symbolized world of Real[1] sensations and perceptions.

In his initial attempts to define the Real, Lacan appropriates Sartre's idea that nothing is lacking in the Real—that the Real is exactly what it is and nothing more. Lacan argues that it is only in the Symbolic order of language that things can be lacking or be missing. Therefore, the subject, who exists solely in the Real, is completely separated from the Symbolic order of social relations.

This primary state of Real, pure existence can be replaced by the secondary level of phenomenological consciousness where the pure experience of sensation becomes superseded by the unity of the ego and the intentionality of the individual.[2] Lacan calls this formation of unity Imaginary, because it is founded on the essential illusion of a totalized body-image. Lacan argues that the subject gains a concept of it only through an ideal representation of a reflected narcissistic image. This image itself represents the organization of the ego's perceptual field into a unified and limited field of consciousness.

The third dimension of experience is the structural level of language and social relations.[3] On this level, the subject is no longer a Being-in-itself (Real), nor a Being-for-itself (Imaginary), but rather a Being-for-Others (Symbolic), who must sacrifice its sensual needs and its egotistical demands for the laws and values of its socio-historical environment.

In his early thesis, Paranoid Psychosis in its Relation to Personality, Lacan attempts to bring together these three different dimensions of human experience by creating a science of personality. "In order for any human manifestation to be related to personality it must imply: 1. a biographical development which we define objectively through a typical evolution and through the relations of comprehension that interpret themselves. This translates itself for the subject by the modes of affectivity in which he lives his history (Erlebnis); 2. a conception of himself, that we define objectively by his vital attitudes and the dialectical progress that one can determine. This is translated by the more or less 'ideal' images of himself that he brings to consciousness; 3. a certain tension of social relations, that we define objectively by the pragmatic autonomy of his conduct and the bonds of ethical participation which are recognized. It translates itself for the subject by the representative value of which he feels himself affected vis-a-vis the Other." (Lacan 1932, 42-3, translation mine) I would like to argue that Lacan's thesis shows that in 1932, he was already struggling with the interrelation among the Real, the Imaginary, and the Symbolic.

On the primary level of the Real, the biographical development of the subject is determined by the existential categories of affectivity and experience (Erlebnis). Next, on the Imaginary level of the phenomenology of consciousness, the experiences of the subject are transformed into ideal images of itself, while on the Symbolic level of social relations, the main emphasis is placed on the relation between the subject and others.

The Ternary Structure of Freud's Thought

These three dimensions of sensual experience (existential), individual consciousness (phenomenological), and social relations (structural) are essential to Freud's thought. For example, the separation of the id, the ego, and the super-ego is structured by the difference between pure, instinctual sensation (the id), individual consciousness (the ego), and social law (the super-ego). This text will attempt to show that Freud's theory of consciousness is phenomenological because it stresses the intentionality of the knowing ego, while his conception of language and social relations is structural because it is based on a theory of differential, transcendental relations.

One of the differences between the realm of the ego and that of language is that with the ego a particular being directs its attention towards a particular object without any outside interference. In the realm of language, one must always account for the mediation of another. Therefore, when the phenomenologists stress the intentionality of consciousness, they highlight the movement of attention from the knowing ego to the known object. However, with the introduction of language and social relations into consciousness, this movement of attention is transformed. Everything becomes mediated by a third element or party that goes beyond the consciousness of the ego. On the level of social reality, it is no longer a question of the simple relationship between the knowing ego and the known object, for now the mediating power of language and social knowledge must be taken into account.

The philosopher Karl Otto Appel argues that there have been three main stages in the history of Western philosophy, the ontological, the epistemological, and the linguistical. For Appel, the ontological period of philosophy stretches from Plato to Descartes, and it is most interested with the understanding of objects themselves and is not concerned with the knowing subject. The next period of philosophy is the epistemological which stretches from Descartes to Kant. During this time, the central concern of philosophy moved away from the existence of objects, to the knowing subject or ego. Questions of consciousness and the intentionality of the ego dominate the discourse of philosophy. At the beginning of the twentieth century, the focus of philosophy switched and became more concerned with the question of language and otherness. In this third, linguistical period of philosophy, knowledge itself becomes an object the must be accounted for. It is during this period that the discipline of linguistic analysis arises, where language is itself taken as an object of study.

This briefly describes the philosophical movement from the ontological concern with the object, to the epistemological exploration of the knowing subject, to the present interest in language. These stages of thought are, of course, generalizations that ignore the particularities of each thinker, but do give a theoretical structure, or tool, that can be used to organize the history of philosophy. It is striking how easily these same categories can be applied to Freud's thought. It is as if Freud was trying to work out the age-old questions of philosophy by creating a new science which turned philosophical theory into a therapeutic practice.

The interactions among objects, subjects, and language are ones which are not only essential to the fields of psychoanalysis and philosophy, but also are essential to all individuals in their daily experiences. Psychoanalysis takes these philosophical relationships and attempts to work them out in analytic theory and practice.

An early example of this is found in one of Freud's first theoretical works, "Project for a Scientific Psychology," where he divides the mind into the three central systems of perception, consciousness, and memory. In this ternary division, Freud attempts to relate the categories of sensation (perception), consciousness, and language (memory). It can be argued that Freud continually divides the psyche into three systems, or agencies, in order to account for the interrelation of Real sensations, Imaginary consciousness, and the Symbolic system of memory and language. By linking Lacan's categories to Freud's concepts, the history of philosophy, or at least Karl Otto Appel's interpretation of it, is repeated, or reproduced, in Freud's structure of the human mind. This argument coincides with Freud's idea that the individual always recapitulates the history of the race.

I can also reverse the way that I've been looking at this question and say that the history of philosophy is determined by the development and structure of the human being, who enters the world as an object amongst other objects, who then becomes a knowing subject, who is later dominated by language and social relations. The existential-ontological level of philosophy is in this way most concerned with the existence of what

I would like to call Real natural objects and experiences. Existence is Real because it is not mediated by anything else.

In developmental terms, what first serves to mediate, or transform, the Real is the Imaginary phenomenology and epistemology of conscious-ness. For Lacan, the Imaginary is dominated by the psychological rela-tionship between an ego and its object. Likewise, in the epistemological period of philosophy, it is the point-of-view of the knowing ego that determines the meaning and essence of the object. If Descartes can state "I think, therefore, I am," it is because, for him, the thinking ego takes precedence over pure existence or being. This reverses the existential claim that existence precedes essence, and the Heideggerian notion that the essential question of philosophy is the question of Being.

The phenomenological level of philosophy is, in this sense, fixated on the second level of psychological development with its concentration on the thinking and knowing ego, while the existential-ontological schools are dominated by the primary level of natural and sensual existence. The current period of philosophy is focused then on the linguistical and social level of development.

Of course, the human being does not simply move from one stage of development to the next. There is always an interaction between these different levels of experience and periods of philosophy, but what I would like to highlight is the way that different schools of thought grow out of different developmental problems and resolutions.

With Freud, a certain developmental structure to his thought can be located that repeats the philosophical movement from natural existence (ontology), to the phenomenology of the knowing ego (epistemology), to the structure of social mediation (linguistics). In *Beyond the Pleasure Principle*, Freud presents a self-reading of the development of his own thought. While introducing his concept of the death drive, Freud states: "I do not dispute the fact that the third step in the theory of instincts [the death drive], which I have taken here, cannot lay claim to the same degree of certainty as the two earlier ones—the extension of the concept of sexuality and the hypothesis of narcissism." (Freud 1920, 53) It can be argued that this passage represents Freud's attempt to read into his own work a certain order of discovery that is determined by the ternary division of the Real (sexuality), the Imaginary (narcissism) and the Symbolic (the death drive).[4]

In his first discovery, Freud expands the common conception of sexuality to include infantile and unconscious manifestations of the libido. This primary discovery can be ascribed to his text of 1905, *Three Essays on the Theory of Sexuality*. The second discovery, the concept of narcissism, can be connected to the text of 1914 entitled "On Narcissism: An Introduction," while the third discovery, the theory of the death drive, is found in *Beyond the Pleasure Principle* (1920). These three discoveries not only define three separate decades of work, but they are determined by the distinction between an existential theory of sexuality and sensation (Real), a phenomenological theory of consciousness and narcissism (Imaginary), and a structural conception of language and the death drive (Symbolic).

The first section of this book presents the first period of Freud's work (1900–1909) in the twentieth century which is dominated by the discovery of a non-phallic and non-social form of sexuality. The concept of infantile sexuality itself is based on the existential argument that the subject first experiences the world in an autistic manner, without language, thought, or any form of social regulation. In fact, Freud's concept of primary auto-erotism demands to be thought of on the level of the 'primitive Real,' where the subject has not yet determined the difference between self and Other, or between male and female.

Furthermore, in his *Introductory Lectures on Psychoanalysis*, Freud equates this primary stage of infantile sexuality with the unconscious itself. "The fact is thus confirmed that what is unconscious in mental life is also what is infantile." (Freud 1916, 210) This connection, between the unconscious and infantile sexuality will be developed by linking together *The Interpretation of Dreams* (1900) with *Three Essays on the Theory of Sexuality* (1905).

The second period of Freud's work (1910–1919) where the concept of narcissism is introduced in relation to the formation of the ego and the phenomenology of consciousness will be discussed in the second section of this book. "Narcissism: An Introduction (1914)" and another text from the same period, *Totem and Taboo* (1913), will be analyzed in order to map out Freud's theory of the Imaginary order. The analysis will attempt to show how this secondary order of consciousness is in opposition to the primary level of pure sexual existence.

The third section will elaborate on the notion of the death drive as it relates to the Symbolic order and to the third period of Freud's work (1920–1929). *Beyond the Pleasure Principle* (1920) and *Group Psychology and the Analysis of the Ego* (1921) will be examined in order to articulate a structural theory of language and social relations.

From the Project of Freud to the Logic of Lacan

The reading of Freud's work presented here will not be simply chronological, but it will also be logical. Lacan's notion of logical time, which serves to determine the relation between 1) the Real order of sexuality and perception, 2) the Imaginary order of consciousness and narcissism, and 3) the Symbolic order of language and the death drive will be developed.

These three dimensions of Being can be mapped onto Lacan's schema L:[5]

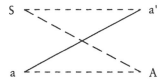

On this diagram, Lacan attempts to develop a logic or algebra of relations. In the position of the S, he places what will be called the existential Subject of infantile sexuality; on the line a – – – – a' he locates the narcissistic relation between an object (a) and its Imaginary representation (a'), and in the position of the Other (A), the social and Symbolic relations of language and law are found.

Lacan often replaced concepts with symbols in order to unite a series of ideas under the heading of one marker. In fact, he argued that the only way that a science makes any advances is by introducing new signs, like the symbol for infinity or the square root. These symbols act as tools that allow ceratin functions to be performed without having to explain how they work each time. They also allow different scientists to communicate with each other by creating a short-hand language.

At first, these symbols might seem alienating, but they do allow a defined, but open, logical structure to be established. Lacan's schema L will be constantly referred to because it enables Lacan to bring together the entirety of Freud's work. An example of this is the way that Lacan returns to Freud's second topic of the id, the ego, and the superego. Lacan equates the id with the "S" or subject. He plays on the fact that both the German word for the id, which is "Es," and the first letter of the word for subject 'S' are pronounced the same. Lacan calls the id the 'subject in his stupid and ineffable existence' in order to stress the way that the natural existence of the sensuous id precedes the structure of language and knowledge.

On a second level, Lacan locates the relation between the ego and its ideal image, or other (autre in French), on the line between (a) and (a'). Lacan uses these mathematical symbols to show that the relation between the ego and its image is defined by the optical relation between a Real point and an Imaginary point. In other words, for every Real representation of an ego there is a corresponding Imaginary representation.

In opposition to the imaginary other (a') or alter ego, Lacan places the Symbolic Other (A) or superego.[6] In French and German philosophy, the term Other has been used to connote various things, such as the other person, the other sex, the social order, or even God. All of these terms represent different elements that serve to show the way that an individual's consciousness is mediated, overcome, or challenged by an external force that is then internalized. For Freud, it is the function of the superego to internalize these external representations and functions.

On Lacan's schema, Freud's different agencies also take on a temporal logic. The Subject (S) or id, is born into the world without relation to the Other (A) in a state of initial autism and auto-erotism. This initial logical period is termed the state of the primitive Real. It is in this initial period of the Real that Freud and Lacan locate the existential subject; both argue that the unity of the ego does not exist at first, but has to be developed. Therefore, on Lacan's schema L, the existential Subject (S) is placed before the narcissistic relation between the ego (a) and the other (a'). It is only in a second logical time that the subject gains access to the stable world of objects and reflexive dual relations. It is, in fact, through relations to other objects and people that a sense of self begins to develop. These Imaginary dual relations are narcissistic and limited because they are based on the need to exclude the third order of social law and regulation.

An interesting anticipation of Lacan's logical categories of the Real, the Imaginary, and the Symbolic can be found in the work of the American philosopher Charles Sanders Peirce. Peirce's categories of Firstness, Secondness, and Thirdness, can help to explain the logical temporality that been developing in relation to Lacan's schema L.

Before these terms can be defined, it must be shown where they can be placed on Lacan's diagram. I will relate Firstness to the position of the Real Subject (S), Secondness to the Imaginary dual relation between the ego (a) and its image (a') and Thirdness to the intervention of the Symbolic Other (A).

The Philosophy of the Real, the Imaginary, and the Symbolic

Peirce argues that there is a primary level of existence that consists solely of pure sensations and feelings. "Firstness is the mode of being which consists in its subject's being positively such as it is regardless of aught else. . . . The idea of First is predominant in the ideas of freshness, life, freedom. The free is that which has not another behind it, determining its actions. . . . By feeling, I mean an instance of that kind of consciousness which involves no analysis, comparison or any process whatsoever, nor consists in whole or in part of any act by which one stretch of consciousness is distinguished from another, which has its own positive quality which consists in nothing else, and which is of itself all that it is." (Peirce, 76–81) For Peirce, like Lacan, the primary state of the Real is defined by its full positivity and its lack of relation or determination. It is equivalent to Sartre's Being-in-itself, which is without any form of lack or negation.

Opposed to this primary form of pure existence, Peirce posits his category of Secondness. "The idea of second is predominant in the ideas of causation and statical force. For cause and effect are two; and statical forces always occur between pairs. Constraint is a Secondness. . . . In sense and will, there are reactions of Secondness between the ego and non-ego (which non-ego may be an object of direct consciousness). . . . Now there can be no resistance where there is nothing of the nature of struggle or forceful action. By struggle I must explain that I mean mutual action between two things regardless of any sort of third or medium, and in particular regardless of any law of action." (Peirce 79–89) In both Lacan's and Peirce's logic, the dual relation between an ego (a) and its object (a') is dependant on the exclusion of the third term (A) of law and order.

The place of the Other (A) thus can be connected to the idea of Thirdness. "The third category of elements of phenomena consists of what we call laws when we contemplate them from the outside only, but which when we see both sides of the shield we call thoughts. Thoughts are neither qualities nor facts." (Peirce, 78) Law introduces into dual relations an element of order and regulation. For Peirce, the possibility of law itself is founded on the possibility of a sign that "stands for something to the idea which it produces, or modifies. Or, it is a vehicle conveying into the mind something from without." (Peirce, 80) This internalization of the external idea and law is located in Freud's concept of the superego and the category of pre-consciousness. Not only can Peirce's categories be used to articulate the logical movement of Lacan's conceptions of the Real, the Imaginary, and the Symbolic, but also to articulate the logic of Freud's two topographical structures: unconscious/conscious/preconscious and id/ego/superego.[7] The id is already attached to the Real (Firstness), the ego to the Imaginary (Secondness), and the superego to the Symbolic (Thirdness). The unconscious must be thought of on the level of Firstness, consciousness on the level of Secondness and the preconscious on the level of Thirdness.[8] Thus, the unconscious id is without relation to any Other, and knows no form of negation, while the ego of consciousness is always taken in a dual relation with an object that excludes the mediation of the preconscious superego of law and language.

Logical Time

Two texts will help to illustrate the logic behind all of these ternary relations. The first being Lacan's text, "Logical Time and the Assertion of Anticipated Certainty," and the second: Freud's "Project for a Scientific Psychology." The goal being to read into these texts the logical relation between the Real, the Imaginary, and the Symbolic orders.

In his text on logical time, Lacan formulates three logical stages: 1) the instant of the look, 2) the time for understanding, and 3) the moment to conclude. The first temporal moment is derived from an existential theory of pure perception, the second temporal stage develops the phenomenological relation of reflexive consciousness, and the third logical time determines a Symbolic law of action.

Lacan begins his text with the elaboration of a logical game that takes the form of a prisoner's dilemma:

> A prison warden has three select prisoners summoned and announces to them the following: "For reasons I need not make known now, gentlemen, I must set one of you free. In order to decide whom, I will entrust the outcome to a test which you will kindly undergo. There are three of you present. I have here five disks differing only in color: three white and two black. Without letting you know which I have chosen, I shall fasten one of them to each of you between his shoulders; outside, that is, your direct visual field—any indirect ways of getting a look at the disk being excluded by the absence here of any means of mirroring. At that point, you will be left at your leisure to consider your companions and their respective discs, without being allowed, of course, to communicate amongst yourselves the results of your inspection. Your own interest would, in any case, proscribe such communication, for the first to be able to deduce his own color will be the one to benefit from the dispensatory measure at our disposal. His conclusion, moreover, must be founded

upon logical and not simply probablistic reasons. Keeping this in mind, it is to be understood that as soon as one of you is ready to formulate such a conclusion, he should pass through this door so that he may be judged individually on the basis of his response." This having been made clear, each of the three subjects is adorned with a white disk, no use being made of the black ones, of which there were, let us recall, but two. (Lacan 1945, 4–5)

This logical puzzle can be solved first translating the black disks into 0's and the white disks into 1's and then by articulating the three possible combinations of disks: 1) 001, 2) 011, and 3) 111.

Lacan argues that in the instant of the look, each subject will say to himself, "Being opposite two blacks (00), one knows that one is white (1)." However, this first possibility (001) is excluded, because each person sees two white disks. Thus, after the first logical moment, there are only two possibilities left (011, 111). The primary time of the Real, therefore, brings no knowledge in itself, but rather, is founded on the exclusion of certain possibilities. Furthermore, in this time of pure perception, no one knows who they are, or if the Other's know who they are.

In the secondary time for understanding, each subject thinks, if "I were black (0), the two whites (11) I see would waste no time realizing they are whites." This second subject is locked into a dual relation of reflection, because the subject must imagine what the other subjects are thinking. "For the two whites in the situation of seeing a white and a black, this time is the time for comprehending, each of the whites finding the key to his own problem in the inertia of his counterpart." (Lacan 1945, 11) What Lacan underlines in this second logical time is not only the reflecting relation between an ego and its alter ego, but also the hesitation of each subject, which points to a subjective element of doubt.

In the third logical time, each subject thinks, "I hasten to declare myself white (1), so that these whites (11), whom I consider in this way, do not precede me in recognizing themselves for what they are." This moment to conclude represents an assertive judgement that the subject makes about himself. It is because the subject realizes that the others do not know what they are, that the subject identifies with them and declares itself to be white.

These three logical moments will be examined by assigning a subject to each logical stage. In the instant of the look, Lacan places the impersonal subject of the Real, with the time for understanding, the subjects are taken in the Imaginary relation of reciprocity and reflection (mirroring), while in the moment to conclude one finds the subjective and Symbolic assertion of the personal "I." "Otherwise stated, the judgement which concludes the sophism can only be borne by a subject who has formulated the assertion about himself, and cannot be imputed to him unreservedly by anyone else—unlike the relation of the impersonal and undefined reciprocal subjects of the first two moments who are essentially transitive. . . ." (Lacan 1945, 13–14) For Lacan, the first subject is a pure, impersonal it (id), which is then replaced by the reflexive ego, and finally by the personal "I."

This movement traces the logical progression from the un-Symbolized, impersonal subject to the personal Symbolic 'I.' In the primary instant of the look, the impersonal subject is equivalent to what Freud calls the "id" or what we can translate as the "it." On Lacan's "schema L," the subject, or id, is located in the position of the "S," representing the place of the existential subject of the unconscious and infantile sexuality.

In his text on logical time, this existential subject is contrasted to the reciprocal dual relation between the ego and its Imaginary other. "The former the impersonal subject expressed in the "one" of the "one knows that," provides but the general form of the noetic subject: he can easily be god, table or washbasin. The latter (the undefined reciprocal subjects) expressed in 'the two whites' who must recognize 'one another,' introduces the form of the other as such, i.e., as pure reciprocity, since the one can only recognize himself in the other. . . ." (Lacan 1945, 14) While on the first level of logical time, the subject is just a thing-in-itself, by the time the second level of understanding is reached, there is a dual mirroring relation between the ego and its object. Lacan adds that the subjects are undefined in this time because they only gain a conception of themselves through what they see reflected back in others.

In clinical terms, this second logical time is best represented by the narcissistic subject who constantly needs the approval and feedback of others. For these subjects, all value is found in an external object or person. However, in this logical game, every subject is a mirror for the other subjects and so there is an infinite series of reflections without any definition or stopping point. Each subject sees that the others are white, but still does not know what it itself is. As a result, if the narcissistic subject only finds value in the reflection of others, then it finds no real value in itself. Its ego is nothing—nothing but what is found in others.

This definition of the ego as nothing helps to anticipate Lacan's later definition of what he calls the object (a). This object is the inverse of narcissism and consciousness. It cannot be perceived, yet it structures the logic of the subject. In this game it is the nothingness of the ego as represented by the black disk that every subject worries about, but which, in the reality of the game, no one has. It allows for the game to be possible because it is the unknown element that causes all of the subjects to desire to know what they are.

However, because this object is only a logical place in the game, it escapes the "time for understanding," which is dominated by the Imaginary world of consciousness and narcissism. Lacan will later argue that the object has no specular image, just as the ego is nothing but the imaginary object that is realized in consciousness.

What then breaks-up this Imaginary dual relation between the ego and its specular reflected other is the intervention of the linguistical subject or "I." "The 'I' subject of the conclusive assertion, is isolated from the other, that is from the relation of reciprocity, by a logical beat. . . . Just as, let us recall, the psychological 'I' emerges from the indeterminate specular transivitism, assisted by an awakened jealous tendency, the 'I' in question defines itself through a subjectification of competition with the other. . . ." (Lacan 1945, 14) The impersonal Subject (S) of the instant of the look exists as a pure Being without a defined attribute, while the reciprocal subject (a – – – –a') of the time for understanding, is trapped in a mirroring game of self-reflection and doubt. Thus, in order for the subject to overcome its non-knowledge of its own attribute and the resulting doubt, it must anticipate its certitude through the affirmation of its "I" in relation to the Other (A) of language and law.

The "I" is a purely linguistical marker that the subject uses in order to represent itself. However, as the philosopher Hegel has pointed out, the "I" is at the same time the most universal and particular pronoun. When we say "I" we refer to ourselves, yet anyone can say I. In this sense, as Rimbaud has stated, "I is an Other."

In this text, Lacan rethinks Descartes by dividing the "cogito" into three logical moments: 1) One thinks, 2) therefore, and 3) I am. These three logical moments are later restated by Lacan as the following: "1) A man knows what is not a man; 2) Men recognize amongst themselves to be men; and 3) I declare myself to be a man for fear of being convinced by men that I am not a man." (Lacan 1945, 18) If the affirmation of masculinity is equated with the affirmation of having a white disk, then the white disk represents the phallus, inasmuch as it is the signifier of masculine sexuality. Thus, in the first logical time, the subject is without the phallic attribute, while in the second time, the subject places the phallus in the other, and finally, in the third time, the subject affirms it for itself.

This logic leads us to state that the initial Subject (S) in the Real is without the attribute of sexuality, while the subject of the second time finds this attribute in the reflected other (a') in an Imaginary dialectic of specular identification. This secondary relationship is then transcended by the Symbolic affirmation of the signifier of sexuality in the Other (A). This final moment of the game is defined by Lacan as an act and a judgment of certitude, which overcomes the doubt of specular identification and the indetermination of the Real. In his second seminar, Lacan simplifies this structure by using the example of the guessing game "odds or evens" in order to demonstrate this logic.

Suppose I told you that I would either place, or not place, a coin in my hand, and you would have to guess if it were there or not. Let us also suppose that we will play the game at least three times. The first time, you would have to make a pure guess, because you would have no prior information other than the rules of the game. On the second turn, you would start thinking about what I did the first time and you would have to decide if I would repeat the same thing or if I would change it. On this second level, you are already thinking about what I am thinking. This represents the Imaginary time for understanding, because you have started to place yourself in my position on a psychological level. During the third turn, you can begin to figure out the different mathematical possibilities of my choice. You now have enough information to start to make a Symbolic conclusion based on the laws and the logic of the game.

For now, what we can derive from this early Lacanian text is the logical relation between the Real, the Imaginary, and the Symbolic orders as it relates to the temporal movement from the originally isolated impersonal id, to the reciprocal and reflexive relation between the ego and its alter ego, to the interpersonal superego.[9]

Perception, Consciousness and Memory

This logical order can be, in turn, related to Freud's early Project which is itself divided into the three dimensions of perception, consciousness, and memory.[10] On a primary level, Freud connects the system of perception to a law of inertia and to the pure discharge of excitation, which he connotes with the symbol "Qn" (the quantity of neuronic energy). "In the first place, the principle of inertia explains the structural dichotomy into motor and sensory as a contrivance for neutralizing the reception of Qn by giving it off. Reflex movement is now intelligible as an established form of giving-off. . . . This discharge represents the primary function of the nervous system." (Freud 1895, 296) Thus, on a primitive level, Freud defines the subject of excitation and perception through the purely physiological process of a stimulus-response or reflex action.

For Freud, the sensuous id is neither a psychological nor a social being, but rather exists in the Real of nature. However, this primary (physiological) response of the subject, to reject all forms of stimulation, is soon replaced by a secondary law of constancy. "The nervous system receives stimuli from the somatic element itself—endogenous stimuli—which have equally to be discharged. These have their origin in the cells of the body and give rise to the major needs: hunger, respiration, sexuality. From these the organism cannot withdraw as it does from external stimuli. . . . In consequence, the nervous system is obliged to abandon its original trend to inertia (that is bringing the level to zero). It must put up with a store of Qn sufficient to meet the demand for a specific action." (Freud 1895, 297) Freud claims here that the "primitive" subject is able to escape all external stimulation through reflex, but is unable to do the same against its internal needs. In order to deal with these needs, the subject must maintain a constant level of stimulation that can be used for a future "specific action."

This accumulation of stimulation demands a secondary form of "resistance" that is set up against the primary discharge of excitation. "The secondary function, however, which calls for the accumulation of Qn, is made possible by the assumption of resistances which oppose discharge; and the structure of neurones makes it probable that the resistances are all to be located in the contacts, which in this way assume the value of barriers." (Freud 1895, 298) This secondary function thus delimits a dual relation (Secondness) between a primary form of stimulation (Real) and a secondary form of resistance and inhibition (Imaginary). Later in Freud's work, this pseudo-physiological process of resistance and inhibition becomes translated into the psychological defenses of the ego.

On the third level of memory, Freud introduces into his Project the structural relationship of difference and overdetermination. For memory to be possible, the original Real stimulation of a perception has to pass beyond the resistances of the contact-barriers. Freud calls these passages of stimulation "facilitations" or "traces" and he adds that, "Memory is represented by the facilitations existing between the psi neurones." (Freud 1895, 300) That is, memory is derived from a series of relations and not from positive elements. Furthermore, Freud connects this system of relations to a system of differences. ". . . Memory is represented by the differences in the facilitations between the psi neurones." (Freud 1895, 300) Freud's theory of memory is structural, because since Saussure, language has been defined as a system of differential relations. "The conceptual side of value is made up solely of relations and differences with respect to the other terms of language, and the same can be said of its material side. . . ." (Saussure, 117) These other terms of language are located in what Lacan calls the Other and can be symbolized by the signifying chain of differential relations.

Furthermore, the signifying chain is itself always overdetermined and Freud relates this to the interconnection of neurones. "Every psi neurone must in general be presumed to have several paths of connection with other neurones. . . ." (Freud 1895, 301) The psi system is thus, in itself, structured like a language where differential elements are related in an overdetermined network of possible connections.

This theory, that memory is structured like a linguistical network, will later reappear in Lacan's argument that the unconscious is structured like a language. Freud anticipated many of the ideas of structuralist linguistics in his early conception of the way that memory works. Unfortunately, too many of Freud's readers have failed to see the metaphoric and Symbolic value of his work, and have therefore taken some of his pseudo-scientific arguments at face value, missing the deeper meaning of his theories. On the other hand, Lacan often extends himself to separate Freud's scientific arguments from his more Symbolic and mythical ideas. The third section of this book will show how the concept of the death drive can only be understood if it is read as a myth and not as a scientific theory.

Thus far, this reading of Freud's Project has attempted to establish the difference between the system of Real perception and the system of Symbolic memory. This difference is mediated by the system of consciousness which introduces the notion of quality into the world. "Where do qualities originate? Not in the external world. For, out there, according to the view of our natural science, to which psychology too must be subjected, there are only masses in motion and nothing else. . . ." (Freud 1895, 308) Here, Freud distinguishes between the Real of perception and physical existence, which is determined by a quantitative relation and his notion of consciousness, which introduces a qualitative dimension.

This qualitative aspect of consciousness is, for Freud, determined by the pleasure principle. "Besides the series of sensory qualities, it [consciousness] exhibits another series very different from that—the series of sensations of pleasure and unpleasure, which now calls for interpretation," (Freud 1895, 312) In this argument, Freud takes a major step in the philosophy of consciousness (phenomenology) by equating consciousness with the pursuit of pleasure and the avoidance of displeasure. Later in his work, the concept of narcissism will account for this connection between consciousness and the pleasure principle.

The Phenomenology of the Ego and of Consciousness

Lacan's theory of the mirror stage will be used in order to determine the relationship between the foundation of the ego, consciousness, and narcissism. For Lacan, the unity of the ego is founded on the Imagined unity of the subject's body. This ideal form or totality (Gestalt) first must be realized in an external object or person. This means that consciousness is always consciousness of an object or other.

To illustrate this relationship between the ego and its perceived unity, Lacan uses the paradigmatic example of the first time that a child sees itself in the mirror and realizes that it is a separate entity with a defined and enclosed body. Lacan argues that this perception of the body as a complete whole is Imaginary because it is based on an ideal form that has no holes or discontinuities. It is a Gestalt because the whole is bigger than the sum of the parts. Furthermore, it is ideal because the child begins to see its body as a complete and controlled form before it has mastered its motor activity. In other words, the subject's conception of his self is first anticipated on the field of vision before it is realized on the level of activity and movement. This phenomenon explains, for Lacan, why Narcissus falls in love with his own reflected image. His self-love is based on his perception of being complete and whole, and therefore lacked nothing.

In his *Ideas Pertaining to a Pure Phenomenology*, Edmund Husserl develops this same relation between consciousness, the ego, and the introduction of unity into the field of perception. "It is equally our concern to characterize the unity of consciousness required, and therefore necessarily required, purely by what belongs to the cogitations as their own such that they could not exist without that unity." (Husserl,

69) For Husserl, consciousness is dependent on the generation of a form of unity.

In his text on narcissism, Freud introduces the ego as precisely this "unity" that is added to the primitive Real. "It is impossible to suppose that a unity comparable to the ego can exist in the individual from the very start; the ego has to develop. But the auto-erotic instincts are primordial; so there must be something added to auto-erotism—some new operation in the mind—in order that narcissism may come into being." (Freud 1914, 59) Freud argues that the subject is born into the world in a state of primordial auto-erotism, and it is only (in a second period) that the unity of the ego comes into being through the secondary state of narcissism.

Lacan's theory of the mirror stage attempts to tie together a phenomenological definition of consciousness with Freud's theory of narcissism by accounting for the imagined unity of the ego. The narcissistic ego sees its perfect image reflected in the Other, and it is this ideal form of unity that gives the subject the possibility of organizing its perceptions and sensations through the development of a unified body image. Thus, consciousness is always for itself, because the ego directs itself towards its own perceptual field in order to appropriate the world and to rediscover the pleasure of unity in its self and in the world.

Husserl connects this "self-centeredness" of consciousness to the way that the subject turns its "mental regard" towards other objects. It is, in fact, the intentionality of the ego, which defines consciousness for Husserl. Yet at the same time, consciousness can only be realized in external objects and thus the ego is nothing in itself.

Returning to the Project, Freud argues that the first object for the ego is always another subject. "Let us suppose that the object which furnishes the perception resembles the subject—a fellow human-being. If so, the theoretical interest is also explained by the fact that an object like this was simultaneously the first satisfying object and further his first hostile object, as well as his sole helping power. For this reason it is in relation to a fellow human-being that a human-being learns to cognize." (Freud 1895, 331) The first object of consciousness for Freud is the mother who simultaneously represents a satisfying, hostile, and helping other. In this sense, consciousness is colored by the initial, ambivalent, reflexive relationship between the mother and the subject's ego.

The subject first loves not only the object that helps and satisfies it, but also the object which allows it to develop a sense of self and consciousness. For Lacan, this mother is not necessarily the actual biological mother, but rather any person or object which plays this role of support and care.

The ambivalence of this Imaginary dual relation between the ego and the (m)other results from the structure of consciousness and narcissism always combining a part of sameness and reflection with an element of difference. ". . . The perceptual complexes proceeding from this fellow human-being will be in part new and non-comparable—his features, for instance, in the visual sphere; but other visual perceptions—e.g. those of the movements of his hands will coincide in the subject with memories of quite similar visual impressions of his own, of his own body. . . ." (Freud 1895, 331) In Lacanian terms, this passage states that the reflecting specular image always contains within itself an element of difference.

This dialectic between the specular narcissistic image in the Other and the object of difference is apparent in the second stage of Lacan's logical time. In the Imaginary time for understanding, each subject is divided between its Imaginary specular identification with the other ("the two whites recognize one another") and its fear that it may be different ("what if I am black.") This division as ascribed to the way that consciousness and narcissism are structured by the opposition between the other who is everything and the ego that is nothing.

This Imaginary division of the subject is only overcome, in Lacan's logic, by the decisive act of self-judgment where each subject declares that it is white in front of the Other. This judgement then requires a speech-act that is made for the Other. On a certain level, this is what the analytic relation creates a space for—the freedom to affirm to another person what one thinks one really is.

The Structure of Judgment and Difference

In Freud's Project, this concept of judgement intervenes in a third logical moment. "This dissection of a perceptual complex is described as cognizing it, it involves a judgement and when this last aim is attained it comes to an end. Judgement, as will be seen, is not a primary function, but presupposes the cathexes from the ego of the disparate portions. . . ." (Freud 1895, 331–2) Judgement, on a Symbolic level, is a judgement of the difference between the perceived object and the wished for object.

Freud articulates three stages to this judgement of difference. In a primary time, the object wished for is perceived through a hallucination. "In the first case: simultaneously with the wishful cathexis of the mnemonic image, the perception of it [the wished-for-object] is present." (Freud 1895, 327) A constant theme in Freud's work is anticipated in this passage, that desire is first satisfied on the level of hallucination. In the first chapter of this book, it will be argued that this theory of hallucination defines Freud's conceptions of the dream-state, the unconscious and psychosis. In terms of logical time, it is in the instant of the look that the subject perceives the lost object through the hallucination of its desire.

In a second logical time, the perception only partially coincides with the wished-for object. "In the second case: the wishful cathexis is present and along with it a perception which does not tally with it wholly but only in part." (Freud 1895, 327) Here is the time for understanding where the subject cannot act because it is plagued by the idea that it may be black. In other words, it fears that there is a part of itself that does not coincide completely with the other. Freud adds that this non-coincidence between the perception and the wish ". . . gives impetus for the activity of thought, which is terminated once more with their coincidence." (Freud 1895, 328) However, on this secondary level of Imaginary consciousness, this coincidence between the object and the desire can occur without an act by the subject. The wished-for object can be imagined merely by the subject in a fantasy.

The second section of this book will demonstrate that one of the predominant features of the neurotic subject is this division between its demand to be like all the others and its fear that it is different. This division of the subject results in the symptom of doubt, which prevents the obsessional subject from acting. In contrast, what seems to define, in part, the clinical category of perversion is precisely the ability of the pervert to act on its desires.

The pervert is dominated by the third logical moment, where the difference between the wished-for object and the perception is affirmed and reproduced. "We now come to the third possibility that can arise in a wishful state; when, that is, there is a wishful cathexis and a perception emerges which does not coincide in any way with the wished-for-mnemic image." (Freud 1895, 330) This absolute difference between the wished-for object and the perception of the object will later be connected to Freud's notions of negation and fetishism. The fetishist "negates" the perception that females have no phallus by creating a Symbolic, substitute phallus. For Lacan, this substitute is a signifier that both affirms and denies the presence of what the Other lacks. The subject's affirmation of having the phallus in the third logical time is then tied to the fear that it does not have it. The play between the presence and the absence of the phallic signifier determines the relation between the subject of sexuality and the Symbolic order of the Other.

Perversion, Drive, and Discourse

In the third section of this book, will be Lacan's argument that the drive represents the dialectic between the subject of sexuality and the signifying chain of the Other. Freud articulates this structure in the Project when he develops a theory of the Symbolic order. "The formation of symbols also takes place normally. A soldier will sacrifice himself for a many-colored scrap of stuff on a pole, because it has become the symbol of his fatherland, and no one thinks that neurotic." (Freud 1895, 349) For the soldier, the flag is a signifier which represents his fatherland. This is the structure of the signifying chain which Lacan defines by the axiom: one signifier (S1) represents the subject ($) for another signifier (S2).

In Freud's example, this means that the flag is a signifier (S1) or a sign that only has meaning when it is put into a relation with another signifier (S2), the fatherland. In other words, signifiers only relate to other signifiers and not directly to things. Furthermore, Lacan adds that subjects only can be represented through these signifying relations which go beyond the consciousness and intentionality of the subject.

Lacan uses what he calls his "discourse of the master" to articulate this structure of the signifying chain or relation:

$$\frac{S1}{\not{S}} - - - - - - - - - - \blacktriangleright S2$$

This formula indicates that the subject ($) is placed below the articulation of the signifying chain (S1 $\longrightarrow$ S2). In Lacan's logic, it is language which is the master and the subject who is "subjected" to the structure. After all, it is not the soldier who decided that the flag would represent his fatherland, nor that a person should die to protect a scrap of colored stuff.

Another example of this structure is given by Freud: "The knight who fights for his lady's glove knows in the first place, that the glove owes its importance to the lady; and secondly, he is in no way prevented by his adoration of the glove from thinking of the lady and serving her in other respects." (Freud 1895, 3) For the knight ($) the glove is a signifier (S1) which represents an Other (S2). Like the flag, the glove derives its signification only because it is related to another signifier which is, in this case, the Lady. However, this signifying chain is socially mediated and thus the desire of the subject is determined by the desire of the Other, and in this way the subject is transcended by the structure of the drive itself. Furthermore, the Lady, who seems to be the object of the drive has her Real being negated and overcome by being translated into the abstract Symbol of the Other.

This pushes Lacan to state that the Other and the Woman do not exist because they represent purely formal or structural categories. In this sense, the pervert is a structuralist at heart, for this subject always attempts to bring the Other of law and love into its sexual activities. The predominance of uniforms, scenarios, and contracts in sadomasochistic relations displays the desire of the pervert to produce its sexuality on the level of the socio-Symbolic order, which serves to challenge the existence of the Other.

Lacan has tied this intervention of the Symbolic order in perversion to the role of the father (père-version). It seems that the sadistic subject attempts to reproduce scenes of castration in his love relations by affirming the law and voice of the superego or father. In perversion there is most often an eroticization of law and language in the subject's attempt to be a father for another. One can say that the sadistic subject affirms in the Symbolic moment to conclude that, "I am the Other of law and desire."

The third section of this text will also tie this position of the Symbolic Other to the death drive and the role of the father in the Oedipus complex. For Lacan, the Symbolic father represents the law that transcends the subject's demand for maternal love. The Oedipal structure itself articulates the relation between the Real Subject (S) of sexuality, the Imaginary (m)other (a') of narcissistic love and the social intervention of the Symbolic father (A) of law and language.

These three dimensions of Being (the Real, the Imaginary, and the Symbolic) can also be used to examine the difference between the three fundamental clinical categories of psychoanalysis: psychosis, neurosis, and perversion. It will be shown that the psychotic subject is dominated by the Real of his perceptions, the neurotic is divided by the Imaginary dialectic between the ego and its object, and the pervert attempts to sexualize the Symbolic structure of language and law. The structure of the psychoanalytic clinic is thus, in itself, Oedipal because the psychotic subject is the subject of sexuality and the unconscious (the child) who, in a second logical time, attempts to establish the stability of its ego through narcissistic love (the mother) and the phenomenology of consciousness which, in a third logical time, is transcended by the Symbolic order of law and regulation (the father). Psychosis, neurosis, and perversion, therefore, represent ways to categorize the fixation of a subject on one of these levels.

The final section of this text will articulate how psychoanalysis offers a fourth alternative to these three dimensions of Being.

The object (a) and the Position of the Analyst

This fourth logical time will be related to Lacan's notion of the object (a) as it represents the presence of the analyst and the end of analysis itself. This object will be defined as a logical element that is simultaneously excluded and included in the three dimensions of the Real, the Imaginary, and the Symbolic.

It is the encounter with this object in the transferential relationship which provides the subject with the opportunity to question its position in relation to the existence of its sexuality, the phenomenology of its narcissistic consciousness, and the structure of the Other which transcends it.

EBERLY LIBRARY
WAYNESBURG UNIVERSITY
WAYNESBURG. PA 15370

EBERLY LIBRARY
WAYNESBURG UNIVERSITY
WAYNESBURG PA 15370

I

The Existence
of the Real

1

The Dream and the Psychotic Subject

Freud's *Interpretation of Dreams* not only attempts to prove the existence of the unconscious, but also serves to articulate the structure of psychosis. This psychotic structure is dominated by the Lacanian axiom: "all that has been rejected in the Symbolic order returns in the Real." In a psychotic state, as in a dream, what is radically rejected is the Symbolic Other (A) or what Lacan calls the Name-of-the-father. This Other represents the socio-Symbolic law of the father, castration, and the desire of the Other. These Symbolic elements, which the subject of the unconscious rejects (forecloses), return in the Real during hallucinations, fantasies, and dreams.

The Structure of the Oedipus Complex

According to Freud and Lacan, the sexuality of every subject is determined in relation to the Symbolic law of the father (the Name-of-the-father). It is through the castration complex that each subject must accept the intervention of the law and the desire of the Other, by either affirming or denying the role of the phallus in the determination of sexual identity. Furthermore, the fear of castration functions to resolve the Oedipus complex and, therefore, to develop the internalized paternal figure of the super-ego.

In Freud's conception of the Oedipus complex, a subject imagines that he is in love with his mother and that the father represents a threat to this Imaginary love relation. If the subject is to overcome the symbiotic love for his mother, his father has to intervene and proscribe the law against incest. This implies that the subject identifies with the father and gives up his desire for his mother at the end of the Oedipus complex. This also implies that the subject has become aware of sexual differences and the possible loss of his own penis.

For many anthropologists, this law against incest represents the defining element between nature and culture. The difference between a natural order and a human cultural society is that humans have an imposed a Symbolic law against incest. The need to prevent incest in a cultural society, in turn, demands a series of laws, rituals, and myths, that serve to keep members of the same family from having sexual relations with each other. For Freud, the whole social network is founded on the incest taboo and the law against patricide.

In his book *Totem and Taboo*, Freud argues that the first laws of society came as the result of the murder of a primal father. The Symbolic law against patricide is tied to the subject's other Oedipal desire; to get rid of his father in order to have his mother for himself. These two Oedipal desires are overcome through the internalization of the superego which represents an identification with the Symbolic law of the father. With the resolution of the Oedipus complex, the subject no longer desires the mother, but identifies with what the father desires.

It should be noted that when Lacan speaks about fathers and mothers in the Oedipus complex and its resolution, he is not necessarily referring to the actual biological mother or father, but rather to the people that play these roles in the Symbolic structure. This means that a female could play the part of the intervening father, just as a male could play the part of the loving and caring mother.

Furthermore, this movement from the Oedipal love of the mother to the intervention of the Symbolic law of the father represents the logical movement from the Imaginary order of love and fantasy to the Symbolic order of desire and law. This movement can be traced on Lacan's schema L:

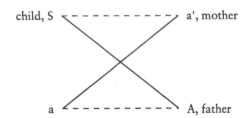

In the position of the Real Subject (S), is the child; in the place of the imaginary other (a'), is the Imaginary love for the mother; and in the position of the Symbolic Other (A), is found the law of the father. This schema can also be read in a developmental logic: in the first stage, the child or Subject (S) exists all by himself, cut off from all others; in the second logical time, the subject enters into a dual symbiotic relation with the mother; in the third logical moment this relation is broken up by the Symbolic law of the father.

The Function of Perversion

For Lacan, the acceptance of the law of the father is tied to the clinical category of perversion and the determination of the desire of the Other.[1] "The whole problem of the perversions consists in conceiving how the child, in his relation to the mother, a relation constituted in analysis not by his vital dependence on her, but by his dependence on her love, that is to say, by the desire for her desire, identifies himself with the imaginary object of this desire in so far as the mother herself symbolizes it in the phallus. The phallocentrism produced by this dialectic is . . . entirely conditioned by the intrusion of the signifier in man's psyche. . . . Freud revealed this Imaginary function of the phallus, then, to be the pivot of the symbolic process that completes in both sexes the questioning of the sex by the castration complex." (Lacan 1966, 197–8) Lacan argues that it is the role of the castration complex and the paternal function to introduce the subject into the Symbolic order of sexual difference, where the desire of one subject (S1) is determined by the desire of the Other (S2). This structure of the castration complex has been formalized, with Lacan's theory of the signifying chain, in order to show that if the phallus is a signifier (S1), it must be related in a differential relation to an Other signifier (S2).

For Lacan, the term "signifying chain" refers to the interrelations between different symbols or words. This relation is called a differential relation because one signifier can never signify itself, it must always refer to other signifiers. For example, the word or concept "up" has no meaning unless it is opposed to the term "down." It is the difference between words, not something inherent in each word, that gives the words their meanings.

Furthermore, every word that is defined by its relation to other words must also be considered within particular historical and cultural contexts. For example, the term "liberal" in the nineteenth century, meant something completely different than what it means in the twentieth century. For Lacan, the Symbolic context of a word is determined by the other signifiers or words to which it is attached. Lacan labels the primary word or signifier S1 and the secondary word or context S2.

In the structure of sexual desire, the primary signifier of every subject is the phallus. However, since there is only one signifier of sexuality (the phallus), the Other signifier of the signifying chain (S2) must represent the absence of the phallus (castration). In this sense, the affirmation of the presence of the phallus is tied to the possibility of its absence.

This dialectic of the absence and the presence of the phallus is in turn determined by the role of the father, who Lacan places in the position of the Other signifier (S2) of castration. For it is the law of the Symbolic Other, through the incest taboo, that serves to regulate and socialize every subject's sexuality and desire. .

Furthermore, because the father of law (the Name-of-the-Father) functions as a signifier, or more precisely as a signifying chain, he is not the Real living father, but rather the dead father of tradition and history. In other words, in Freud's and Lacan's Oedipal logic, the father is a pure social function, whose living presence is transcended by his Symbolic role. "How, indeed, could Freud fail to recognize such an affinity [between death and the father], when the necessity of his reflection led him to link the appearance of the signifier of the father, as the author of the Law, with death, even to the murder of the father—thus showing that if this murder is the fruitful moment of debt through which the subject binds himself for life to the Law, the symbolic Father is, in so far as he signifies this Law, the dead Father." (Lacan 1966, 199) In order for the father to be internalized as the superego, his word and law must become detached from his personal presence, then he can become a pure signifier of social regulation. This also means that the position of the father is not based on biology—whether he has a penis or not—but on the Symbolic position that he holds in the family structure.

In Freud's myth of the primal hord, in *Totem and Taboo*, the father must be killed in order for a society to be born. Freud implies there can be no social order without law, and no law without guilt and respect. It is the role of the paternal superego to represent the acceptance of society and the link between guilt and legality by standing in for the dead father. Lacan calls this function of the Symbolic Other, the Name-of-the-Father in order to stress the connection between the signifier and paternity.

Psychotic Foreclosure

In psychoses, it is precisely this function of the Name-of-the-father, that the subject rejects (forecloses). "We will take *Verwerfung*, then, to be the *foreclosure* of the signifier. To the point at which the Name-of-the-Father is called—we shall see how—may correspond in the Other, then, a mere hole, which by the inadequacy of the metaphoric effect will provide a corresponding hole at the place of the phallic signification." (Lacan 1966, 201) The rejection of the function of the Symbolic father also results in the rejection of the phallic function and the social Other. The Name-of-the-Father can be equated to the Other and the signification of the phallus. It is the role of these Symbolic attributes to lead the subject beyond his initial state of autistic and auto-erotic existence towards the affirmation of the desire of the Other, which transcends the *jouissance* (unconscious sexual excitation) of the individual subject.

In psychoses, the rejection of the Other not only results in a transformation of the subject's sexuality, but also in a distortion of the subject's relation to language and the social order. This allows an affirmation of a strict relation between the regulation of sexuality and the structure of language. It is the rejection of the Symbolic Other of language and law that results in the disappearance of the phallic function, which in turn can lead to the subject's loss of sexual identity.

This same distortion of the Symbolic order of language and sexuality is manifested during dreams. In *Introductory Lectures on Psychoanalysis*, Freud declares that the mode of expression in dreams is totally cut off from the desire to be understood and is equivalent to a rejection of the social Other. "A dream does not want to say anything to anyone. It is not a vehicle for communication; on the contrary, it is meant to remain ununderstood." (Freud 1916, 231) The dream is itself autistic because it is cut off from the recognition of the Other and the desire to be understood.

This non-relation with the Other is evident in the lack of relations within the discourse of the psychotic and the dream. "Thus the language consists, one might say, solely of the raw material, just as our thought-language is resolved by the dream-work into its raw material, and any expression of relations is omitted." (Freud 1916, 231) The symbol S2 represents these relations within language, but which are rejected in the dream, and which result in a return to a primitive state of language.

In this same text, Freud points out that in the dream there is also a return to the period of infantile sexuality. "Let us now being together what our researches into child-psychology have contributed to our understanding of dreams. We have not only found that the material of the forgotten experiences of childhood is accessible to dreams, but we have also seen that the mental life of children with all its characteristics, its egoism, its incestuous choice of love-objects, and so on, still persists in dreams—that is, in the unconscious, and that dreams carry us back every night to this infantile level." (Freud 1916, 210) Here Freud draws an equivalency between the unconscious, infantile sexuality, and dreams.

This equivalency is explained in *The Interpretation of Dreams* where Freud articulates his notion of regression. "Three kinds of regression are thus to be distinguished: (a) *topographical* regression, in the sense of the schematic pictures of the psi-systems . . . ; (b) *temporal* regression, in so far as what is in question is a harking back to older psychical structures; and (c) *formal* regression, where primitive methods of expression and representation take the place of the usual ones. All these three kinds of regression are, however, one at bottom and occur together as a rule; for what is older in time is more primitive in form and in psychical topography lies nearer to the perceptual end." (Freud 1900, 587) On the level of topographical regression, Freud is referring to the primary system of perception which implies a temporal regression to the state of infantile sexuality and a formal regression to the unconscious mode of expression.

This structure of regression can be inscribed onto Freud's schema of the mental apparatus that he develops in the final chapter of *The Interpretation of Dreams*:

Pct   Mnem   Mnem'   Ucs   Pcs

The logical order of this diagram goes from 1) the system of perception (Pct) to 2) the primary memory system (Mnem) and 3) finally to the secondary memory system (Mnem').[2] The initial system of perception represents the primitive Real of the mental apparatus which refers to the unconscious, (Ucs) infantile sexuality, and primitive language.

The primary state of the Real is replaced, in a second logical time, by an initial memory system (Mnem), which serves to generate perception-signs that in a third logical moment are organized into a Symbolic system of verbal associations. This secondary memory system (Mnem') can be equated, in turn, with the preconscious chain of signifiers (S2). Freud's schema can be rewritten by adding Lacan's symbols and by equating the system of the unconscious with the primary system of perception, and the preconscious with the secondary memory system (Mnem'):

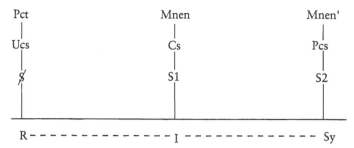

Freud's diagram is transformed in order to articulate the logical progression that begins with 1) the Real (R) subject ($) of the unconscious (Ucs) and perception (Pct), which 2) in a second logical moment is replaced by the Imaginary (I) system of consciousness (Cs) and the primary signifier of difference (S1), and 3) in a third time enters into the preconscious (Pcs) system of Symbolic (Sy) relations (S2).

This movement from the Real order of perception to the Symbolic order of differential relations is determined by Freud's theory of the generation of thought. "Now our thoughts originally arose from sensory images of that kind: their first material and their preliminary stages were sense impressions, or more properly mnemic images of such impressions. Only later were words attached to them and the words in turn linked up into thoughts." (Freud 1916, 180–1) This logical progression from perception to words to thoughts traces the movement from the Real order of sensual and perceptual existence to the Symbolic order of language and what Freud will call the death drive.[3]

The connection between the death drive and language is one of Lacan's essential interpretations of Freud's work. Lacan turns to the field of German philosophy, in particular the works of Heidegger and Hegel, to show that there is an inherent association between death and language. From Hegel he takes the idea that "the word is the death of the Thing" because language replaces lived experiences with the dead letter of representation.[4] In other words, because a "tree" can be discussed without the tree being present, the actual tree itself becomes unimportant.

From Heidegger, Lacan borrows the concept of "Being-towards-death" in order to argue that the essential meaning of the subject only comes into being through an encounter with death. However, since we can never remember and discuss our own death, we only encounter death through the death of the Other.

Furthermore, as will be seen in the third section of this book, Freud's theory of the death drive, as it is articulated in *Beyond the Pleasure Principle*, is tied to his elaboration of children's games and other forms of symbolic representation, which attempt to master the absence of the Other. Lacan argues that desire becomes humanized by being separated from the dependence on actual things and people.

For Lacan, the Symbolic order of language and law is devoid of both existence and jouissance (unconscious sexual excitement).[5] In a sense, this is simply another way of stating Freud's theoretical opposition between sexuality and civilization. For Freud, the sexual experience is fundamentally without law and regulation, and maintains itself on an auto-erotic and autistic level without relation to the social Other. If we equate life to this primary level of the primitive Real, we must infer that the opposing order of Symbolic representation can be equated to the concept of death.

The Anxiety of Death in the Real

It is precisely this signifier of death that is often refused in the formation of a dream. In one of the central dreams of *The Interpretation of Dreams* Freud recounts how a father sees his recently dead son, who now appears alive and who questions the father, asking, "Father, can't you see that I'm burning?"[6] This dream serves to fulfill the wish of the father to deny the death of the Other.

This rejection of death is made possible by the father's ability to forget the past and to fit his desired object into a perception in the present. "When the glare of light fell on the eyes of the sleeping father, he drew the worrying conclusion that a candle had fallen over and might have set the dead body on fire. He turned this conclusion into a dream by clothing it in a sensory situation and in the present tense." (Freud 1900, 589) This dream represents the reversal of the structure of the mental apparatus that we have just presented. The logical Symbolic conclusion (S2) is no longer at the end of the mental process but rather at the beginning, and the perceptual system which Freud defines as the primary stage of thought is now placed at the end. Furthermore, what aids this process of dream distortion is the transformation of a memory of the past into a present perception. Returning to the schema developed out of Freud's diagram of the mental apparatus, its temporal characteristics now can be determined:

36 All narrower goods are to be subordinated to the good of this very broad realm. And so, on the basis of utilitarian considerations, we may now bring some clarity into the area that was previously obscure; for we are now in a position to say something more positive about the standard that ought to be applicable to any particular choice.* Even if there is no way of comparing the intrinsic value of acts of insight, say, with acts of high-minded love, it is clear, at least, that neither type of act is to be entirely neglected for the sake of the other. If one person had complete knowledge but felt no exalted love, and another felt the love but did not have the knowledge, neither would be able to put his gifts to the service of the larger collective good. From this point of view, it is clear that we should try to realize and harmonize all our noblest capacities.[44]

37 Now that we have been able to see how so many duties toward the highest practical good arise, let us turn to the source

[44] We may be more disturbed, however, by the fact that it is often impossible to measure the remote consequences of our actions.

But this type of uncertainty need not discourage us, if we really do love what is best on the whole. Of those possible consequences which are equally unknown, any one has as many chances in its favour as any of the others. According to the law of large numbers, results will balance out in the long run. Hence if we choose a good that we are sure of, then a plus will remain on the side of the good and our choice will be justified, just as it would be if it were to stand alone.

We mentioned another type of uncertainty in the lecture (at the end of section 27)—the uncertainty arising out of the possibility that some good things may not be experienced by us as good. Similar considerations show that this type of uncertainty need not disturb us either.

* [Editor's note: Since the time of Kant, the term "utilitarian" has had an unfortunate connotation in Germany. The realm of value toward which, according to Brentano, we should endeavour to make ourselves as useful as possible is not restricted, of course, to pleasure or to oneself.]

wise counsel, follows from the same precept. But it does *not* mean that my future happiness should be of less value to me than the happiness of the present moment.

These considerations also indicate that there is no justification for the communistic doctrines which some have tried to deduce, much too rashly, from the lofty principles of universal brotherhood.

of our legal duties. One indispensable condition for bringing about the highest practical good is that we so live that a division of labour will be possible. It is morally necessary, therefore, that man live in society. From this it follows that each person should be to a certain extent restricted in his activities; otherwise he will bring more harm than good to those around him. [45] These restrictions can be made definite only by positive legislation (though much can be accomplished merely by the simple exercises of good sense), and they need the security and support of public authority.

And just as our natural insight requires and sanctions the existence of a positive law, it may also make particular demands which must be fulfilled if the legal order is to bestow upon us its full store of blessings.

Thus truth, which bears the highest crown, may sanction or refuse to sanction the products of positive legislation. It is from this sanction that they derive their true binding force. [46] The old sage of Ephesus observed, in one of his Sibyl-like utterances that are so full of meaning: "All human laws are nourished from the *one* divine law." [47]

[45] [This note, "Criticism of Ihering", may be found on page 93ff.]

[46] Reason may yet give provisional sanction to a law that is essentially bad and contrary to nature, no matter how much the law is to be condemned from a moral point of view and no matter how urgently it may require amendment. This has long been recognized and often been pointed out; see for example Bentham's *Theory of Legislation*. Socrates, who deemed himself worthy to be feasted in the Prytaneum, died for the sake of this conviction. The positive legal code, despite its defects, establishes a condition that is better than anarchy. Since each violation of the law threatens to weaken the force of law in general, it may well be that in order to preserve the existence of the legal order a rational man must occasionally pursue a course of action which would not otherwise deserve our approbation. This is a logical consequence of the relativity of secondary ethical rules— a matter which will be taken up later.

Errors in the prevailing moral codes must be looked upon in a similar way (this point is to be touched upon in the lecture).

But there are limits, and it is necessary to give heed to the sublime saying, "We owe greater obedience to God than to man".

[47] Heraclitus of Ephesus (500 B.C.), the first of the Greek philosophers from whose writings we have extensive fragments.

38 In addition to those laws that set limits on our rights, every society has positive stipulations about the way in which the individual should act within his own sphere of rights, stipulations as to how he should make use of his own freedom and property. Public opinion approves diligence, generosity, and economy, each in its proper place, and disapproves indolence, greed, extravagance, and many other things. These prescriptions do not appear in any law books, but, as we may put it, they stand written within the hearts of the people. And they carry with them their own characteristic rewards and punishments—namely, the advantages and disadvantages, respectively, of good and of bad reputation. Thus we have, so to speak, a prevailing positive code of morality that supplements the prevailing positive code of law. This code of morality, like the code of law, may contain correct and incorrect precepts. If the precepts are to be truly binding, then, as we have seen, they must accord with what reason sees to be our duties toward the highest practical good.

And so we have found what we were looking for—the natural sanction for law and morality.

39 I shall not pause to discuss the way in which this sanction makes itself felt. Everyone prefers to say "I am acting rightly", and not "I am acting wrongly". No one who is capable of recognizing what is better can be entirely indifferent to this fact when he comes to make a decision. For some, though not for others, it is a consideration of supreme importance. Natural endowments vary from one person to another, but much can be accomplished by means of education and self-guidance. Truth speaks, and whoever is of the truth hears its voice.

40 We have seen that utilitarian considerations set the standard, so far as concerns the multiplicity of subordinate rules which nature engraves upon the tables of law. Just as we resort to different means in different situations, so, too, we should follow different precepts in different situations. Some of these may seem to conflict with others, but they do not conflict in fact, since they are intended to be applied to different types of situation. In *this* sense, it is correct to say that there is a kind of relativity in ethics.

Ihering has emphasized this type of relativity, but he is not, as he seems to think, one of the first to do so.[48] The doctrine was known in antiquity and Plato takes note of it in the *Republic*.[49] Aristotle emphasized it in the *Ethics* and made even more of it in the *Politics*.[50] It was acknowledged by the scholastics, and in modern times even Bentham, with his strong ethical and political convictions, has not denied it.[51] The fanatics of the French Revolution may have misconceived such relativity, but this is not true of the more circumspect among their compatriots. Laplace, for example, takes note of it in his *Essai philosophique sur les probabilités* and raises his voice in warning.[52]

The distinguished investigator who has disclosed to us the spirit of Roman law has given us much for which we should be grateful in *Der Zweck im Recht*. But he has obscured the true doctrine of ethical relativity by confounding it with a false doctrine of ethical relativism. According to the latter doctrine, *no* proposition in ethics has unexceptionable validity—not even the proposition that one ought to bring about the best within the widest area that one is capable of influencing. Ihering explicitly says that, in primitive times and for long periods afterwards, such a course of action would have been *immoral*, just as it is *moral* now. If we look back to the days of cannibalism, Ihering would have us sympathize with the cannibals instead of with those people who, in advance of their time, preached the universal love of one's neighbour.[53] These errors have been conclusively refuted, not only by philosophical reflection upon the principles of our knowledge of ethics, but also by the success of our Christian missionaries.

[48] Ihering, *Der Zweck im Recht*, Vol. II, p. 119 and elsewhere.

[49] Plato, *The Republic*, Book I, 331c.

[50] Aristotle, *Nichomachaean Ethics*, Book V, Chapter 10, 1137b 13; *Politics*, Books III and IV.

[51] See the Preliminary Discourse to Bentham's *Theory of Legislation*, as well as the "Essay on the influence of time and place upon the matter of legislation", in *Works of Jeremy Bentham*, ed. Bowring, London, William Tait, 1873; Vol. I, pp. 169–197.

[52] Pierre Simon Laplace, *Essai philosophique sur les probabilités*, Part II, Chapter 10 ("Application of the Calculus of Probabilities to the Moral Sciences").

[53] Cf. his article in *Allgem, Juristenzeitung*, Seventh Year, p. 171, and *Zweck im Recht*, Vol. II, pp. 118 and 122ff.

41 We have now reached the end of the road leading to the goal we had set before us. The road took us through strange and unfamiliar territory. But the results we have finally attained seem like old acquaintances. In saying that love of one's neighbour and self-sacrifice for one's country and for mankind are duties, we are merely repeating what is proclaimed all around us. A more detailed investigation would also show that deceit, treachery, murder, lasciviousness, along with countless other such things that are held to be morally reprehensible, are also to be condemned as being either unjust or immoral on the basis of the principle of moral knowledge that we have set forth.*

And so we find ourselves returning to familiar territory, as though we had returned from a distant voyage and could see at last the outlines of our homeland and the smoke rising from our own chimney.

42 We have a right to take pleasure in the familiarity of what we have found. The indubitable clarity with which everything follows is a good indication of the success of our undertaking. For the manner in which each step follows from the previous one is the most essential aspect of what we have said. Otherwise what advantage would the present inquiry have over any other? Even Kant, whose conception of our knowledge of right and wrong is very different from ours, arrived eventually at the most familiar views. But what we miss in his work is strict logical coherence. Beneke has shown that the Categorical Imperative, as Kant conceived it, may be used to prove contradictory propositions about one and the same thing and therefore to prove everything and nothing.[54] If we find, all the same, that Kant keeps drawing correct conclusions, we may attribute this to the fact that he had held them all along. Similarly, if Hegel had not known independently that the sky was blue, he would never have been able to deduce it *a priori* by means of his

[54] The reference is to Kant's *Grundlegung zur Metaphysik der Sitten*; see note 15 ("Kant's Categorical Imperative").

* [Editor's note: See Appendix V ("Epicurus and the War"). It may be noted that Brentano took very seriously the importance of sexual ethics and contributed a preface to the German edition of A. Herzen's, *Wissenschaft und Sittlichkeit: ein Wort an die männliche Jugend*, a manual that had been widely distributed in Germany.]

dialectic. (He also managed to deduce that there are exactly seven planets, the number accepted in his day—a view falsified by later scientific discoveries.)

The causes of the phenomenon are thus easily understood.

43 But there is another point that is puzzling. How does it happen that the prevailing public opinion about what is right and what is moral is in so many respects correct? If such a philosopher as Kant failed in the attempt to find the source of our knowledge of right and wrong, is it conceivable that ordinary people succeeded in drawing from this source? And if it is not, how does it happen that they have so often arrived at the proper conclusions without having the necessary premises? One cannot possibly explain the fact by saying that the correct view was established long ago.

But this difficulty, too, is easily resolved, We have only to reflect that much of what is present in our store of knowledge contributes toward the attainment of new knowledge without our being clearly conscious of the process.

One must not infer that in saying this I am subscribing to the celebrated "philosophy of the unconscious". I am referring only to certain familiar and indisputable facts. It is well known that men were able to reason correctly for thousands of years without having reflected upon the principles of valid reason and even without knowing anything about them. Indeed, when Plato first contemplated these principles, he was led to adopt the erroneous view that inference always involves a process of reminiscence.[55] He thought that what we perceive and experience on earth enables us to recall what we had learned in some pre-terrestrial life. Of course no one believes this now. But we continue to encounter erroneous theories about the source of our knowledge of the syllogism. Albert Lange, for example, thinks that this knowledge arises out of a combination of spatial intuition and the synthetic *a priori*. Alexander Bain, on the other hand, says it arises out of the fact that our experience up to the present shows that whenever any of the moods, Barbara, Celarent, and the others, have true premises, they also have true conclusions.[56]

[55] See, for example, Plato's *Meno*.

[56] Friedrich Albert Lange, *Logische Studien: ein Beitrag zur Neubegründung der formalen Logik und der Erkenntnislehre* (Iserlohn, 1887); and Alexander Bain, *Logic* (London, 1870), Part I, "Deduction", p. 159.

These are the crudest possible erors about the kind of insight that such knowledge really involves; but they did not prevent Plato, Lange, and Bain from reasoning just the way that other people do. Despite their failure to recognize the true principles of knowledge, their reasoning none the less has conformed to these principles.

But why go so far to find our examples? All we need to do is to question any ordinary person who makes a correct inference. If we ask him to tell us the premises upon which his inference was based, we are likely to find that he is unable to do so and that he will give us an entirely inaccurate account of the way in which he has actually reasoned. Or if we ask him to define some concept that is very familiar to him, he is likely to make the most glaring of errors, thus demonstrating once again that he cannot correctly describe his own processes of thought.

44 The road to ethical knowledge may seem obscure to the layman and also to the philosopher. The process is complex and there are many different principles working together. One would expect that some effects of each of these principles would be discernible throughout the course of history. This fact will do even more to confirm the correct theory than does the general agreement with respect to final results.

And what a multitude of examples could be cited if only there were time! Who would refuse to look upon joy (so long as it is not joy in what is bad) as an evident good? Many writers on ethics have even said that the concept of pleasure and the concept of good are one and the same.[57] But there have been others who in opposition bore witness to the intrinsic value of an insight, and anyone who has not had his head turned by theories must agree with them. Some have even wished to exalt knowledge to the position of being the highest good, elevated above all others.[58] But they also see a certain intrinsic value in every act of virtue. And others have said that virtuous action is the highest good.[59]

[57] For example, Bentham and, in antiquity, Epicurus.

[58] For example, Plato and Aristotle and, following them, Thomas Aquinas.

[59] For example, the Stoics and, in the middle ages, the followers of Scotus.

On these points, then, there is sufficient confirmation for our views.

And let us also consider the principles of preference. Do we not see the principle of summation exemplified in the dictum that the measure of happiness should be taken to be life as a whole and not merely the passing moment?[60] And passing beyond the limits of the self, we see the same principle exemplified in Aristotle's observation that the happiness of a whole people is a higher end than the happiness of oneself.[61] We find the same thing, he said, in a work of art, or in an organism, or in a household: the part exists for the sake of the whole, and everything is subordinate to the good of the whole ("εἰς τὸ κοινόν").[62] He even applies the same principle to the whole creation. He asks: "Where are we to look for the good and the best, which is the ultimate end of all created things? Is it immanent or is it transcendent?" And he answers, "Both", saying that the transcendent end is the divine first cause which all things strive to emulate and that the immanent end is the whole world-order.[63] The Stoics give similar testimony to the principle of summation.[64] Indeed, the principle reappears in every attempt to construct a theodicy, from Plato to Leibniz and even later.[65]

[60] Even Epicurus does not deny this—despite the fact that it conflicts with the assertion of his referred to in Section 31.

[61] Aristotle, *Nicomachaean Ethics*, Book I, Chapter 2.

[62] Aristotle, *Metaphysics*, Book XII, Chapter 10.

[63] Aristotle, *Metaphysics*, Book XII, Chapter 10. [Editor's note: compare the discussion in Brentano's *Aristoteles und seine Weltanschauung* (Leipzig: Quelle & Meyer), 1911.]

[64] They appealed to it when they argued that the life of the person who devotes himself to practical affairs is superior to the theoretical life.

[65] Appeal to the principle of summation is also made whenever the notion of God is employed in the construction of an ethical theory based on egoism and eudaemonism; for example, in Locke, in Fechner's work on the highest good, and in Leibniz (see Adolph Trendelenburg, *Historische Beiträge*, Vol. II, p. 245). God loves each of his creatures and therefore—so the argument goes—he loves them in their totality more than he loves each of them individually; hence he approves and rewards the sacrifice of the individual for the sake of this totality, while disapproving and punishing misdeeds committed for selfish purposes.

The influence of the principle of summation also shows itself in

It also appears in the precepts of our popular religion. The commandment to love our neighbour as ourselves tells us that we should give equal weight to every good, whether it be found in ourselves or in others. And this means that the individual should subordinate his own interests to that of the collective whole, just as the Saviour—the ethical ideal of Christianity—sacrificed himself for the salvation of the world.*

The commandment, "Love God above all else", is also a particular application of the law of summation. (As Aristotle said, God rather than the world as a whole is what is to be called the best.)[66] For do we not think of God as though he were the epitome of everything that is good, but raised to an infinite degree?

And so the two commandments—to love our neighbour as ourselves and to love God above all else—turn out to be so closely related that it is no longer surprising also to hear that the one is "like unto the other". It is very important to note that the commandment to love our neighbour is neither subordinate to nor in any way derivative from the commandment to love God. According to the Christian, the commandment to love our neighbour is right not in virtue of the fact that God requires it; God requires it in virtue of the fact that it is naturally

[66] Aristotle, *Metaphysics*, Book XII, Chapter 10, 1075a.

* [Editor's note: See Brentano's posthumous, *Die Lehre Jesu und ihre bleibende Bedeutung*, ed., Alfred Kastil (Leipzig: Felix Meiner, 1921).]

---

the desire for immortality. Thus Helmholtz, in seeking to offer hope to those who have this desire, writes: "If our achievements can enrich the lives of our descendants . . . then the individual may face without fear the thought that the threat of his own consciousness will some day be broken. But even such great and independent spirits as Lessing and David Strauss could not reconcile themselves to the thought that all living things, and therefore the fruits of the work of all past generations, might some day be annihilated." (See his "*Über die Entstehung des Planetensystems*", a lecture given at Heidelberg and Cologne, 1871). He believes that, if it is ever shown scientifically that the earth will one day be incapable of supporting life, then the need for immortality will once again establish itself, and people will then feel compelled to look for something which will show that belief in it is acceptable.

right.[67] The two commandments are alike in that their correctness is revealed in the same way, with the same clarity, and, so to speak, by means of the same light of natural knowledge.

Perhaps we now have sufficient evidence of the influence of some of the principles we have emphasized. And so on the one hand we have a kind of corroboration of our theory; and on the other hand we are able to explain those puzzling anticipations of philosophical results that are to be found in ordinary life.

45 We are not to suppose, however, that everything has now been settled. Even when concealed, the pure and exalted sources of knowledge that we have discussed send forth their product in great abundance. But there are also opinions regarding law and morality that are accepted by society and have the sanction of ethics which do not in fact arise from these sources. Many of them have arisen in a way that is quite unjustifiable from the point of view of logic. Investigation shows that many have their origin in certain lower impulses, in self-centred desires that then underwent a transformation. It is true, as so many utilitarians have emphasized, that egoism gives men an incentive to make themselves agreeable to others and that such conduct, continually practised, finally develops into a habit which is no longer referred back to its original purpose. This is primarily a result of the narrowness of our intellect, the so-called limits of consciousness which make us lose sight of our more distant ends when some more immediate question is at hand. Thus the blind force of habit may lead many people to have a certain selfless regard for the well-being of others. It is also true, as many have pointed out, that there have been powerful personalities throughout the course of history who were able to subjugate certain weaker individuals and transform them through habit into willing slaves. Ultimately in these poor slave-souls there comes to operate an

[67] This is the orthodox view of the great theologians, for example, Thomas Aquinas in the *Summa Theologica*. Only certain nominalists—for example, Robert Holcot—held that divine commands are completely arbitrary. See my *"Geschichte der kirchlichen Wissenschaften"*, in Volume II of Johann Adam Möhler's *Kirchengeschichte*, edited by P. B. Gams (Regensburg: G. J. Manz, 1867), pp. 526–84; I would also call the reader's attention to the list of typographical errors to be found in Volume III of that work (pp. 103–4).

αὐτὸς ἔφα with a blind though powerful force; they come to hear a compelling "You ought" just as though it were a revelation of nature about good and evil. When the individual violates the command, he is inwardly tormented, just as a well-trained dog would be. The tyrant is well-advised, in his own interests, to issue commands conducive to maintaining his horde. His subjects will learn to obey these commands as slavishly and habitually as they do any others. Concern for the whole society will then become a goal towards which every subject feels himself impelled as though by nature. And the tyrant himself, because of his concern for his possessions, will also form habits favouring the collective welfare. Indeed, like the miser who sacrificed himself in order to preserve his treasure, the tyrant may be ready to die for the sake of his people. Throughout this entire process, ethical principles exercise next to no influence. The compulsions and attitudes which arise in this way have no connection with the natural sanction for morality and no intrinsic ethical value. Yet consider what happens when one such tribe enters into relations with another and finds that here, too, considerations of friendliness begin to prove advantageous. The kind of training to which the people have been submitted will be certain sooner or later to lead to the acceptance of principles which accord with those that arise out of the true source of our knowledge of right and wrong.

46 Consider now an analogous situation. Men and animals have the blind habit of expecting similar events to recur under similar circumstances. This habit, which is exercised in countless instances, very often coincides with what one would do if one were to act in accordance with an induction fully conforming to the principles of the probability calculus. Indeed the similarity of the results has sometimes led even people with a knowledge of psychology to assume that the habitual instinctive process is no different from the one illuminated by mathematical insight, despite the fact that the two processes are as different as night and day.[68] We should take care not to suppose, therefore, that the true ethical sanction exerts any influence upon the pseudo-ethical developments we have described.

[68] [This note, "Mill's Conception of the Evident", may be found on page 96ff.]

47 Of course these lower processes have their use. As is often pointed out, nature does well to leave so much that pertains to our welfare to instinctive drives such as hunger and thirst instead of to our reason.[69]

I had earlier conceded to Ihering (perhaps the justification for the concession is now more clear) that there have been periods of history in which there was practically no trace of ethical thought or feeling. But even then much occurred which was a preparation for true virtue. Public law and order, for whatever motives they may originally have been established, were preconditions for the unfolding of our noblest capacities.

Under the influence of such training some passions were checked and some dispositions were implanted which made it easier for people to conform to the true moral law. Catiline's courage was not the true virtue of courage—if Aristotle was right in saying that the truly courageous man is the one who faces danger and death τοῦ καλοῦ ἕνεκαι; that is to say, "for the sake of the morally beautiful".[70] Augustine might have appealed to his case when he said: "Virtutes ethnicorum splendida vitia". Yet one cannot deny that if Catiline had been converted then the dispositions he had acquired would have made it easier for him also to take the greatest risks for the sake of what is good. It is in this way that the ground was laid for the reception of genuine ethical insights. These preparatory steps greatly encouraged those who, acquiring for the first time knowledge of right and wrong and hearing within themselves the voice of the natural sanction, were then impelled to make the truth known to others. This is what Aristotle meant when he said that not everyone can study ethics: anyone who is to learn about law and morality must first be disposed toward what is good. It is a waste of effort, he said, for anyone else to study the subject.[71]

Indeed, those pre-ethical, though not pre-historic, times rendered still other services to the knowledge of natural law and morality. The legal ordinances and customs then established approached so very closely to what ethics demands, for the reasons

[69] Compare Hume, *Enquiry concerning Human Understanding*, Section 5, Part 2.

[70] Aristotle, *Nicomachaean Ethics*, Book III, Chapter 7; compare the subtle discussion in Chapter 8 of the five kinds of false courage.

[71] Aristotle, *Nicomachaean Ethics*, Book I, Chapter 3.

already discussed, that the similarity has led many to the mistaken belief that there was a deep and thorough-going relationship between these ordinances and customs, on the one hand, and ethics on the other. The precepts which are thus made into law by blind impulse often coincide in content with those which would be established on the basis of a knowledge of the good. In these codified laws and customs there are rough drafts, so to speak, of laws that ethics itself could sanction. And they were all the more valuable because they were adapted to the special circumstances of the people, as utilitarian considerations would require. Comparison of different laws and customs makes this latter point clear, just as, long ago, it helped lead to the important recognition of the correct sense in which one may speak of the relativity of natural law and morality. If Aristotle had not made such comparisons, would he have succeeded as he did in keeping himself free from stereotyped and doctrinaire theories?

So much, then, in order to give the pre-ethical ages their due.

48 Nevertheless, it was then night. But it was a night that heralded the coming day, a day which will witness the most significant dawn in the history of the world. The day is yet to come; the forces of light are still struggling against the powers of darkness. Genuine ethical motives are by no means the generally accepted standard, either in private or in public life. These forces—to use the language of the poet—are not yet strong enough to hold the world together. We may be thankful that nature keeps us going by means of hunger and love and all those other obscure drives and strivings which are capable of being developed from self-seeking desires.

49 The jurist, then, must take account of these drives and strivings and of the psychological laws that govern them if he is to understand his times and work for what is good. And he must also take into account those precepts of natural law and natural morality which, as we have suggested, were not the first to have emerged in the history of the subject, but which, if we may hope for a complete realization of the ideal, will be the last.

Here, then, we have in all its diversity the intimate relationship which, as Leibniz had seen, jurisprudence and politics bear to philosophy.

Plato said that the state will never thrive until the true philosopher is king, or until kings are able to philosophize in the proper way. In our own times we might put the point better by saying that the many defects of our political system will not begin to be corrected until our students of law, instead of being deprived of what little stimulus they now have to inform themselves about philosophy, are given a philosophical training that is adequate to their noble calling.

SUPPLEMENTARY NOTES

On Kant's Categorical Imperative
(Note 14 to page 11)

In the *Grundlegung zur Metaphysik der Sitten*, (*Foundations of Morals*)* Kant formulates his categorical imperative in these two ways: "Act only in accordance with that maxim which you can at the same time will should become a universal law"; and "Act as if the maxim of your action were to become by your will a universal law of nature" (IV, 421 in the Akademie edition). In the *Critique of Practical Reason*,* he says: "Act so that the maxim of your will can always at the same time hold good as a principle of universal legislation" (V, 31). In other words, as Kant himself puts it, act upon a maxim which is such that, if it were to become a universal law, it would not lead to contradictions and thus nullify itself. Consciousness of this fundamental imperative, according to Kant, is a fact of pure reason, which thereby proclaims itself to be legislative (sic volo sic jubeo). But Beneke has long since observed that this supposed consciousness is only a "poetic, psychological fiction". (See his *Grundlinien der Sittenlehre*, 1841, Vol. II, p. xviii; compare his *Grundlegung zur Physik der Sitten*, which is a counterpart to Kant's *Grundlegung zur Metaphysik der Sitten*.) There is probably no longer anyone of sound judgement who would disagree with Beneke on this point. It is noteworthy that even philosophers such as Mansel, who have the highest esteem for Kant, concede that the categorical imperative is a fiction and manifestly untenable.

And the categorical imperative has still another defect which is no less serious. Even if one were to accept it, one could not use it to deduce any ethical consequences. As Mill correctly observes (*Utilitarianism*, Chapter 1), the deductions Kant himself attempts to make fail "in an almost grotesque fashion". The following is

* [Translations of these works appear in *Critique of Practical Reason and other writings in Moral Philosophy*, ed. and trans. Lewis White Beck; University of Chicago Press, 1949.]

Kant's favourite example of the way in which the categorical imperative is to be applied; it is to be found in the *Grundlegung zur Metaphysik der Sitten* (IV, 722) as well as in the *Critique of Practical Reason*. If a person has been entrusted with some possession, without giving a receipt or any other acknowledgement, is it right for him to keep it for himself? Kant answers: "No!" For, he says, if the contrary maxim were to become a universal law, then no one would entrust anything to anyone without a receipt. In this case, Kant says, the law could not be put into effect since there would be no instances to which it applied, and therefore it would nullify itself.

It is easy to see that Kant's reasoning is invalid and in fact absurd. If in consequence of a law certain actions cease to be performed, the law *does* exert an influence. It is therefore still effective and it has in no way nullified itself. To see the absurdity of what Kant says, we have only to deal with the following question in an analogous way: "Should I give in to a man who tries to bribe me?" The answer would have to be this: "Yes!" For if the contrary maxim were to become a universal law, then people would no longer attempt bribery. Therefore the law could not be put into effect since there would be no instances to which it applied, and therefore it would nullify itself.

Descartes' Classification of Psychological Phenomena
(Note 21 to page 15)

Descartes writes in the third Meditation: "It is requisite that I should here divide my thoughts (all mental acts) into certain kinds. . . . Of my thoughts some are, so to speak, images of the things, and to these alone is the title 'idea' properly applied; examples are my thought of a man or of a chimera, of heaven, of an angel, or of God. But other thoughts possess other forms as well. For example, in willing, fearing, approving, denying, though I always perceive something as the subject of the action of my mind, yet by this action I always add something else to the idea which I have of that thing; and of the thoughts of this kind some are called *volitions* or *affections*, and others *judgements*."[1]

[1] Nunc autem ordo videtur exigere, ut prius omnes meas cogitationes in certa genera distribuam. . . . Quaedam ex his tanquam

Despite this clear statement, we find Windelband saying that, according to Descartes, to judge is to will.[2] What misled him is Descartes' treatment, in the fourth Meditation, of the influence of the will in the formation of our judgements. Scholastic philosophers—Suarez, for example—were already attributing too much to this influence, and Descartes himself exaggerates it to the point of considering every judgement, even those which are evident, as the product of an act of will. But it is one thing to *produce* the judgement and quite another thing to *be* that judgement. The view that judgement is a product of the act of will does appear in the passage cited above, and it is probably what led Descartes to assign judgement to the third place in his classification of psychological phenomena. And yet he can add, quite consistently, concerning such phenomena, "Some are called volitions and *others* are called judgements".

There are two passages in Descartes' later writings which are more likely to lead us astray. One of these appeared in the *Principles of Philosophy* (Part I, Principle 32), written three years after the *Meditations*, and the other three years after that, in the *Notae in Programma*.[3] It is strange that Windelband did not appeal to the passage from the *Principles*, instead of to the one in the *Meditations*, for the former could easily lead one to suppose that Descartes had changed his views. The passage reads: "All the modes of thinking that we observed in ourselves may be related to two general modes, the one of which consists in perception, or in the operation of the understanding, and the other in volition,

[2] *Strassburger Abhandlungen zur Philosophie* (1884), p. 171.

[3] "Notes directed against a Certain Programme, published in Belgium at the end of the year 1647, under the title 'An Explanation of the Human Mind or Rational Soul: What it is and What it May be'."

---

rerum imagines sunt, quibus solis proprie convenit ideae nomen, ut cum hominem, vel chimaeram, vel coelum, vel angelum, vel Deum cogito; aliae vero alias quasdam practerea formas habent, ut cum volo, cum timeo, cum affirmo, cum nego, semper quiden aliquam rem ut subjectum meae cogitationis apprehendo, sed aliquid etiam amplius quam istius rei similitudinem cogitatione complector; et ex his aliae voluntates sive affectus, aliae autem judicia appellantur. [English trans. from the *Philosophical Works of Descartes*, trans. E. S. Haldane and G. R. T. Ross, Vol. I, p. 159.]

or the operation of the will. Thus sense-perception, imagining, and conceiving things that are purely intelligible, are just different modes of perceiving; but desiring, holding in aversion, affirming, denying, doubting, all these are the different modes of willing."[4]

This passage, which could easily be taken to conflict with what Descartes says in the third Meditation, may tempt one to suppose that he has abandoned his threefold classification, thus giving up Scylla for Charybdis. Has he avoided the older mistake of confusing judgement and idea only now to confuse judgement and will? A closer examination will show that this is not the proper interpretation and that Descartes has made no such mistake. Let us note the following points. (1) There is not the slightest indication that Descartes was ever aware of abandoning the views he had expressed in the third Meditation. (2) Moreover, in 1647—three years after the publication of the *Meditations* and shortly before the conception of *Notae in Programma*— Descartes published his revised translation of the *Meditations*, and he made no change whatever in the crucial passage in the third Meditation.[5] (3) In the *Principles* (Part I, Principle 42), just after the passage we have cited, he says that all our errors depend upon the will, but far from saying that our errors are themselves acts of will, he says that there is no one who would err voluntarily ("there is no one who expressly desires to err"). And there is an even more decisive indication of the fact that he views our judgements not as inner acts of will comparable to our desires and aversions, but as only the effects of the acts of will. For he immediately adds: "There is a great deal of difference between willing to be deceived and willing to give one's assent

[4] Ordines modi cogitandi, quos in nobis experimur, ad duos generales referri possunt: Quorum unus est perceptio sive operatio intellectus; alius vero volitio sive operatio voluntatis. Nam sentire, imaginari et pure intelligere, sunt tantum diversi modi percipiendi; ut et cupere, aversari, affirmare, negare, dubitare sunt diversi modi volendi. [Trans. Haldane and Ross, Vol. I, p. 232.]

[5] Entre mes pensées quelques-unes sont comme les images des choses, et c'est à celles-là seules que convient proprement le nom d'idée; ... D'autres, outre cela, ont quelques autres formes; ... et de ce genre de pensées, les unes sont appelées volontés ou affections, et les autres jugements.

to opinions in which error is sometimes found." He says of will, not that *it* affirms or assents, in the way in which it desires, but rather that it *wills* assent. Just as he says, not that it is itself true, but that it desires the truth ("it is the very desire for knowing the truth which causes . . . judgement on things").[6]

There can be no doubt about Descartes' real view; in the respects concerned it did not undergo any change at all. But we do have to explain the fact that he did alter the way in which he expressed his views. I think the solution is clearly as follows. Although he recognized that will and judgement are two fundamentally different types of mental phenomenon, he also saw that they have one feature in common which distinguishes them both from ideas. In the passage from the third Meditation, he notes that both will and judgement *add* something to the ideas on which they are based. And in the fourth Meditation he refers to another common character: the will decides with respect to both—it can initiate and withhold, not only its own acts, but also the acts of judgement. It is this feature which seems to him to be all-important in the first part of the *Principles* (numbers 29 to 42), and thus he contrasts ideas, which he takes to be operations of the understanding ("operationes intellectus"), with both judgement and will, which he takes to be operations of the will ("operationes voluntatis"). In the *Notae in Programma*, he again describes the acts of both judgement and will as being determinations of the will. "When I saw that over and above perception, which is required as a basis for judgement, there must needs be affirmation, or negation, to constitute the form of the judgement, and that *it is frequently open to us to withhold our assent*, even if we perceive a thing, I referred the act of judging which consists in nothing but assent, i.e., affirmation or negation, not to the perception of the understanding, but to the determination of the will."[7] Indeed, he does not hesitate to say in the *Principles* that both

---

[6] Nemo est que velit falli . . . Sed longe aliud est velle falli, quam velle assentiri iis, in quibus contingit errorem reperiri . . . Veritatis assequendae cupiditas . . . efficit, ut . . . judicium ferant. [Trans. Haldane and Ross, Vol. I, pp. 235-6.]

[7] Ego enim, cum viderem, praeter perceptionem, quae praerequiritur ut judicemus, opus esse affirmatione vel negatione ad formam judicii constituendam, nobisque saepe esse liberum ut cohibeamus assensionem; etiamsi rem percipiamus, ipsum actum judicandi, qui non

of these "modes of thinking" are "modes of willing", but from the context it is clear that he wishes only to say that both fall within the *domain* of the will.

We find additional support for this explanation if we consider the scholastic terminology with which Descartes had been familiar in his youth. It was customary to designate as *actus voluntatis* not only the motion of the will itself, but also anything performed under the control of the will. Hence there were said to be two kinds of acts of will—*actus elicitus voluntatis*, the acts of the will itself, and *actus imperatus voluntatis*, the acts that are performed under the control of the will. In the same way Descartes includes under one category both the *actus elicitus* of the will and what, according to him, can only be an *actus imperatus* of the will. But his classification must not be taken to imply that the intentional relation is the same in the two cases.

This explanation is clear enough if we consider all sides of the matter; yet we find Spinoza anticipating Windelband's misconception of the Cartesian doctrine. (It is more likely that Spinoza was misled by the passage in the *Principles* than by the one which Windelband cites from the *Meditations*.) In Proposition 49 of the Second Book of the *Ethics*, Spinoza himself interprets affirmation and negation as being, in the strictest sense, "volitions of the mind" ("volitiones mentis"), and then, as a result of still further confusion, he abolishes the distinction between the class of ideas and that of acts of will. The thesis now reads, "Will and understanding are one and the same",[8] so that the three-fold classification of Descartes and the twofold classification of Aristotle are both discarded altogether. Here, as usual, Spinoza has served only to corrupt the doctrines of his great teacher.

In Defence of a Theory of Judgement
(Note 22 to page 15)

All states of consciousness fall into one or the other of three groups: (i) merely contemplating something, having the thing

[8] Voluntas et intellectus unum et idem sunt.

---

nisi in assensu, hoc est in affirmatione vel negatione consistit, non rettuli ad perceptionem intellectus sed ad determinationem voluntatis. [English trans. from Haldane and Ross, Vol. I, p. 446.]

before the mind [*Vorstellen*]; (ii) judging [*Urteilen*]; and (iii) feeling or having an emotion [*Gemütstätigkeiten*]. I do not wish to claim, however, that there is now general agreement on this point. After all, if we had to wait for universal agreement, we could not even be sure of the law of contradiction; and in the present case there are some old prejudices that are not easily given up. Nevertheless no one has found it possible to bring forward a single serious objection to this conception of psychological phenomena, and this fact itself is a significant confirmation.

There are some—for example Windelband—who concede that judging and mere having before the mind should not be thought of as constituting one and the same type of phenomenon, but who do contend that judging and the feelings of emotions should be classified together. They make the mistake that Hume made in his discussion of belief. The act of affirming is taken to be an instance of approval, or valuing or prizing, on the part of the feelings, and the act of denying is taken to be an instance of disapproval, a rejection on the part of the feelings.

There is some analogy, to be sure, but it is difficult to see how this confusion could be made. There are people who affirm the goodness of God and the wickedness of the devil—the being of Ormuzd and that of Ahriman—with the same degree of conviction, yet they value and prize the being of the one, while feeling nothing but aversion and repulsion towards that of the other. Or again: we love knowledge and we hate error; hence it is entirely proper that we approve those *judgements* which we hold to be correct—and every judgement we make, after all, is one that we hold to be correct. Judging is related to feeling, then, in that we do thus approve of the judgements we make. But why would one confuse the judgement, which we may thus be said to approve, with the activity or feeling which is the approval itself? It is as though a man who loves his wife and child and material possessions came to confuse these objects with the love that he feels for them. Compare again what I have just said [in Note 21] about Windelband's mistake in ascribing such a doctrine to Descartes. One might also compare Sigwart's note about Windelband, parts of which are very much to the point.[1] Perhaps I may be permitted to refer anyone who needs further grounds for

---

[1] Sigwart's *Logik*, 2nd edn., Book I, pp. 156ff.

distinguishing the second and third of these basic types of phenomena to my forthcoming *Deskriptive Psychologie*. This work, which is almost completed, will be a further development, and not just a continuation, of my *Psychologie vom empirischen Standpunkt.**

I have just a few more remarks, in opposition to what Windelband has to say.

(1) He writes, on page 172, that according to me "love and hate" is not an appropriate designation for this third class of psychological phenomena; indeed, he attributes to me a quotation to this effect. But he is entirely mistaken and has made a serious oversight—as he could verify for himself by re-reading Vol. I, page 262, of my *Psychologie*.[2]

(2) On page 178, he says that, according to me, the only classification of judgements which pertains to the act of judging itself is the classification according to *quality*; but this too is a mistake, and one which is entirely unjustified. My own belief is just the contrary; unlike Windelband, I believe that both the distinction between assertoric and apodictic judgements and the distinction between evident and blind judgements pertain to the act of judgement itself, and also that these distinctions are of basic importance. And I could cite still other distinctions—for example, the distinction between simple and compound acts of judgement. For it is not possible to resolve every compound judgement into entirely simple elements. The same can be said of certain compound concepts, as Aristotle saw. What is it to be red? To be coloured red. What is it to be coloured? To have the quality of being coloured. In each case the concept of the genus is contained in that of the specific difference; the separability of the one logical element from the other is thus one-sided. And we find the same situation, I believe, with respect to certain compound judgements. J. S. Mill said that to classify judgements as simple and complex would be like classifying horses as single horses and teams of horses.[3] But he is quite wrong in ridi-

[2] [Second edition, Vol. II, p. 35ff.]
[3] J. S. Mill. *Logic*, Vol. I, Bk. I, Chap. 4, Sec. 3.
* [Editor's note: The *Deskriptive Psychologie* that Brentano here announces exists only in the form of lecture notes. But see Volume II of his *Psychology from an Empirical Standpoint*, as well as his *Vom sinnlichen und noetischen Bewusstsein* (Leipzig: Felix Meiner, 1928).]

culing this traditional classification; for his argument would apply equally well to the distinction between simple and compound concepts.

(3) Still another mistake—which almost everyone has made and which I, too, made in the first volume of the *Psychologie*—is that of supposing that one's "degree of conviction", so-called, is a kind of intensity analogous to the intensity of pleasure and pain. Were Windelband to accuse me of *this* mistake, his accusation would be entirely just. Instead, however, he criticizes me because I say that the so-called intensity of conviction is only analogous to, and not the same as, the variety of intensity experienced in pleasure and pain, and because I say that the (supposed) intensity of conviction and the (real) intensity of feeling are not comparable with respect to magnitude. This is one of the consequences of what Windelband takes to be his improved theory of judgement!

If a man's belief that $2+1 = 3$ had a degree of conviction which was literally an intensity, consider how powerful it would be! And if, as Windelband would have it (p. 186), the belief were a *feeling* in the strict sense of the word, and not merely something bearing a certain analogy to feeling, consider the havoc and violence to which the nervous system would be submitted! Our doctors might well tell us that, for the sake of our health, we should avoid the study of mathematics. (Compare what J. H. Newman has to say about the so-called degree of conviction in *An Essay in Aid of a Grammar of Assent*—an interesting work which has received but little notice in Germany.)

(4) Windelband wonders how I could think that the word "is" has one and the same meaning in such sentences as "There is a God", "There is a human being", "There is a deprivation", "There is a possibility", and "There is something which is true" (p. 183). Referring to my *Von der mannigfachen Bedeutung des Seienden nach Aristoteles*, he finds it odd that anyone who writes on the manifold significance of being should fail to take account of this manifold significance himself (p. 184). I can only say that if Windelband cannot see what my theory of judgement obviously implies in this case, then he has not understood the theory at all. Aristotle, in treating this question, divides being (ὄν) in the sense of being a thing into different categories and into actuality (ὄν ἐνεργείᾳ), and potentiality (ὄν δυνάμει), but it never occurs to

him to do the same with "is" (ἔστιν), which transforms the expression of an idea into that of a judgement, or with what he calls being in the sense of the true (ὂν ὡς ἀληθές). No one would think of making such a distinction unless, like Herbart and so many after him, he had failed to distinguish the concept of being in the sense of the true, and being in the sense of being a thing. (Compare the following discussion of Sigwart's doctrine.)

(5) I have said above that there are simple and compound judgements, and that there are some compound judgements which cannot be resolved without remainder into judgements which are simple. We must consider this fact when we try to reduce to existential form those judgements which have a different linguistic formulation. For it is obvious that only simple judgements—those which are truly unitary—can be so reduced. It goes without saying that this qualification should be made, and therefore I did not mention it in the *Psychologie*. And if the qualification holds generally, it also holds for the categorical forms of traditional logic. The A, E, I, and O statements are interpreted by the formal logician as expressions of judgements which are strictly unitary, and therefore they can be reduced to existential form.[4] But such reduction is not possible when the ambiguity of our language allows us to use a single categorical statement to express a plurality of judgements.[5] An existential formula can be used to express a unitary categorical judgement which is equivalent to the compound judgement, but it cannot adequately express this compound judgement itself.

Windelband should have taken these facts into consideration when, on page 184, he asks whether the statement "The rose is a flower" can be put into existential form. He is quite right in saying that the statement cannot be formulated as "There is no rose which is not a flower", but he is mistaken in thinking that I would disagree. I have never said—in the passage cited or anywhere else—that it *could* be so expressed. "The rose is a flower" cannot be expressed in *this* way, nor can it be expressed in the the way in which Windelband and so many others would have it. For the statement expresses *two* judgements, one of which consists in the acceptance or affirmation of the subject of the judgement—which could be "the rose", in the usual sense of

[4] See my *Psychologie*, Vol. II, pp. 53ff.

[5] See my *Psychologie*, Vol. II, p. 183 and pp. 158ff., esp. pp. 164ff.

this word, or "that which is called a rose", or "that which is understood as a rose". But, as we have remarked above, there are statements of the form "All A are B" which do *not* express any judgement accepting or affirming the subject.

Unfortunately this point has also been overlooked by Land—the only one of my critics who has understood what Windelband has called my "mysterious" suggestions for reforming elementary logic; he has seen their necessary connection with the principle which I have used and he has been able to derive them correctly from this principle.*

Let me call attention finally to a certain curio which Steinthal has recently provided for us, in his *Zeitschrift fur Völkerpsychologie* (Vol. xviii, p. 175). Here I am amazed to read: "Brentano completely separates judgements from ideas and from thinking [!], and classifies judgements, as acts of acceptance or rejection, with love and hate [!!]—a confusion which is instantly dispelled, if one interprets any such judgement [?] as being rather a matter of taking an aesthetic [!] stand or position." Probably Steinthal read only Windelband's review, and did not look at my *Psychologie* itself. But he must have read the review in such a cursory fashion that perhaps he will appreciate my forwarding his lines to Windelband for correction.

On Existential and Negative Judgements
(Note 23 to page 16)

Sigwart has published a monograph, *Die Impersonalien*, attacking Miklosich.[1] Marty wrote a penetrating criticism of the monograph in the *Vierteljahrsschrift für wissenschaftliche Philosophie*; he had previously criticized the relevant portions of Sigwart's

---

[1] Franz Miklosich, *Subjektlose Sätze*, Second Edition (Vienna: Braumüller, 1883). If the reader wishes to acquaint himself with this valuable work, I may suggest that he read the notice of it I prepared for the *Wiener Abendpost*. Through a misunderstanding it was published as a *feuilleton* in the *Wiener Zeitung*, where no one would think of looking for it, and so I include it in the present book.

* See J. P. N. Land, "On a supposed Improvement in Formal Logic", *Abhandlungen der Königl. Niederländischen Akademie der Wissenschaften*, 1876.

*Logik.** Quite unreasonably, Sigwart seems to have been considerably annoyed. "Il se fache", as the French would say, "donc il a tort". Steinthal burns thick clouds of incense on behalf of Sigwart in his *Zeitschrift* (Vol. xviii, pp. 170ff.), and in the foreword to the fourth edition of his own *Ursprung der Sprache* we find him approving what any true friend of the deserving Sigwart can only regret; yet even Steinthal admits that Sigwart's view is mistaken in its essentials. After the high praise with which he begins his review, we end up feeling somewhat disillusioned. Steinthal (pp. 177–180) rejects the grammatical implications of Sigwart's theory; hence the only real achievement Steinthal attributes to the monograph must be its contributions to psychology. But psychology is not the area in which Steinthal's judgement is authoritative. If it were, one would have to be serious even about the following remark: "On hearing the lines 'Da bückt sich's hinunter mit liebendem Blick' (from Schiller's *Taucher*), no one can fail to think of the daughter of the king. It is not she who comes before the mind, however; it is only a subjectless bow or curtsey. And now I feel myself even more with her. According to my [i.e., Steinthal's] psychology, the idea of the king's daughter hovers in the background, but does not enter consciousness." The wise man knows when he has had enough.

I

The limitations of Sigwart's psychological theory become glaringly apparent when he tries to come to terms with the concept "existence". Aristotle realized that this is a concept we acquire through reflection upon the affirmative judgement.[2]

---

[2] The concepts of existence and non-existence are correlatives to the concepts of the truth of (simple) affirmative and negative judgements. The judgement is correlative with that which is judged; the affirmative judgement with that which is judged affirmatively, the negative judgement with that which is judged negatively. So, too, the correctness of the affirmative judgement is correlated with the existence of that which is affirmatively judged, and that of the negative judgement with the non-existence of that which is negatively judged. We may say either that an affirmative judgement is true or

* [Editor's note: See Anton Marty, *Gesammelte Schriften* (Halle: May Niemeyer, 1918), Vol. II, Section 1.]

But Sigwart, like most modern logicians, fails to follow the lead of Aristotle on this point. He does not say that the existent comprises everything of which the affirmative judgement is true. Instead of this, he goes into a lengthy discussion of the concept of being and the existential proposition. But Sigwart is on the wrong track altogether, and his views on these questions—which he sets forth again in the second edition of his *Logik* (pp. 88–95)—do not throw light on anything at all.

"To be", according to Sigwart, expresses a relation (pp. 88, 95). What kind of a relation? At first consideration (p. 92), one might suppose it to be a "relation to me as one who is thinking". But this will not do, for the existential proposition is said to assert precisely the fact that "that which has being exists apart from its relation to me or to any other thinking being". But if the relation in question is not "a relation to me as one who is thinking", what could it be? We do not find out until page 94. Here we are told that the relation is (to be sure, Sigwart adds: "to begin with") an "agreement of the thing thought about with a possible perception"; he also says it is an "identity" (p. 94) of the thing thought about with something "perceivable", or with "something which can be perceived by me" (p. 90, note).

We can see at once that his concept of existence is too narrow. For much of what exists cannot be perceived; for example, a past and a future, an empty space, any kind of deprivation, a possibility, an impossibility, and so on. It is not surprising,

———

that its object is existent; *in both cases we are saying precisely the same thing.* Similarly for saying that a negative judgement is true, and saying that its object is non-existent. We may say that, for every (simple) affirmative judgement, either it or the corresponding negative judgement is true; and we may express precisely the same logical principle by saying that, for every such affirmative judgement, either its object is existent or its object is non-existent.

The assertion of the truth of the judgement, that there is a learned man, is thus correlative to the assertion of the existence of its object, viz., a learned man. The assertion of the truth of the judgement, that no stone is alive, is similarly correlative to the assertion of the non-existence of its object, viz., a living stone. Correlative assertions, here as elsewhere, are inseparable. Compare such correlatives as "*A* is greater than *B*" and "*B* is less than *A*", or "*A* produces *B*" and "*B* is produced by *A*".

therefore, that Sigwart himself makes an effort to widen his concept. But what he does is very difficult for me to understand. First, he seems to say that, in order for a thing to be counted as existing, the thing need not be capable of being perceived by me; it is necessary only that it be capable of being perceived by someone or other. At least this seems to be what he means when, after saying that existence is an agreement between the thing thought about and a possible perception, he goes on to say: "That which exists bears *this relation* not only to me but also to everything else that has being." Surely Sigwart does not mean to say that everything that exists is capable of perceiving everything. Perhaps he means only that everything that exists stands in the relation of existence to every other being, in which case his empty-sounding phrase might be taken to mean that to say something exists is to attribute to it the capacity of acting and being acted upon. (Thus he tells us that "what exists . . . stands in causal relations to the rest of the world", and, in a footnote on page 91, that the existent is that which "can exercise effects upon me and others".) By the time we reach the end, however, there is some ground for supposing that what Sigwart wants to say is something like this: the existent is that which can be perceived or that which can be inferred as capable of being perceived. For he adds that "in consequence [i.e., in consequence of this causal relation] a merely *inferred* existence may be ascribed to that which is *capable of being perceived*".

But it is plain to see that these various assertions are equally unacceptable.

For (1) "to infer the existence of something" does not mean the same as "to infer that it is capable of being perceived". Thus if we were warranted in inferring, say, the existence of atoms and empty spaces, we would not thereby become warranted in inferring that these things could be perceived by us or by any other creature. Or if we were to infer that God exists, but resist the temptation to "enliven" our concept anthropomorphically, we would not therefore suppose that God can be perceived by any of his creatures or even by himself.

(2) Given Sigwart's point of view, it would be self-contradictory for a person to say: "I am convinced that there are many things the existence of which can never be perceived or even inferred by anyone." For he would be saying only: "I am con-

vinced that many of the things which can be perceived, or which can be inferred to be perceivable, can never be perceived or even inferred by anyone." Who could fail to see that Sigwart has left the true concept of existence far behind!

(3) Or did Sigwart, in the passage cited, intend to extend his concept of existence in such a way that what exists could be said to be that which is either capable of being perceived, or that which can be inferred from that which is capable of being perceived, or that which stands in some sort of causal relation to that which is capable of being perceived? If so, we would have to reply that the concept is still too narrow—if such a monstrous determination of the concept of existence requires refutation. Suppose I say, for example: "Perhaps there is an empty space, but this can never be known with certainty." I would be saying that perhaps empty space exists, but I would be denying that it is capable of being perceived, or that it can be inferred from what is capable of being perceived. An empty space (since it is not itself a thing) cannot be related as cause or effect to anything that is capable of being perceived. And so Sigwart's view, once again, would transform a perfectly sensible assertion into one that is utter nonsense.

The extent of Sigwart's error, in his analysis of the concept of existence, may be indicated very simply by the following: no real centaur exists; but a *contemplated* or *thought-about* centaur [*ein vorgestellter Zentaure*] does exist, and indeed it exists as often as I think of it. If there is anyone who fails to see, in this instance, the distinction between the ὂν ὡς ἀληθές (*being* in the sense of the true or of the existing) and the ὂν in the sense of the real (thinghood), I am afraid that he would be unable to appreciate the abundance of other illustrations to which we might also appeal.

But let us also consider the following. According to Sigwart, knowledge of the existence of anything must consist in the knowledge of an agreement between the content of an idea and something else. I do not clearly understand what this something else is, so let us call it simply x. What, now, is required in order to know that one thing is in agreement with another thing? Obviously, a knowledge of everything which is necessary in order for there to be such an agreement. It is necessary, first, that there be the one thing, secondly that there be the other thing, and thirdly that there be a relation of identity holding between them; for that which is not can neither be the same as nor be different from that which is. But the knowledge of the first of these three items is itself already the knowledge of an existence. Hence the knowledge of the other two is no longer required in order for us to have any knowledge of existence; and therefore Sigwart's theory leads to a contradiction. (Compare what is said here with Sigwart's polemic against my *Psychologie*, Book II, Chapter 7, [Vol. I] in his *Die Impersonalien*, pp. 5off., and his *Logik*, 2nd ed., Vol. I, pp. 89ff. See also Marty's polemic against Sigwart in the articles, "Über subjektlose Sätze", in the *Vierteljahrsschrift für wissenschaftliche Philosophie*, Vol. VIII.)*

II

If Sigwart misconceives the nature of judgement in general, then we can hardly expect that he will understand the nature of the negative judgement in particular. And indeed he goes so far astray that he refuses to regard the negative judgement as being a species of judgement on an equal footing alongside the positive or affirmative judgement. No negative judgement is direct, he says; its object is always some other judgement or an attempt to make some other judgement (*Logik*, 2nd edn., Vol. I, p. 150).

With this assertion, Sigwart contradicts certain important psychological theses which I have defended. It seems appropriate, therefore, for me to counter his attack. I wish to show three things. (1) Sigwart's own theory is without adequate foundation. (2) It leads to hopeless confusion: for Sigwart's affirmative

* I had already written my critique of Sigwart's concept of existence when I came across a certain note in his *Logik*, 2nd edn., Vol. I, p. 390. The note does not make it necessary to change anything, but I shall add it here for purposes of comparison. " 'Being' in general", Sigwart says, "cannot be regarded as a true generic concept which applies to particular individuals; conceptually regarded it is only a common name. Since 'being' is for us a relational predicate, it cannot be a common characteristic; if it were, it would have to be shown that the ground of this predicate lies in a determination common to the concept of everything that there is." I am afraid that this passage will no more enlighten my readers about Sigwart's concept of existence than it did me; it may help to show, however, why all my efforts to understand his concept have been in vain.

judgement is negative; his negative judgement—if it *is* a judgement and not merely the lack of a judgement—is positive; and his positive judgement actually involves a negative judgement. Such confusions are compounded. Finally (3) I wish to show the genesis of Sigwart's mistake; Sigwart's detailed discussions make it possible to do this.

(1) The first question that arises in the face of such a novel and outlandish assertion is: What kind of basis does it have? Sigwart emphasizes above all else (p. 150) that a negative judgement would have no meaning unless it were preceded by the thought of the positive attribution of a predicate. But what is this assertion supposed to mean? Unless it is a simple *petitio principii*, it tells us only that a connection of ideas must have preceded the negative judgement. If we suppose for the moment that the latter proposition is true (though I have shown in my *Psychologie* that it is not true), then the thesis in question would still not be established. For Sigwart himself (p. 89n. and elsewhere) realizes that no such "subjective connection of ideas" constitutes a judgement; there must be in addition (he would say) a certain feeling of compulsion.

Sigwart subsequently formulates another argument (p. 151), but I find it equally difficult to follow. He notes, quite correctly, that there are countless predicates which we have the right to deny of any given thing; and he adds, equally correctly, that we do not in fact make all of these negative judgements. But now —what are we to infer from these premises? That the fact that a given negative judgement is justified is not itself sufficient to account for the fact that the judgement is made? This, of course, we may admit without pause. But what Sigwart infers is quite different. A necessary condition for making a negative judgement, he says, is that we first attempt to make the corresponding positive judgement; hence if we do not make the attempt at the positive judgement, we do not make the negative judgement. This is a bold leap indeed, which *my* logic, at least, is unable to follow. What if we were now to ask, "And why is it that all the corresponding positive judgements are not attempted?" Sigwart's examples ("This stone reads, writes, sings, composes verses", "Justice is blue, green, heptagonal, moves in circles") would require the following answer: the reason that we do not attempt the positive judgement is that we have already made the negative judgement, and found it to be evident and certain. This is what would best explain why there is no "danger" of "anyone wanting to attribute such predicates to the stone or to justice". Another acceptable explanation of why we do not attempt all the relevant positive judgements would be that our consciousness, after all, has its limitations. But if this is Sigwart's line, why didn't he appeal directly to this fact earlier in his discussion? He says himself that there is an "unlimited number" of possible negative judgements.

Sigwart makes still another curious mistake (as Marty has already noted). Affirmative judgements, he says, differ from negative judgements in that "only a finite number of predicates can be affirmed of any subject". How so? Aren't we justified in saying, for example, that a whole hour is greater than a half an hour, greater than a third of an hour, greater than a fourth of an hour, and so on, *ad infinitum*? If now I do not in fact make each one of these judgements, there must be a good reason. After all, the limitations of consciousness would hardly permit it. But these same considerations may be applied equally well to negative judgements.

We find a third argument somewhat later on. We may treat it briefly here, for I have already refuted it in my *Psychologie* (Book II, Chapter 7, Section 5). Sigwart reasons as follows (p. 155f.): suppose the negative judgement is direct and, as a species of judgement, co-ordinate with the affirmative judgement; then, if the affirmation of the subject is involved in an affirmative categorical proposition, it follows that the denial of the subject is involved in a negative categorical proposition; but it is not. The latter observation is correct. (The denial of the subject need not be involved in the affirmation of a negative proposition.) But the observation that precedes it (viz., if one thinks that the affirmation of the subject is involved in an affirmative categorical proposition, one should also think that the denial of the subject is involved in a negative proposition) is entirely untenable and, indeed, self-contradictory. Precisely because of the fact that the existence of a whole involves the existence of each of its parts, all that is needed, if a given whole is *not* to exist, is that at least one of its parts be lacking.

There is, finally, a linguistic consideration which Sigwart believes will confirm his view. He says that we symbolize a negative judgement by adding a certain complication to the way in which we symbolize an affirmative judgement; we add the word "not" to the copula. To evaluate this, let us for a moment consider the emotions. Sigwart agrees with me, and with everyone else, that pleasures and displeasure, rejoicing and sorrowing, loving and hating, and the like are co-ordinate with each other. Yet we have a large group of expressions which are such that the names for feelings of disinclination are dependent upon the names for feelings of inclination. Thus we have: "inclination" and "disinclination"; "pleasure" and "displeasure"; "fortunate" and "unfortunate"; "happy" and "unhappy"; "agreeable" and "disagreeable"; and (in German) *"lieb"* and *"unlieb"*, *"schön"* and *"unschön"*, and even *"ungut"*. I believe that the psychologist will not find this fact difficult to explain, despite the fact that we have here two co-ordinate species of emotive phenomena. But if this is so, why should there be a difficulty in reconciling the corresponding fact, about the way in which negative judgements are expressed, with the fact that there are two co-ordinate species of intellectual phenomena?

If a thinker of Sigwart's calibre must take refuge in this type of argument to defend an important and unorthodox doctrine, then his case must be very poor indeed!

(2) There is no tenable basis, then, for Sigwart's theory of the negative judgement. And this is as it should be. One should not expect to be able to demonstrate a theory which seems to plunge everything into the greatest possible confusion.

Sigwart now finds himself compelled to distinguish a *positive* judgement and an *affirmative* judgement. And he goes on to say (this new terminology is dumbfounding!) that the *affirmative* judgement is, strictly speaking, a negative judgement! In his own words: "The original and primordial judgement should not be called affirmative; it would be better to say that it is a positive judgement. The simple assertion, that *A* is *B*, should be called *affirmative* only in opposition to a negative judgement and only *insofar* as it may be said to *reject* the possibility of a negation (p. 150)." Insofar as it "rejects"? What can this mean other than "insofar as it *denies*"? And so it really is true that, given this strange new use of words, only denials are to be called affirmations! But all this—especially if one is also going to say that the assertion, *A* is *B*, is sometimes such a denial (compare the words cited above)—multiplies linguistic confusion beyond necessity and beyond endurance.

Not only does the affirmative judgement turn out to be strictly negative, on Sigwart's account; we also find, paradoxical as it may seem, that his *negative* judgement, when closely examined, is a *positive* judgement. He does protest against the view of Hobbes and others, according to which negative judgements are really positive judgements with negative predicates. On *his* view, however, they have to be positive judgements with positive predicates; for he says that the subject of a negative judgement is always a judgement and that its predicate is the concept "invalid". Thus he says (p. 160n.) that negation serves to cancel out a supposition and to reject it as invalid (*spreche ihr die Gültigkeit ab*); these words would suggest that Sigwart does suppose that there is a special function of rejecting which is contrary to that of affirming. But no; according to him (see p. 153) there is no such thing as a negative copula. How on earth are we to interpret his "rejection", then? Could it be the simple "cessation" of the positive judgement about the corresponding subject-matter—and thus (on Sigwart's view) the disappearance of the feeling of compulsion which had previously existed along with a joining of concepts? This could not possibly be; for if the feeling of compulsion disappears, then, on Sigwart's view, there remains only a joining of ideas without any affirmation or negation. Consider how often it happens that something previously certain becomes uncertain—without our therefore rejecting or denying it. What is it, then, to reject or deny? Could we say that just as, for Sigwart, affirmation is a feeling of being compelled to posit, denial or negation is a feeling of being compelled to cancel out? In this case we should have to say that, whenever we make a negative judgement, we have found ourselves frustrated in a previous attempt to make the corresponding positive judgement. But he who finds simply that there is no ground for the positive judgement is in a similar state of mind; whoever could bring himself to believe a proposition he holds to be totally groundless? Certainly, such an attempt would be inconceivable on Sigwart's own definition of judgement; it would always end in failure. And so we have not yet been able to get the negative judgement clearly before us. If there is no negative copula, then rejection or denial would have to be a matter of attributing the predicate "false" to something, or, in Sigwart's terms, a matter of inserting this predicate into a judgement having the judgement in question as its subject. But this "false" cannot be said simply to mean the same as "not true". For we can say of countless things that they are "not true", where it would hardly be appropriate to say of them that they are "false". If judgements are the only things that can be said to be true, then "not true" applies to everything that is not a judgement; but "false" does not at all apply to everything that is not a judgement. Thus "false" must be conceived as a positive predicate. Hence, given Sigwart's point of view, which is inherently wrong, just as we must say that negation or denial is something other than mere failure to be convinced, we must say that every negative judgement is a positive judgement with a positive predicate. And thus we have a paradox which is even more striking than the first one we encountered.

But there is a third paradox, which serves to make the confusion complete. If we consider the way in which Sigwart conceives the nature of judgement in general, we can easily see that his simple positive judgement involves, again, a negative judgement. According to him, every judgement involves, not only a certain connection of ideas, but also a consciousness of the necessity of our putting them together and of the impossibility of the opposite (see in particular p. 102), and, indeed, it involves the consciousness of such a necessity and impossibility for every thinking being (pp. 102, 107)—which, incidentally, is just as much mistaken as is Sigwart's whole concept of the nature of judgement. Because of this characteristic, then, Sigwart says that *every* judgement without exception is apodictic; there is no valid distinction, according to him (see pp. 229ff.), between assertoric and apodictic judgements. I would ask, therefore: Do we not have here that which obviously involves a negative judgement? Otherwise what sense could we give to Sigwart's "consciousness of the impossibility of the opposite"? And there is still more! I have already shown in my *Psychologie* [Bk. II, Chap. VII (p. 59 in Vol. II)] that every universal judgement is negative; for to be convinced of universality is no more nor less than to be convinced that there is no exception. Without this latter negation, no accumulation of positive assertions, however extensive, would be sufficient to constitute a belief in universality. Hence when Sigwart says that every judgement involves the awareness that such-and-such a way of thinking must be universal, we have additional confirmation for our contention that, according to Sigwart's theory of judgement, even the simplest positive judgement has to involve a negative judgement. Are we really supposed to believe, then, that the negative judgement shows up relatively late (as we are told on pp. 159ff.) and that, on the basis of these and other considerations, the negative judgement should be thought unworthy of being placed on an equal footing with the positive judgement as being an independent species of judgement? The more one considers Sigwart's views the clearer it becomes that they do involve the implications developed here; surely Sigwart would never have maintained such things had he thought them through. There are passages, of course, in which he contradicts one or another of these theses which I have shown his views to imply. But what else are we to expect when everything is in such great confusion and when the attempt to clear up things serves only to uncover a multiplicity of contradictions?

(3) We have, then, a highly respected logician, misconceiving the nature of judgement and then becoming entangled in hopeless confusion with respect to a relatively simple question. What is the origin of the error? The *proton pseudos* consists of a mistake which has been handed down from the older logic; it is the mistake of supposing that a relation between two ideas is a part of the essence of a judgement. Aristotle had described the relation as being one of combining or separating (σύνθεσις καὶ διαίρεσις); he realized, however, that the terminology is not entirely appropriate, and he noted that there is a sense in which both relations could be said to be a matter of combining (σύνθεσις); see *De Anima*, Bk. III, chap. 6. Scholastic logic and modern logic have retained the two terms "combining" and "separating", but in grammar both relations are called "combining" and the symbol for combining is called the "copula". Now Sigwart takes these expressions "combining" and "separating" literally. Hence a negative copula appears to him to be a contradiction (see p. 153); and the negative judgement is said to presuppose a positive judgement. For how can we separate any two things unless they have first been combined? Thus we find that, according to Sigwart (p. 150 and the passages cited above), it makes no sense to speak of a negative judgement which does not presuppose a positive judgement. The consequence is that

all the efforts of this distinguished thinker turn out to be in vain; the negative judgement is no longer even comprehensible.

There is a note, beginning on p. 150, in which Sigwart tells us what finally confirmed him in his endeavours. What we have here is a remarkable description of the process by means of which we are supposed to arrive at the negative judgement. The attentive reader will be able to see the whole series of errors in succession, and he will find that the negative judgement is actually presupposed long before the point at which it is finally supposed to emerge.

Sigwart proceeds from the correct observation that our first judgements are all positive. These judgements are evident and made with complete confidence. "But now", he says, "our thought goes out beyond the given; as a result of recollections and associations, other judgements are formed, also with the thought that they express what is real." (This means that the ideas are connected with a consciousness of objective validity, this being of the essence of judgement, according to Sigwart; sect. 14, p. 98.) These other judgements, he continues, might be exemplified by our "expecting to find some familiar thing in its usual place, or our assumption that we will be able to smell a certain flower. But now some part of what we thus suppose comes into *conflict* with what it is that we immediately know". (Sigwart does not attempt to show how we are able to recognize that something "conflicts" with what we know, if we are not yet able to make negative judgements and are not in possession of negative concepts. The difficulty becomes even more apparent as he continues.) "In such cases, when we do *not find* what we had expected, we become aware of the *difference* between what is *merely* thought about and what is real." (What does "not find" mean here? The phrase is one which, prior to this point, is not to be found. Clearly what I find, in the cases in question, is that something which I had expected to be accompanied by something else is in fact *without* that something else; but this is possible only to the extent that I am able to affirm the one and deny the other—i.e., affirm that the other does *not* accompany the one. And how are we to interpret the term "difference"? To be aware of a difference is to be aware, with respect to two things, that one of them is *not* the other. And, finally, what is the meaning of the phrase "*merely* thought about"? Clearly: something which is thought about but which is *not* at the same time real. Sigwart does not seem to realize that he has already allowed the negative judgement to come into play). He continues: "What we are immediately certain of is something *other* than that which we had expected." (Something other—i.e., something which is *not* the same, something which cannot possibly be the same.) "And now" (because of the fact that we have already made so many negative judgements) "negation finally enters into the picture, cancelling out the assumption in question and rejecting it as invalid. With this we have something *entirely new*; the subjective combination is separated from the consciousness of certainty. This subjective combination is contrasted with one that is certain and we recognize the difference between them; out of this the concept of invalidity arises." The final sentence would seem to result from sheer carelessness of expression. If the word "invalid" is to mean *false*, and not merely *uncertain*, then the concept of invalidity cannot be acquired by comparing a combination of ideas which is uncertain; what we need is a contrast between a combination which has been accepted and one which has been rejected. But actually the conflicting affirmative judgement is not at all required. The conflict—the incompatibility of certain characteristics—is already apparent from the relation between the concepts of the conflicting characteristics. Even Sigwart himself, if I may be permitted to repeat it, is aware that his conflict cannot be grasped by any attempt at a positive judgement (see p. 89n. and pp. 98ff.). It may well be that we often make negative judgements as a result of having first made the opposing positive judgement, but this is by no means the way in which *every* negative judgement comes about. Suppose, for example, I am asked: "Is there a regular figure with a thousand angles and a thousand and one sides?" It will have occurred to me previously, as may be the case with most people, that I cannot be at all sure that there is such a thing as a regular figure with a thousand angles. Hence I may make the negative judgement, on the basis of a conflict of characteristics, that there is no such figure—*without* having previously made an attempt at a positive judgement. It is not at all necessary, as Sigwart thinks it is, that I must first make a "confident assumption" that there is a regular figure with a thousand angles and a thousand and one sides.

The application of negation or denial is by no means restricted in the way in which Sigwart says it is. Sigwart betrays the fact that he realizes this too (see, e.g., p. 152 and even p. 150), despite his insistence that there can be no negative copula which performs a function of judgement on the same footing as affirmation or acceptance. It is false that, whenever a thing is denied, what it is that is denied is always the property "valid". Even in the case of a judgement, we can deny not only its validity, but also, among other things, its certainty, or its being *a priori*. The subject of the judgement may be treated in a similar way. One can deny certainty or validity of a judgement; one can deny modesty of a request; and, more generally, one can deny, of any *A*, a *B*. Sigwart himself makes such denials, just as everyone else does. Indeed, he often speaks with far more correctness than his theory would allow, thus instinctively bearing witness to the truth. According to his theory, the only thing that can be denied is validity, and this can only be denied of judgement; but he tells us, on p. 151 for example, that "of any subject, an *unlimited number of predicates* may be denied". This is certainly correct, and it is precisely for this reason that we are justified in retaining the ancient doctrine that there are two co-ordinate species of judgement.

On the Concepts of Truth and Existence
(Note 25 to page 18)

We use the expressions "true" and "false" in a number of quite different ways. Taking them in their strict and proper sense, we speak of true and false *judgements*; then (modifying the meanings somewhat) we also speak of true and false *things*, as when we speak of "a true friend" or "false gold." It is hardly necessary to observe that when I spoke in the lecture of *things* being true or false, I was using the terms in their derivative sense and not in their strict and proper sense. In this derivative use, we may say that the true is that which is, and the false that which is not. Just as Aristotle spoke of "ὄν ὡς ἀληθές," i.e., a being in the sense of the true, we might thus speak of a "ἀληθὲς ὡς ὄν," i.e., a true in the sense of a being.

It is often said that truth, in its strict sense, consists in a correspondence between a judgement and its object (in an *adequatio rei et intellectus*, as the scholastics had put it). This dictum is right in a certain sense, but it is easily misunderstood and has in fact led to serious errors. Some have taken the correspondence to be a kind of *identity* which holds between something in the judgement, or in the thought or idea at the base of the judgement, and something to be found outside the mind. But this cannot be the meaning of "to correspond" in the present context. It means rather "to be appropriate," "to be in harmony with", "to suit", "to be fitting to".

One could propose a similar view about the correctness of the emotions. In other words, one could say that the correctness of emotion also consists in a kind of correspondence between the emotion and its object. And this would also be right, if it were not misinterpreted. One loves or hates correctly provided that one's feelings are adequate to their object—adequate in the sense of being appropriate, suitable, or fitting. But it would be manifestly absurd to say that the correctness of love and hate consists in a kind of *identity* that holds between these feelings, or in the thought or idea on which they are based, and something lying outside the feelings; and it would be equally absurd to say that when such feelings are incorrect it is because of the absence of such identity. This misconception of the notion of adequacy or correspondence, along with a number of other errors, has brought the theory of judgement to the present unhappy state from which psychologists and logicians are trying so hard to free it.

The concepts of *existence* and *non-existence*, respectively, are correlates of the concepts of the truth of the (unitary) affirmative judgement and the truth of the (unitary) negative judgement. Judgement is correlated with what is judged, the affirmative judgement with what is judged affirmatively, the negative judgement with what is judged negatively; so, too, the correctness of the affirmative judgement is correlated with the *existence* of what is judged, and the correctness of the negative judgement is correlated with the *non-existence* of what is judged. To say that an affirmative judgement is true is to say no more nor less than that its object is existent; to say that a negative judgement is true is to say no more nor less than that its object is non-existent. It is one and the same logical principle that tells us, in the one case, that either the simple affirmative judgement or the simple negative judgement is true, and in the other case, that the object of the judgement is either existent or non-existent.

Thus, for example, the assertion of the truth of the judgement, "Some man is learned", is the correlate of the assertion of the existence of its object—namely, a learned man. And the correlate of the assertion of the truth of the judgement, "No stone is alive", is the assertion of the non-existence of its object—i.e., the non-existence of a living stone. Here, as elsewhere, correlative assertions are inseparable. The judgement "A is greater than B" and "B is smaller than A" are related in the same way, as are the judgements "A causes B" and "B is the effect of A".*

On the Unity of the Concept of the Good
(Note 26 to page 18)

The concept of what is good in itself is thus univocal in the strict sense and not, as Aristotle taught, univocal only in an analogous sense. (Aristotle had been the victim of a confusion of which we shall speak later). German philosophers—for example, Kant, and more recently, Windelband—have also failed to grasp the unity of the concept. There is a defect in ordinary German that is likely to be misleading: We have no single expression to serve as the contrary of *"gut"*. We must appeal to a variety of terms—for example, *"übel"* (evil), *"böse"* (wicked), *"arg"* (ill),

* [Editor's note: Brentano's later conception of truth is quite different. The thought that true judgements are correlated with "the existence of objects" and with "the non-existence of objects" is dropped altogether. He came to hold that the expressions "the existence of such-and-such" and "the non-existence of such-and-such" are only synsemantic and do not refer to anything at all. His later view is substantially this: an affirmative judgement is true provided its object is such that anyone who judged about it with evidence would accept or affirm it; and a negative judgement is true provided its object is such that anyone who judged about it with evidence would reject or deny it. For further details, see Brentano's *Wahrheit und Evidenz* (Hamburg: Felix Meiner, 1958), ed. Oskar Kraus; English translation, *The True and the Evident* (London: Routledge & Kegan Paul, 1966), ed., Roderick M. Chisholm. On the concept of a "unitary" [*einheitlich*] judgement, see Brentano's addendum to the second part of "Miklosich on Subjectless Propositions", below.]

"*schlimm*" (annoying), "*abscheulich*" (loathsome), "*schlecht*" (bad), and the like. And thus one is misled into thinking that, as is so often the case, the absence of a single term for the contrary of a concept indicates that the concept is not univocal. If there is no common concept for those things that are the opposite of what can be called "good", then one may wonder whether "good" is equivocal.

Of the various expressions I have mentioned, it seems to me that "*schlecht*" (bad), like the Latin "*malum*", is the one that is most generally applicable to designate the contrary of what is good (philologists whom I have consulted are of the same opinion), and I shall use it therefore as the contrary of "*gut*".

I have said that particular instances of the intentional relation of love and of hate all have something in common. This does not mean, however, that there are no *subspecies* of these relations. Thus even if "*schlecht*" (bad) is a truly general concept, applicable to anything that is the contrary of what is good, there may yet be subspecies within the general domain to which it applies, of which the one may suitably be called "*böse*" (wicked), another "*übel*" (evil), and so on.*

On the Evident
(Note 27 to page 20)

The distinction between judgements which are evident and judgements which are blind is much too striking to have escaped notice altogether. Even the sceptical Hume is far from denying the distinction. According to what he says in the *Enquiry Concerning Human Understanding* (Section IV), the *evident* comprises analytic judgements (which are supposed to include the axioms and proofs of mathematics) and certain impressions; but these

---

* [Editor's note: According to Brentano's later view, such terms as "good" and "bad", like "true" and "false", are synsemantic and have no independent meaning. The point, expressed above, that "good" is a univocal term could be put, in accordance with the later view, by saying: the term "good" performs a uniform function in discourse; sentences in which "good" is ostensibly predicated of some thing all serve to indicate that any correct emotion that is directed upon the thing must be positive. See Brentano's *The True and the Evident*.]

latter do not include the so-called inferences from experience. Inferences from experience, according to Hume, are not the effects of reason, but the effects of a habit or custom which is entirely unreasonable; such beliefs are instinctive and mechanical. (See Section V.)

It is one thing, however, to take note of a fact, and another thing to provide a clear and distinct account of its nature. Given that the nature of judgement has been almost universally misconceived until very recent times, it is hardly to be expected that the nature of the evident would be properly understood. Even Descartes' usual discernment fails him here. He was very much concerned with the problem, however, as we may see from the following passage taken from the third of his Meditations: "When I say that I am so instructed by nature [he is referring to so-called external perception], I mean merely a certain *spontaneous inclination* which impels me to believe in this connection, and not a *natural light* which makes me recognize that it is true. But these two things are very different. For I cannot doubt that which the *natural light* causes me to believe to be true; as for example, it has shown me that I *am* from the fact that I doubt, or other facts of the same kind. And I possess no other faculty whereby to distinguish truth from falsehood, which can teach me that what this light shows me to be true is not really true, and no other faculty that is equally trustworthy. But as far as neutral impulses are concerned, I have frequently remarked, when I had to make active choice between virtue and vice, that they often led me to the part that was worse; and this is why I do not see any reason for following them in what regards truth and error."[1]

---

[1] Cum hic dico me ita doctum esse a natura intelligo tantum spontaneo quodam impetu me ferri ad hoc credendum, non lumine aliquo naturali mihi ostendi esse verum, quae duo multum discrepant. Nam quaecunque lumine naturali mihi ostenduntur (ut quod ex eo quod dubitem sequatur me esse, et similia) nullo modo dubia esse possunt, quia nulla alia facultas esse potest, cui aeque fidam ac lumini isti, quaeque illa non vera esse possit docere: sed quantum ad impetus naturales jam saepe olim judicavi me ab illis in deteriorem partem fuisse impulsum cum de bono eligendo ageretur, nec video cur iisdem in ulla alia re magis fidam. [English translation from the *Philosophical Works of Descartes*, trans. E. S. Haldane and G. R. T. Ross, Vol. I, pp. 160–1.]

We certainly cannot conclude from this passage that the concept of the evident escaped Descartes or that he failed to take note of the distinction between an insight (*Einsicht*) and a judgement which is blind. Yet, despite the fact that he took care to distinguish the class of judgements from that of ideas, he misplaces the distinguishing characteristic, evidence, which pertains always to the insightful judgement, and classifies it with ideas instead of with judgements. That form of perception which he called the *idea*—the presentation, that which is before the mind—is the basis of the judgement, and Descartes assumes that the idea is that which is evident. He even goes so far as to call this idea a "cognoscere"—an instance of knowing. A matter of knowing something and yet not a judgement! One might say that what we have here are vestigial organs in the development of psychology. After the great advances which Descartes himself made in the theory of judgement, they survive to remind us of a stage long since past. There is one point, however, with respect to which this phenomenon is to be distinguished from similar phenomena in the evolution of species. In the present case, the vestigial organs, not having adapted themselves to the stages that follow, become highly troublesome, with the result that Descartes' additional efforts on behalf of the theory of knowledge turn out to be in vain. To quote Leibniz, Descartes remains in the "antechamber of truth". It is only from this point of view that we are able to understand the peculiar hybrid character of Descartes' *clara et distincta perceptio*, of which it is so difficult to obtain a clear and distinct idea. If we are to find that which distinguishes insights from all other judgements, we must look for it in the inner peculiarities of the *act of insight* itself.

To be sure, there are those who have looked in the right place without having found what they were looking for. We have seen how Sigwart misconceives the nature of judgement. Judgement, according to him (*Logik*, sections 14 and 31, esp. 4 and 5), involves a relation between ideas and also a feeling of compulsion, or an irresistible impulse, which pertains to the ideas. This feeling, according to him, is to be found even in connection with the most blind of prejudices. In such cases it is not normative, but (Sigwart says explicitly) it is taken to be normative and universal. How do these cases differ, then, from insights? Sigwart says (in *op. cit.*, section 3, for example) that the evident character of a genuine insight is constituted by such a feeling. But the feeling which pertains to the insight is not merely one that is *taken* to be normative and universal; it must be one that *is* normative and universal.

The untenability of this theory seems to me to be obvious; there are many reasons for not accepting it.

(1) The peculiar nature of insight—the clarity and evidence of certain judgements which is inseparable from their truth—has little or nothing to do with a feeling of compulsion. It may well be that, at a given moment, I cannot help but judge in the way in which I do judge. But the clarity in question does not consist in any feeling of compulsion; no awareness of a compulsion to judge in a certain way could, as such, guarantee the truth of the judgement. One may reject indeterminism and thus hold that every judgement, given the circumstances under which it is made, is necessary; and yet one may deny, with perfect right, that every such judgement is true.

(2) In trying to locate the consciousness of an insight in the feeling of a compulsion to believe, Sigwart asserts that the consciousness of one's own compulsion is at the same time a consciousness of a similar necessity for every thinker to whom the same grounds are present. If he means that the one conviction is indubitably connected with the other, then he is mistaken. Given that on the basis of certain data one thinker is compelled to make a certain judgement, why should it be that every thinker on the basis of the same data would have a similar compulsion? One may be tempted, in this connection, to appeal to the general causal law according to which, if all the relevant conditions are the same, the effects will also be the same. But this general law is not applicable in the present case. For the relevant causal conditions will include all those psychical dispositions which may not enter directly into consciousness at all but which will exercise their effects upon one's judging; and these dispositions are different for different people. Misled by paralogisms, Hegel and his school have even denied the law of contradiction; and Trendelenburg, who opposes Hegel, has at least restricted its validity (Trendelenburg, *Abhandlungen über Herbarts Metaphysik*). Hence we can no longer say, as Aristotle did, that it is impossible for anyone inwardly to deny the principle—although for Aristotle himself,

to whom the principle was clearly evident, its denial was certainly impossible.

But it is true that anything that is seen to be evident by one person is certain, not only for him, but also for anyone else who sees it in a similar way. Moreover, any judgement which is thus seen by one person to be true is universally valid; its contradictory cannot be seen to be evident by any other person; and anyone who accepts its contradictory is *ipso facto* mistaken. What I am saying here pertains to the nature of truth: anyone who perceives something as true is also able to see that he is justified in regarding it as true for all. But it would be a gross confusion to suppose that this awareness of something being true for everyone implies an awareness of a universal compulsion to believe.*

(3) Sigwart entangles himself in a multiplicity of contradictions. He says—as he must if he is not to give in to scepticism or to abandon his entire logic—that judgements which are evident may be distinguished from judgements which are not, and that we can make the distinction in our own consciousness. Thus the one class of judgements, but not the other, must appear as normative and universal. But he also says that both classes of judgements—those which are evident and those which are not— are made with a consciousness of universal validity. The two types of judgement, therefore, would seem to present themselves in precisely the same way. If this were true, then one could make out the distinction between those of the first kind and those of the second only by further reflection—taking place either at the same time or later than the judgements—during the course of which one would appeal to some *criterion* or other as a kind of measuring rod. There are actually passages in which Sigwart says that there is an awareness of agreement with universal rules and that this awareness accompanies every perfectly evident judgement (cf., e.g., *op. cit.*, 2nd edn., section 39, p. 311). But this is hardly in agreement with our experience—it was possible to reason syllogistically with perfect evidence long before the discovery of the rules of the syllogism. And in any case, we must reject what Sigwart is saying here, for the rule to which he appeals is itself

* [Editor's note: This criticism, and this work in general, make clear that the refutation of so-called "psychologism" goes back to Brentano, and especially to the *Ursprung*.]

something that must be assured; such assurance would require either an infinite regress or a vicious circle.

(4) In his theory of self-consciousness, Sigwart becomes involved in still another contradiction (but one which, it seems to me, he could have avoided even after arriving at his erroneous conceptions of the nature of judgement and of evidence). What is expressed by "I exist" is said to be *merely* evident and to be quite unaccompanied by any feeling of compulsion or of universal necessity. (At any rate, this is the only way I am able to interpret the following passage from his *Logik*, 2nd edn., Vol. I, p. 310: "The certainty that I exist and that I think is basic and fundamental, the condition of all thought and of all certainty. Here one can speak only of direct evidence; one cannot even say that the thought is necessary, for it is prior to all necessity. Equally direct and evident is the conscious certainty that I think this or that; it is inextricably interwoven with my self-conscious in such a way that the one is give with the other.") Given the doctrines previously considered, this would seem to be a *contradictio in adjecto* and thus incapable of defence.

(5) Still more contradictions are to be found in Sigwart's peculiar and dubious theory of "postulates", which he contrasts with axioms. The certainty of axioms is said to lie in the compulsion we have to think in a certain way. But the certainty of postulates, according to Sigwart, is based upon our practical needs and not upon any purely intellectual motive (*op. cit.*, pp. 412ff.). Thus the law of causality, in his view, is a mere postulate and not an axiom; we take it to be certain because we find that, if we were not to accept it, we would be unable to investigate nature. But consider now the consequences, for Sigwart, of his accepting the law of causality in this way: out of sheer good will, he decrees that like conditions produce like effects; thus he is taking something to be true without any consciousness of being compelled to do so. But to say this is to contradict Sigwart's theory of judgement— unless, of course, taking something to be true is not the same as making a judgement. So far as I can see, Sigwart has only one way out: he ought to say that he does *not* believe any of the postulates, such as that of causation in nature, which he assumes to be "certain". But in such a case, he could no longer be serious.*

* [Editor's note: Brentano's conception of the universal validity of causation is set forth in detail in his *Vom Dasein Gottes* (Leipzig:

(6) The doctrine of postulates becomes even more questionable if we consider it along with what we have discussed under (2) above. The consciousness of a universal necessity to think in a certain way, according to Sigwart, is an axiom and not a postulate. But this universal necessity to think in a given way is obvious to us only if we apply the law of causality to our own compulsion to think in that way. And then the law of causality itself is said to be a mere postulate and hence to be without evidence. The mark of axioms, according to Sigwart, is that they involve a universal compulsion or necessity to believe; hence it is only a postulate that there are such axioms. And therefore what Sigwart calls axioms are deprived of what they must have, according to him, if they are to be distinguished from his postulates. All this accords with Sigwart's remark (*op. cit.*, section 3) that the belief in the reliability of evidence is a "postulate". But given his interpretation of "postulate", I cannot imagine how such a remark is to fit in with the rest of the theory.

(7) Sigwart denies that there is any distinction between assertoric and apodictic judgements (*Logik*, section 31) for, he says, every judgement involves the feeling of necessity. This assertion must also be attributed to his erroneous conception of judgement; he would seem to identify the feeling, which he sometimes calls the feeling of evidence, with the nature of apodicity. But this is to overlook the *modal* characteristic which distinguishes some evident judgements from the evident judgements of self-awareness; the law of contradiction would be an instance of the former, the judgement that I exist an instance of the latter. The former exemplifies what is "necessarily true or necessarily false", the latter what is only "actually true or false". Both are evident, however, and in the same sense of the word, and they do not differ with respect to certainty. It is only from judgements of the former sort, not from those of the latter sort, that we acquire the concepts of impossibility and necessity.*

Despite his polemic against conceiving apodictic judgements as a special class of judgement, Sigwart occasionally bears witness to the contrary view, as is clear from what was discussed under

* [Editor's note: See Appendix I.]

Felix Meiner, 1929), ed. Alfred Kastil, and his *Versuch über die Erkenntnis* (Leipzig: Felix Meiner, 1925), ed. Alfred Kastil.]

(4) above. The knowledge expressed by "I exist", according to him (*op. cit.*, p. 312), is to be contrasted with our knowledge of axioms in that it pertains to a simple factual truth. Here he speaks more soundly than his general theory would allow.

Sigwart's theory of the evident, then, is essentially wrong. Like Descartes, he certainly took note of the phenomenon; and it must be said to his credit that he exercised great zeal in trying to analyze it. But like many others who have been concerned with the analysis of psychological phenomena, he seems not to have stopped at the right place in his eagerness to complete the analysis; the result was that he attempted to reduce one set of phenomena to another set of entirely different phenomena.

Obviously any mistake about the nature of the evident must be full of dire consequences for the logician. We could say that Sigwart's theory of the evident is the basic defect of his logic— were it not for his misconception of the nature of judgement in general. Again and again we find the unhappy results of his theory; an example is his inability to understand the general causes of error. The principal cause, he says in his *Logik* (Vol. I, 2nd edn., p. 103n), is the imperfection of our language; and this, surely, is a one-sided account.

Many other prominent logicians, of recent years, have fared no better than Sigwart with the theory of the evident. The views of the excellent John Stuart Mill—to cite only one example —are discussed in Note 68.

The fact that the nature of the evident is almost universally misunderstood explains why it is that we often hear the expression "more or less evident". Even Descartes and Pascal spoke in this way; but the expression is completely inappropriate. What is evident is certain; and certainty in the strict sense of the term knows no distinctions of degree. In a recent issue of the *Viertel-jahrsschrift für wissenschaftliche Philosophie*, we are even told, in all seriousness, that there are *evident presumptions* which, despite their evidence, may well be *false*. Needless to say, I regard this as nonsense. I regret that my own lectures, given at a time when I took degrees of conviction to be a matter of intensity of judgement, seem to have been the occasion for such confusions.*

* [Editor's note: Brentano is here referring to A. Meinong's "Zur erkenntnistheoretischen Würdigung des Gedächtnis", *Vierteljahrsschrift für wissenschaftliche Philosophie*, Tenth Year (1886), pp. 7–33.]

Ethical Subjectivism
(Note 28 to page 21)

Compare Hume's *Enquiry concerning the Principles of Morals*, which has already been cited. Some philosophers who have attempted to base ethics upon the feelings have shown more insight than Hume. (For example, Beneke and Überweg, who follows him; see the account of Beneke's ethical views in Volume III of Überweg's *Grundriss der Geschichte der Philosophie*.) Herbart comes closer to the truth when he speaks of "evident judgements of taste" and when he contrasts the beautiful with what is merely pleasing, ascribing universal validity and indubitable worth only to the former. (Strictly speaking, however, one should not use the expression "evident judgements of taste". For what we have here are really *feelings* and not *judgements* at all. And feelings, as such, are not evident but only analogous to what is evident.) Unfortunately, Herbart's views are mistaken in other respects, and he soon strays from the proper path, with the result that his practical philosophy is much farther from the truth than that of Hume.

Those who overlook the distinction between pleasure that is experienced as being correct and pleasure that is not so experienced are likely to fall into one or the other of two opposing errors. Thus some speak as though *all* pleasure is experienced as being correct, and others as though *no* pleasure is experienced as being correct. Those who take the latter course abandon altogether the concept of the good as being that which rightly pleases; "worthy of being desired" as distinguished from "capable of being desired" is said to be an expression without sense. But for those who take the former course, the expression "worthy of being desired" does at least remain an independent concept. When they say, "Whatever is capable of being desired for its own sake is something that is worthy of being desired for its own sake, something that is good in itself", they believe that they are not expressing a tautology. And obviously this is something they should say if they are to be consistent, and in fact many did say it. In the middle ages, for example, it was even taught by the great Thomas Aquinas, to whom Ihering has paid fresh tribute. (See for example, the *Summa Theologica*, I, Q. 80 and 82, Art. 2, ad 1, and elsewhere.)

84

But this doctrine cannot be made to fit the facts unless the concepts of good and bad are given an incorrect subjective interpretation, similar to the Protagorean interpretation of the concepts of truth and falsehood. According to such subjectivism within the sphere of judgement, each man is the measure of all things; hence it often happens that what is true for one man is false for another. Analogously, those who hold that only the good can be loved and only the bad can be hated must assume that, within the sphere of the emotions, each man is the measure of all things, of things that are good in themselves, that they are good, and of things that are bad in themselves that they are bad. If this assumption is correct, then it will often happen that one and the same thing is both good and bad in itself; it will be good in itself for those who love it for its own sake, and it will be bad in itself for those who hate it for its own sake. But this is absurd. The subjective falsification of the concept of the good is just as untenable as is the subjective falsification of the concepts of truth and existence which Protagoras defended. But it is much easier to slip into the subjectivistic error in the former case, where we are concerned with what is rightly pleasing or displeasing. The error infects most ethical systems today. Some embrace it openly, as Sigwart has recently done (see the *Vorfragen der Ethik*, p. 6); others fall into it without being clearly conscious of the subjectivistic nature of their views.[1]

[1] Some thinkers teach that each person's knowledge, pleasure, and perfection are the things that are good for him: their opposites are bad for him, and everything else indifferent in itself. Possibly they will object to my counting them among the subjectivists, since it may seem upon superficial consideration that they are advocating a theory of the good that is equally valid for all. But a more careful examination will show that according to this view there is *nothing* that is universally good. Thus my own knowledge would be said to be worthy of *my* love, but it would be said to be intrinsically indifferent for everyone else; and the knowledge that any other person has would be intrinsically indifferent for me. It is especially strange to find that theists often advocate a subjectivistic view of loving and willing in the case of mortals, while assuming that God, and God alone, applies an objective standard and is thus able to estimate each perfection without regard to person. And then they suppose that by setting up God as an objective and eternal judge, they can make their egoistic principles harmless in practice.

As I have said, once one accepts the view that nothing can please except to the extent that it is really good in itself, and nothing can displease except to the extent that it is really bad in itself, one has taken a path which, if followed consistently, can lead only to subjectivism.

In the celebrated controversy between Bossuet and Fenélon, the great Bishop of Meaux advocated what might be called a version of subjectivism. Though Fenélon's moral precepts were neither base nor unchristian, his theses were finally condemned by Rome, but without being declared to be heretical. Indeed, if his teachings were heretical, then so, too, would be the thought underlying those beautiful and inspired lines, sometimes attributed to St. Theresa, which have not only escaped ecclesiastical censure, but have also found their way into many Catholic prayer books, in an inadequate Latin translation. I translate them here directly from the Spanish:

> Nicht Hoffnung auf des Himmels sel'ge Freuden
> Hat Dir, mein Gott, zum Dienste mich verbunden,
> Nicht Furcht, die ich vor ew'gem Graus empfunden,
> Hat mich bewegt, der Sünder Pfad zu meiden.
>
> Du, Herr, bewegst mich, mich bewegt Dein Leiden,
> Dein Anblick in den letzten, bangen Stunden,
> Der Geisseln Wut, Dein Haupt von Dorn umwunden,
> Dein schweres Kreuz und—ach!—Dein bittres Scheiden.
>
> Herr, Du bewegest mich mit solchem Triebe,
> Dass ich Dich liebte, wär' kein Himmel offen,
> Dich fürchtete, wenn auch kein Abgrund schreckte;
> Nichts kannst Du geben, was mir Liebe weckte;
> Denn würd' ich auch nicht, wie ich hoffe, hoffen,
> Ich würde dennoch lieben, wie ich liebe.

[This poem may be paraphrased as follows:

> It is not hopes of heavenly bliss
> That have bound me to your service, O God;
> It was not fear of eternal torment
> That persuaded me to avoid the path of the sinner.
>
> It was you and your sufferings that moved me, Lord:
> Your visage in the last fearful hours.
> The fury of the scourge, the crown of thorns on your brow,
> Your heavy cross—and your bitter farewell.

This becomes evident once one concedes (as at first one may not) that one and the same phenomenon may give rise to contrary tastes—to pleasure in one case and to displeasure in another. One may be tempted to argue that in such cases, although the external stimuli are the same, the corresponding subjective ideas or presentations must be essentially different. But this is impossible in the cases where we repeatedly experience one and the same phenomenon and then, as a result of an increase in age or a change in our habits, come to feel quite differently about it, experiencing it now with displeasure instead of with pleasure,

> Lord, you move me so strongly
> That I would love you if there were no entrance to heaven
> And would fear you if there were no threat of hell.
> You cannot give me anything to make me love you:
> If you had nothing to give, I would not hope as I do,
> But I would love you just as I do now.]

The views of Thomas Aquinas have often been presented as though they were pure subjectivism. It is true that much of what he says has a subjectivistic tone. (See for example, *Summa Theologica*, I, Q. 80, Art. 1, and note in particular the objections and replies, as well as the passages in which he states that one's own happiness is the highest final end for each person. He even says that each of the saints in heaven rightly desires his own blessedness more than that of all others.) But there are also statements showing that he rises above this subjectivistic viewpoint. For example, he says (as Plato and Aristotle had said before him, and as Descartes and Leibniz were to say afterwards) that everything that exists is as such something that is good, and good not merely as a means but also in itself. This last is a point the pure subjectivist explicitly denies (as Sigwart has recently done in his *Vorfragen der Ethik*, p. 6). Aquinas also says that if—what is in fact impossible—one had to choose between one's own eternal damnation and an injury to the divine love, then it would be right to prefer one's own eternal unhappiness.

In this latter instance, the moral feelings of Western Christianity are the same as those of the heathen Hindu, expressed in the rather strange story of the maiden who renounced her own eternal blessedness for the salvation of the rest of the world. The positivistic philosopher, Mill, expresses the same sentiment when he writes that, rather than bow in prayer before a being who is not truly good, "to hell I will go". I knew a Catholic priest who voted for Mill in a parliamentary election just because of this remark.

87

or conversely (see Section 25 of the lecture). There is no doubt but that contrary feelings may be directed upon one and the same phenomenon. This is also confirmed where an idea or presentation is instinctively repellent to us and yet arouses at the same time a higher type of pleasure (see Note 32 of the lecture).

If it were reasonable to suppose that every positive feeling or emotion is correct and that no such feeling or emotion ever contradicts another, then it would also be reasonable to suppose that the same is true of acts of preference. But this latter is so obviously false that those who hold the former view explicitly deny it and insist that, so far as contrary preferences are concerned, one is correct and the other incorrect.

Looking away from the medieval Aristotelians and going back to the master himself, we find that his own doctrine was quite different. He was aware of the distinction between correct and incorrect desires (ὄρεξις ὀρθὴ καὶ οὐκ ὀρθή) and knew that what is desired (ὀρεκτόν) is not always what is good (ἀγαθόν) (De Anima, Book III, Chapter 10). In the Nicomachaean Ethics (Book X, Chapter 3), he says that not every pleasure (ἡδονή) is good; there is such a thing as taking pleasure in the bad, and this is itself bad. In the Metaphysics (Book XII, Chapter 7, 1072a 28), he distinguishes between a lower and a higher type of desire (ἐπιθυμία and βούλησις); what is desired for its own sake by the higher type of desire is truly good. Here we are very close to the correct conception. It is especially interesting to find (as I did after presenting the lecture) that Aristotle had observed the analogy between ethical subjectivism and the logical subjectivism of Protagoras and that he repudiates both (Metaphysics, Book XI, Chapter 6, 1062b 12 and 1063a 10). But in the lines that immediately follow this passage, he seems to say, incorrectly, that we can recognize the good as good without any excitation of the emotions (compare De Anima, Book III, Chapters 9 and 10).

The temptation leading to such an error is easy to understand. It undoubtedly explains why Aristotle denies in the Nichomachaean Ethics (Book I, Chapter 6) that there is a univocal concept of the good (meaning thereby the concept of what is good in itself) and why he says that the goodness of rational thinking, of seeing, of joy, are united only by analogy. And it also explains why he says in the Metaphysics (Book VI, Chapter 4, 1027b 25) that the true and the false, unlike the good and the bad, are not in things. The former predicates, he says, are ascribed to things only in relation to certain psychological acts—namely, true and false judgements—as when we say "a true God" or "a false friend". But the predicates good and bad, he continues, are not thus ascribed to things merely in relation to a particular class of psychological activities. This is all incorrect, but it is an inevitable consequence of the error we have noted. Aristotle is closer to the correct view of the source of our concept and knowledge of the good when, in the *Nichomachaean Ethics* (Book X, Chapter 3), he argues against the doctrine that pleasure cannot be good. His argument is that everyone desires it. He adds: "If only irrational beings desired it, there might be something in what is said. But if rational creatures do so as well, what sense can there be in this view?" And this assertion can also be reconciled with the erroneous part of Aristotle's theory. In this respect, then, the moralists of sentiment, such as Hume, have an advantage over Aristotle, for they may correctly ask: How is one to know that a thing is worthy of being loved if one does not have the experience of love?

I have said that the temptation into which Aristotle fell seems quite understandable. It may be traced to the fact that whenever we have a positive emotion that is experienced as being correct, we also acquire the knowledge that the object of the emotion is something that is good. It is easy to confuse the relation between the emotion and the knowledge. One may then assume, mistakenly, that the love of the good thing is a consequence of the knowledge that it is good, and that the love is seen to be correct because it is seen to be appropriate to the knowledge.

It is interesting to compare this error of Aristotle concerning the experience of correct emotion with the analogous error that Descartes had made in the case of judgement (see Note 27, "On the Evident"). In each case, the philosopher in question tries to find the distinguishing mark in some peculiarity of the *idea* or presentation that lies at the basis of the psychological act, instead of looking, as he should have, toward the *act* itself which is experienced as being correct. Indeed, it seems clear to me from various passages in Descartes' book, "*Les Passions*", that he viewed correct emotion in substantially the same way that Aristotle did and that he held an analogous theory of the evident.

At the present time, there are many who come close to making the error that Descartes had made with respect to the nature of the evident (or perhaps we should say, they *do* make this error, implicitly). They seem to hold that every evident judgement can be seen to be evident upon the basis of some criterion, which would have to be given in advance. Either the criterion itself would have to be *known*, in which case there would be an infinite regress, or—and this is the only alternative—it would have to be given in the idea or presentation that underlies the judgement. As in the previous case, the temptation to make this error is easy to understand, and doubtless it had its effect upon Descartes. Aristotle's error is less common, though probably only because the phenomenon of an emotion being experienced as correct has received less attention than the evident judgement. Many have misconceived the latter, but few have even given the former enough consideration to be able to misconceive it.

Two Unique Cases of Preferability
(Note 37 to page 29)

If our account of preferability is to be exact and exhaustive, we should consider two further important cases that were not mentioned in the lecture. The one case may be described as feeling pleasure in the bad, and the other as feeling displeasure in the bad.

What of pleasure in the bad? Is it itself something that is good? Aristotle says that it is not, and in a certain sense he is undoubtedly right. He writes in the *Nichomachaean Ethics* (Book X, Chapter 3, 1174a, 1–4): "No one would wish to feel joy in what is base, even if he were assured that no harm would come from it". The hedonists expressed the contrary view, and they include even such high-minded men as Fechner (see his work on the highest good). But their view is to be rejected. As Hume remarked, their practice is happily much better than their theory. Yet there is a grain of truth in what they say.

Pleasure in the bad is, as pleasure, something that is good, but at the same time, as an incorrect emotion, it is something that is bad. Even if it is predominantly bad, because of this incorrectness, it cannot be said to be purely bad. If, therefore, we reject it as bad, we are performing an act of preference in which freedom from what is bad is given preference over something else that is good. If we are able to see that it is correct to reject such pleasure as being bad, it must be because the act of preference is experienced as being correct.

What of displeasure in the bad? If displeasure in the bad is experienced as being correct, is it itself something that is good? Consider what occurs when a magnanimous person is pained at the sight of innocent victims of injustice, or when a man feels remorse about some misdeed that he has committed in the past. Now we have the reverse of the situation previously considered. Here we have a feeling that strikes us as being predominantly but not purely good. Its goodness is not like that of the exalted joy we would feel if the object of our emotion were the contrary of what it is that pains us or makes us feel regret. And this offers a justification for Descartes' advice that we ought rather to direct our attention and emotions upon the good. All this we recognize easily. Thus we have yet another case in which a preference that is experienced as being correct enables us to know what things are preferable to others.

In order not to introduce too many complications, I did not discuss these cases in the lecture. I felt that the omission was justifiable, since for all practical purposes the same results could be obtained if the hate that is experienced in these cases as being correct were treated simply as an instance of disliking or aversion (this is what Aristotle had done in the case of shameful joy), and if the love that is experienced as being correct were treated simply as an instance of liking or attraction.

Here, then, we have two rather special cases pertaining to the possible quantitative relations between the goodness and badness of pleasure and displeasure, on the one hand, and the correctness and incorrectness of emotion, on the other (compare also what is said in Note 31). These make clear that there is little hope of finding a generally valid way of filling in the great gaps in our ethical knowledge that were referred to in the lecture.*

* [Editor's note: These points are refined in Brentano's *Untersuchungen zur Sinnespsychologie* (Leipzig: Duncker & Humblot, 1907). Brentano there distinguishes between nonsensuous emotions (simple evaluations and preferences) and the sensuous side-effects (*Redundanzen*) which they cause (the sensations of pleasure and pain which may vary in their intensities). These blend into a single consciousness, but the different elements can be separated by conceptual analysis. The

On the Charge of Excessive Rigorism
(Note 42 to page 32)

In his *Vorfragen der Ethik* (p. 42), Sigwart insists that one must not demand more of the human will than it is capable of performing. This doctrine, which is most surprising coming from the lips of so decided an indeterminist (compare his *Logik*, Vol. II, p. 592), hangs together with his subjectivistic conception of the good—a combination that can hardly be satisfactory to anyone who takes these questions seriously. (Note the way in which Sigwart himself, on page 15, slides over from egoism to a concern for the general good.)

But others have expressed similar opinions. One might really begin to wonder whether the sublime command to order all our actions by reference to the highest practical good is the correct ethical principle. For, aside from cases of insufficient reflection, which are not here to the point, the demand that we surrender ourselves completely to the highest good may well seem too severe. There is no one—no matter how upright his conduct may be—who can honestly look into his heart and deny these words of Horace:

> Nunc in Aristippi furtim praecepta relabor,
> Et mihi res, non me rebus subiungere conor.

But the doubt is unfounded. A comparison may make things clear. It is certain that no man can entirely avoid error. Nevertheless, avoidable or not, every erroneous judgement is a judgement that ought not to have been made, a judgement in conflict with the requirements of logic, and these cannot be modified. The rules of logic are not to be given up merely because of the weakness of our powers of reasoning. Similarly, the rules of ethics are not to be given up because of weakness of will. If a man is weak willed, ethics cannot cease to demand from him

---

purely sensuous constituents are to be evaluated separately from the nonsensuous constituents that cause them. In the case of remorse, for example, the nonsensuous emotion of regret is something that is in itself correct; but the sensuous "pangs of regret" to which the remorse gives rise are sensations which are not in themselves correct—they are useful, but in and for themselves they are an evil. See sections 25 and 26 of "Loving and Hating", Appendix IX of the present book.]

that he love what is known to be good, prefer what is known to be better, and place the highest good above all else. Even if one could show (and one cannot) that there are circumstances under which no one could remain true to the highest good, there would not be the slightest justification for setting aside the requirements of ethics. The one and only correct rule would remain evident and unalterably true: Give preference in every case to that which is better.

J. S. Mill feared that this demand would lead to endless self-reproach which would embitter the life of every individual. But such self-reproach is not itself one of the requirements of ethics; indeed the rule excludes it. Goethe was aware of this. These lines of his were not intended to encourage laxity:

> Nichts taugt Ungeduld,
> Noch weniger Reue,
> Jene vermehrt die Schuld,
> Diese schafft neue.

> [Impatience does us no good;
> Even less does rue.
> The first increases the old fault;
> The second creates a new.]

He refers here to impatience with one's own limitations; one should not submit to pangs of conscience when only a fresh and cheerful resolution will avail.

The same sentiment is expressed in the following lines, which I once found in an album, written in the hand of the pious Abbott Haneberg, who later became Bishop of Spires:

> Sonne dich mit Lust an Gottes Huld,
> Hab' mit allen,—auch mit dir Geduld!

> [Bask with pleasure in the grace of God;
> Have patience with everyone—including yourself.]

Criticism of Ihering
(Note 45 to page 34)

Philosophers and jurists alike have emphasized that the law imposes restrictions in order to protect those spheres which should be at the disposal of the individual will. See, for example, Herbart's

Idee des Rechts. Ihering confirms this with numerous citations in his *Geist des römischen Rechts* (Book III, Chapter 1, p. 320n.). Arndt, in his *Handbuch der Pandekten*, defines law as "the supremacy of the will with respect to an object"; Sintenis defines law as "the will of one person elevated to the general will"; Windschneid defines it as "the content of a certain volition which the legal code declares shall be given expression in a given case in preference to any other". And Puchta, who may have expressed the thought in the greatest variety of ways, writes in his *Pandekten* (Section 22): "Men are called persons to the extent that they are potentially subject to such a will. . . . Personality is therefore the subjective possibility of a legal will, of a legal power." When speaking in the same work (Section 118, Note b) of the absence of personality, he observes that "the principle of modern law is the ability to dispose of one's own powers". He makes the same point in many other ways.

These legal authorities have concentrated their attention exclusively upon legal duties, not touching upon the ethical question as to how the individual will should manage its affairs within its own legitimate sphere. But Ihering has taken them to mean that the highest good, and the true end at which the legal code aims, is the pleasure that the individual takes in the activities of his own will. And so he writes: "The final goal of all law is, for them, willing" (*op. cit.*, pp. 320, 325); "The end of law (according to them) consists ultimately in the power and supremacy of the will" (p. 326). Given this interpretation of what the legal authorities have said, it is easy to understand why Ihering rejects it and succeeds in making it appear ridiculous. "According to this view", he says (p. 320), "the whole domain of individual rights is nothing more than an arena in which the will moves and exercises itself. The will is supposed to be the faculty by means of which the individual enjoys the law. This enjoyment is thought to consist in the satisfaction and glory of power that the individual feels when he exercises his legal rights—for example, when he arranges a mortgage or brings legal action, thus documenting the fact that he is a legal personality. What a poor thing the will would be if its proper 'sphere of activity' were restricted to these pedestrian legal activities!"

The legal authorities in question do regard the *immediate* aim of law as the setting of limits to what is at the disposal of the individual will. Had they intended thereby to disavow all concern for the *ultimate ethical end*, namely, the promotion of the highest practical good, they would deserve to be ridiculed. But there is no ground at all for this charge. If there is anything ridiculous here, it would seem to be the zeal with which Ihering has conducted his attack upon an army of straw men.

And his own proposal is hardly a satisfactory substitute. According to him, the sphere that the law assigns to the individual is simply one in which the individual's egoism is given free reign (a view which, as author of the later *Zweck im Recht*, he may no longer hold). He thus proposes this definition: "Law is the legal security for enjoyment" (p. 338). It would have been much better had he said: "Law is the legal security for the undisturbed exercise of individual power in the advancement of the highest good." Are violations of law the only type of bad conduct? Not at all. Our legal duties have their limits, but duty in general has jurisdiction over *all* our actions. This is emphasized by our popular religion—when it says, for example, that the individual must render an account for every idle word.

Ihering's first objection, then, was based upon a simple misunderstanding of what was intended. He also made other objections, but these seem to have been occasioned merely by imperfections in the use of language. He points out that if law is essentially a matter of setting limits to the activity of the individual will, so that one person will not disturb another in his efforts to promote the good, then one could say, of those persons who have, or have had, or will have no will, that they also have no legal rights. I say "have, or have had, or will have", since we must consider the past and the future as well as the present. A man who is dead often exercises an influence extending into the distant future. As Comte well said: "The living are increasingly dominated by the dead". There are circumstances, similarly, under which we may leave a decision to the future, thus renouncing the domain of our will, so to speak, in favour of some future will. This fact alone is sufficient to resolve a number of the paradoxes urged by Ihering (see pp. 320–325), but it does not resolve them all. Concern for the highest practical good does not require that an incurable imbecile be assigned a domain for the exercise of his will, for he has no will to exercise. Strictly speaking, therefore, he cannot be said to have any legal rights, according to our conception. Yet he is said to have a right to his own life. And sometimes we refer to such a person as the owner of a great estate and even say that he has a right to the crown and to the powers that go along with it. But if we examine the situation carefully, we will see that a subject incapable of responsibility is not hereby assigned legal rights. The legal rights and duties pertain to certain *other* individuals. Thus there are the rights and duties of the father who in his will makes provisions with respect to his property which will provide for the imbecile child. And when the imbecile is considered to have a right to his life, the legal domain that is involved is actually that of the state itself. For, in addition to the fact that murder is a violation of our duty to love, the state permits no one else to take a human life, and thus it sometimes even imposes a punishment in the case of attempted suicide.

Ihering makes still a third objection, saying that if legal rights are determined by reference to the spheres of individual wills, then the most foolish dispositions of will must be given legal validity. But it is easy to deal with this objection in the light of what we have said. Certainly, the state will permit its citizens to exercise their wills in foolish and senseless ways. Otherwise the state alone would have the right of making final decisions and there would be no individual rights. Those who hold the power of government are also capable of making foolish and senseless decisions, and as long as this is so, the state should not have all the power in its hands. But all secondary moral principles admit of exceptions, and it is often necessary for the state to expropriate the property of private individuals. And at times the state may annul senseless arrangements, or arrangements that have lost all relevance to the highest practical good. Here, as in every other so-called collision of duties, concern for the highest practical good is what must be decisive.

Mill's Conception of the Evident
(Note 68 to page 43)

It is not surprising that Hume would be guilty of this confusion [between expectation that is instinctive and habitual, and expectation that is justified by the principles of the calculus of probability]. For at the time he wrote, psychology was far less developed than it is now and study of the probability calculus had not yet sufficiently clarified the process of rational induction. But it is surprising to find that James Mill and Herbert Spencer did not advance in the slightest beyond Hume (see James Mill's *Analysis of the Phenomena of the Human Mind*, Vol. I, Chapter 9 and note 108) and that even the excellent J. S. Mill never saw the essential distinction between the two procedures—this despite the fact that Laplace's *Essai Philosophique sur les Probabilités* was at his disposal. Mill's failure to recognize the purely analytic character of mathematics and the general significance of the deductive procedure is connected with the same point. He had even denied that the syllogism leads to new knowledge. If one bases mathematics upon induction, then, of course, one cannot justify induction mathematically, for this would lead to a vicious circle. So far as this point is concerned, Jevons' *Logic* is beyond question the more nearly adequate.

But there is reason to believe that Mill had some inkling of the distinction we have referred to. In a note to his edition of James Mill's *Analysis of the Phenomena of the Human Mind* (Volume I, Chapter 11, p. 407), he criticizes his father's theory in the following terms: ". . . if belief is only an inseparable association, belief is a matter of *habit* and accident, and not of *reason*. Assuredly an association, however close, is not a sufficient *ground* of belief*; it is not *evidence* that the corresponding facts are united in external nature. The theory seems to annihilate all distinction between the belief of the wise, which is *regulated by evidence*, and conforms to the real successions and co-existences of the facts of the universe, and the belief of fools, which is *mechanically produced* by any accidental association that suggests the idea of a succession or co-existence to the mind; a belief aptly characterized by the popular expression, 'believing a thing because they have taken it into their heads". This is all excellent. But it is robbed of its essential worth when Mill writes in a subsequent note (*op. cit.*, p. 438, note 110): "It must be conceded to him [the author of the *Analysis*] that an association, sufficiently strong to exclude all ideas that would exclude itself, *produces a kind of mechanical belief*; and that the processes by which the belief is corrected, or reduced to rational

* [The italics up to this point are Mill's; the remaining ones are Brentano's.]

grounds, *all consist in the growth of a counter-association* tending to raise the idea of a disappointment of the first expectation, and as the one or the other prevails in the particular case, the belief or expectation exists or does not exist exactly as if the belief were the the same thing with the association."

There is much here to give one pause. Mill refers to ideas that mutually exclude one another. What sort of ideas could these be? Mill tells us elsewhere that he knows "no case of absolute incompatibility of thought . . . except between the presence of something and its absence" (*op. cit.*, Vol. I, pp. 98–9, note 30). But are even these thoughts incompatible? Mill himself tells us the opposite elsewhere. He says that along with the thought of being there is always given at the same time the thought of non-being: "We are only conscious of the presence [of objects] by comparison with their absence" (p. 26, note 39). But aside from all this, how strange it is that Mill here allows the distinctive nature of the evident to escape him entirely and retains only that blind and mechanical formation of judgement which he had rightly looked down upon! So far as this point is concerned, the sceptic Hume stands far higher than Mill. For Hume sees at least that no such empirical conception of induction can satisfy the requirements of reason. Sigwart's criticism of Mill's theory of induction (*Logik*, Vol. II, p. 371) is basically sound. But in turning to his own "postulates", he does not provide us with any satisfactory alternative.

*Miklosich on Subjectless Propositions**

I

"*Subjektlose Sätze*" is the title which the distinguished linguist has now given this little work which was originally entitled, "*Die Verba Impersonalia im Slavischen*".

The change of title may well be connected with the significant additions to be found in the second edition, but actually it would have been more suitable for the first edition, too. For the author is not concerned with the nature of just *one* group of languages;

* [Discussion of Franz Miklosich, *Subjektlose Sätz* (Vienna: Braumüller, 1883); reprinted from the *Wiener Zeitung*, November 13 and 14, 1883, and included as an appendix to the first edition of *Vom Ursprung sittlicher Erkenntnis.*]

he is concerned with a thesis that is of much more extensive significance. If it is in conflict with the prevailing view, it is all the more worthy of investigation. The question is of interest, not only for philology, but also for psychology and metaphysics. What the author has to say should be welcomed, not only by those who are investigating these learned areas, but also by the schoolboy who is now tormented by his schoolmaster with impossible and incomprehensible theories (see Miklosich, p. 23ff.).

But actually the treatise has not had the influence it deserves. The contrary views still hold sway. The reappearance of the monograph indicates that the work is of interest to certain wider circles, but this is not to be attributed to the fact that the work is thought to have thrown light upon previous doubts and errors. Thus Darwin's epoch-making work, quite apart from the question of whether or not its hypothesis was correct, had incontestable value even for those who rejected it. One could only admire the wealth of important observations and ingenious conjectures that it contained. So, too, in the case of Miklosich. He has compressed into a few pages a rich store of learning, interspersed with the most subtle perceptions. Those who reject his principle thesis may yet be greatly indebted to him for points of detail.

Let us first consider the central question with which the work is concerned, and indicate briefly its significance.

According to an ancient doctrine of logic, all judgement is a matter of relating ideas; some judgements were said to combine ideas and others to separate them. This doctrine, which has been accepted almost unanimously for the past few thousand years, has exercised considerable influence upon disciplines other than logic. Thus grammarians have long held that the categorical judgement, in which a subject is combined with a predicate, is the simplest form that a judgement can take.

When we ask ourselves whether this doctrine is really true, we find that it involves certain difficulties. These difficulties could not permanently be kept out of sight, but most investigators held to the doctrine so firmly that they felt no inclination to question its universal validity. Propositions such as "It is raining" and "It is lightening" look as though they had no wish to conform to the doctrine. It was necessary, therefore, to conduct a search—to find subjects for these propositions so that they, too, might be put into categorical form. And many thought that they had found the proper subjects. But then, in strange contrast to the unity that had prevailed up to that point, they headed off in a great variety of directions. If we examine the various hypotheses that were proposed, we can readily see why there was no general agreement and why none of them could really be permanently satisfactory.

Science explains by conceiving a multiplicity as a unity. Attempts were made to do the same thing here, but none of the attempts was satisfactory. Thus it was held that when we say, "It is raining", the unnamed subject designated by means of the indefinite "it" is in fact Zeus; the proposition tells us that Zeus rains. But in "It is noisy", it would seem obvious that Zeus cannot be the subject. And so others assumed that in this latter case the subject is actually noise; what the proposition tells us is that the noise is noisy. Applied to the previous example, this hypothesis would have it that raining, or the rain, is what rains.

When we say in German, "*Es fehlt an Geld*", the meaning would have to be "*Das Fehlen an Geld fehlt an Geld*" ["There lacks money" would tell us that the lack of money is what lacks money]. But this is absurd. So it was said that in this case "*Geld*" was the real subject; hence the proposition would tell us that money is what lacks money. But if this type of proposition requires special handling, then the desired unity of explanation is threatened. Perhaps by closing one eye we may partially conceal this fact from ourselves. But then what are we to do with "*Es gibt einen Gott*" ["There is a God", or, literally, "It gives a God"]? We can hardly render "It gives a God" as "The giving of a God gives a God", or "The giving gives a God", or "God gives a God".

And so the philologists had to look for an entirely different type of explanation. But where was it to be found? Perhaps, they thought, some new expedient could be found for dealing with the last example. But if we have to modify our hypothesis for each new case that comes along, we have produced only a caricature of a genuinely scientific explanation. No single hypothesis was advanced which could deal with all these cases—with the possible exception of a hint by Schleiermacher. If this learned man really said, as has been reported (Miklosich, page 16), that the subject of these propositions is *Chaos*, we have to assume, not that he was offering still another hypothesis, but only that he was ridiculing what the philologists had been able to do with their problem.

Some hold that the true subjects of such propositions as "It is raining" and "It is lightening" have not yet been discovered and think that science still faces the task of finding the subjects. But if these propositions really do have subjects which people think of but leave unexpressed when they assert them, why should they be so difficult to find? Steinthal tries to explain this by saying that the grammatical subject which is denoted by these propositions is a certain Something, which is not thinkable but is somehow alluded to. Many will prefer to say with Miklosich (p. 23): "We are not going too far when we say that grammar is not concerned with the unthinkable."

Miklosich says that the supposed subject in the case of these propositions is a delusion. The propositions do not involve combining a subject and a predicate; they are, as he puts it, subjectless. He bases his assertion on the totality of phenomena that are involved and upon the grotesque failures of the various attempts, often highly ingenious, to find subjects for these propositions.

There are other observations that will confirm his view. Among these is one consideration about the nature of judgement that is of special significance. Miklosich opposes those who, like Steinthal, think there is no real relationship between grammar and logic. He also defends his views against those who have attacked them on the basis of psychological and logical considerations. And he arrives at the conclusion that, because of the peculiar characteristics of one type of judgement, we should expect to find subjectless propositions in language. As he points out, it is not true that every judgement is a matter of relating one concept to another. A judgement is often merely the affirmation or denial of a simple fact. In such a case, the proper linguistic expression clearly cannot be one in which there is a combination of a subject and a predicate. Miklosich notes that there have been philosophers who were aware of this fact but, as he observes, they did not usually appreciate its significance. They were not entirely clear about the matter and, despite some indecision, they were disinclined to give up the traditional view and ended up by denying what it was that they first affirmed. Thus Trendelenburg concluded that "It is lightening", strictly speaking, does not express a judgement. It expresses only the rudiments of a judgement, he said; it makes way for the concept of lightning and serves to fix it, thus providing a ground for the complete judgement, "Lightning is conducted by iron". And Herbart concluded that judgements such as "It is noisy" are not judgements in the ordinary sense, nor are they, strictly speaking, what is meant in logic by judgement. There is an excellent passage (p. 21f.) in which Miklosich shows that these philosophers actually contradict themselves and traces their mistakes back to a misunderstanding of the nature of judgement and to an inadequate definition of it.

Miklosich concludes from all this that the existence of sub-jectless propositions is beyond doubt. And he shows that they are by no means as uncommon as the controversy about them might lead one to believe. There is a great variety of them, which he classifies in the second part of his treatise (pp. 33 to 72). Thus he lists subjectless propositions with a *Verbum activum*, subject-less propositions with a *Verbum reflexivum*, subjectless proposi-tions with a *Verbum passivum*, and subjectless propositions with the *Verbum esse*, and he cites countless examples of each type from a great variety of languages. In connection with the first type in particular, he makes an eightfold division, grouping the propositions with respect to differences of content. He notes as a general principle (p. 6) that the *Verbum finitum* of subjectless propositions is always in the third person singular and, where differences in gender are utilized, it is always neuter.

He also considers the matter in many other connections. He shows that, historically, subjectless propositions did not come into being after subject-predicate propositions; they existed from the very first (p. 13ff., p. 19), but in the course of time they disap-peared from some languages (p. 26). He notes that the languages in which they are preserved have an advantage, since the use of subjectless propositions can enliven the language (p. 26). And he cites still other reasons for denying that these propositions can be put into the subject-predicate form that is supposed to be equivalent to them. The German "*Mich friert*" [It makes me cold] cannot be identified with "*Ich friere*" [I am cold]; otherwise we would have to identify "*Was frierst du draussen? Komme doch herein!*" [What are you doing freezing out there? Come right in!]

with "*Was friert dich's draussen? Komme doch herein!*" [What is it that is making you freeze out there? Come right in!] "The expression '*Mich friert*' cannot be used if I expose myself voluntarily to the cold" (p. 37).

II

This, in brief, is the content of the book. I shall now permit myself a few critical remarks.

It should be clear that I not only approve of this treatise in general, but also that I accept its basic theses. The proofs are put so cogently that even those who are putting up a struggle will be unable to resist the truth. Quite independently of these proofs, I arrived long ago at the same view of the basis of a purely psychological analysis, and I gave it unequivocal public expression when I published my *Psychologie* in 1874.

I took great pains to put the view in a clear light and to show that the previous theories were untenable. But up to now what I said does not seem to have had much effect. A few have agreed with me, but for the most part I have had no more success in convincing philosophers than Miklosich, in his first edition, had had in convincing philologists. We are confronted here with a prejudice that has been sending out roots for thousands of years; it has forced its way into our elementary schools, and it is now looked upon as a fundamental principle upon which a host of others depend. We should not expect, therefore, that the error will simply disappear once it has been refuted. It is more likely that the new point of view will be distrusted and that the grounds upon which it is based will not be properly evaluated. But now two investigators have arrived at this point of view, working entirely independently of each other and approaching the topic from quite different directions. Perhaps we have a right to hope that this fact will not be looked upon as a mere coincidence and that due attention will be given to the evidence, particularly to the new edition of Miklosich's treatise, in which I am happy to find my own work considered.

Since I am in agreement with respect to the principal theses of the treatise, my disagreement with respect to certain subordinate points is of no great significance. But I shall mention some of these.

Miklosich uses the expression "subjectless propositions" to

refer to those simple propositions in which there is no combination of subject and predicate. I agree entirely that there are such propositions, but I am not happy with the expression "subjectless proposition" in this context or with the reasons that Miklosich has given for using it.

Subject and predicate are correlative concepts and they stand and fall together. If a proposition is truly subjectless, then, by the same token, it is also truly predicateless. For this reason it does not seem to me to be appropriate to describe the propositions in question merely as "subjectless"; and it is quite incorrect to describe them, as Miklosich sometimes does (see pp. 3, 25, 26, and elsewhere), by saying they are merely "predicate propositions" [*Prädikatsätze*]. This manner of speaking might lead one to think that Miklosich, too, thinks that in these propositions there is a concept, namely the subject, which is understood and left unexpressed; but of course he explicitly denies this (p. 3f., and elsewhere). Or one might assume that he looked upon these propositions as a type of stunted subject-predicate proposition which were originally of the subject-predicate form; but he explicitly denies this, too (p. 13ff.). Actually, his view may be put in the following way: In thought and language there is a natural development from simple propositions to subject-predicate propositions, so that the concept which appears alone in the former type of proposition is combined with a second concept in the latter type of proposition, the second concept then serving as subject. Thus he writes (p. 25): "The subjectless propositions . . . are propositions which consist only of a predicate. In a great number of propositions, this predicate is to be thought of as being prior in the natural process of thought formation. It is then possible, though not at all necessary, to seek out some subject which may then be added to the predicate."

But this latter claim can hardly be correct; the word "subject", moreover, is not the one to use for the concept that may thus be added. Surely that which lays the basis for the judgement is what stands first in the construction of the judgement. The temporal sequence of words does not accord with what Miklosich says here, for normally we begin the categorical judgement with the subject. It is to be noted, moreover, that in categorical judgements the emphasis is usually upon the predicate. (This latter led Trendelenburg to describe the predicate as the principal concept and to say, with some exaggeration, "We think in predicates"; see Miklosich, p. 19.) If the subject concept, as Miklosich suggests, is the one that is added on to the concept that is first given, then we would hardly expect the predicate to be the object of greater interest; but if the predicate concept is the one that is added, then we would expect it to be of greater interest.

Where we say "A bird is black" we could also say "A black thing is a bird [ein Schwarzes ist ein Vogel]"; where we say "Socrates is a man", we could also say "Some man is Socrates". But Aristotle noted that only the former type of predication is natural, while the latter is opposed to the natural order. This is right insofar as we naturally take as the subject the term that we first consider when we make the judgement, or the term which the hearer must first attend to in order to understand the proposition or to find out whether or not it is true. If we wish to decide whether or not there is a black bird, we may look among birds to see whether there is one that is black, or we may look among black things to see whether there is one that is a bird, but it is preferable to take the former course. And if we wish to decide whether a given individual belongs to a certain genus or species, it is much easier to analyze the nature of that particular individual than it is to run through the extension of the relevant general concept. The apparent exceptions actually confirm the rule and the reasons that have been given for it. Suppose, for example, that I say: "There is a black thing; oh, the black thing is a bird." What I am aware of first in this case is simply a black thing, and therefore when I make a subject-predicate judgement it is natural for me to let the black thing be the subject.

In the Aristotelian sorites, the term that a premise has in common with its predecessor is taken to be the subject of that premise, but in the Goclenian sorites it is taken to be the predicate. For this reason, the Aristotelian sorites seems the more natural. It is said to exhibit the normal way of reasoning in a chain, whereas the Goclenian sorites reverses the normal order.

Again, consider what happens when we begin with a simple proposition, which does not combine a subject and predicate, and then proceed to a subject-predicate proposition in which one of the terms is the one that occurred in the simple proposition. Ordinarily, the term that is common to the two propositions would become the *subject* of the second proposition, and it would seem more natural to say that we have sought out a predicate for the subject than to say that we have sought out a subject for the predicate. For example: "There is noise; the noise comes from a brook"; "It is thundering; the thunder is a sign of an approaching storm"; "It smells of roses; the smell is coming from the neighbour's garden"; "There is laughter; the laughter comes from the clown"; "There is no money; the absence of money is the cause of the business depression"; "There is a God; this God is the creator of heaven and earth"; and so on.

It seems to me, therefore, that there is only *one* respect in which the expression "subjectless proposition" may be justified and perhaps even recommended. The expression takes account of the fact that the term which is contained in the propositions in question is the only term and therefore, obviously, the term which is of principal interest; and in propositions which have a subject and predicate the term which is of principal interest is the predicate and not the subject. Compare the relation that holds between categorical propositions and hypothetical propositions. If we had to choose, it would be much better to say that the categorical proposition is a "proposition without an antecedent" than to say that it is a "proposition without a consequent". But this would not mean that where there is no antecedent there may yet be a consequent; it means only that in a hypothetical proposition the consequent is the principal component. Looking at the matter this way, then, I might be able to go along with the author's "subjectless proposition".

But there is another point of disagreement. This concerns the extent to which we can make use of subjectless propositions. Miklosich is right in emphasizing that the limits must not be made too narrow. But he thinks that there *are* limits, as is shown by the fact that he attempts to survey and classify the sort of thing that can be expressed by these propositions. And here he seems to me to be mistaken. Strictly speaking, we may say that there is no limit to the applicability of the subjectless form. I think I have shown in my *Psychology* that *every* judgement, whether it be expressed in categorical, hypothetical, or disjunctive form, may be expressed without loss of meaning in the form of a subjectless proposition, or, as I would prefer to put it, in the form of an existential proposition. Thus the proposition "Some man is sick" is synonymous with "There is a sick man"; the proposition "All men are mortal" is synonymous with "There are no immortal men"; and so on.[1]

There is another respect in which what Miklosich has to say about the applicability of subjectless propositions would seem to be overly restrictive. He says that these propositions are "a great advantage to a language" and that "it is by no means true that all languages can boast of this advantage" (p. 26). But this is hardly plausible if, as he himself demonstrates so persuasively, there have always been judgements which are not formed by combining two different concepts, and which therefore cannot be expressed in subject-predicate form (p. 16). It follows that Miklosich is right when he says there are such things as subjectless propositions, and wrong when he says these propositions are not to be found in all languages.

I think that the author's mistake on this point may be traced in part to the fact that he was much too cautious. He wanted to be certain that his examples could not be objected to, and in consequence he leaves unmentioned certain types of subjectless

---

[1] Addendum: What I have said here about the general applicability of the existential form obviously is true only if we restrict ourselves to those judgements that are genuinely and perfectly unitary [einheitlich]. The tradition in logic is to express these judgements in categorical form, as subject-predicate propositions. But in ordinary life we often use the categorical, subject-predicate form to express a multiplicity of judgements, one built upon another. The proposition, "That is a man", is a clear example. Use of the demonstrative "that" already presupposes belief in the existence of the thing in question; a second judgement then ascribes to it the predicate "man". This happens very frequently. I would say that the original purpose of the categorical form was to express these double-judgements [Doppel-urteilen]—judgements in which something is first accepted as existing and in which something else is then either affirmed or denied of the first thing. I would also say that existential and impersonal forms then grew out of this categorical form as a result of the change in function. But this fact does not alter their essential nature. Thus a lung is not a fish-bladder even if it did grow out of one. Again, the origin of the German preposition "kraft" ["by dint of"] may be traced to a substantive ["Kraft", meaning power]; nevertheless the word is syncategorematic and not a substantive (see Mill's Logic, Book I, Chapter 2, Section 2).

proposition. According to Miklosich, as we have already noted, the finite verb of subjectless propositions is always in the third person singular and, where differences in gender are utilized, it is always in the neuter. This is much too restrictive, and Miklosich himself has provided us with exceptions, though in a much later passage. He writes in the second part of his treatise: "In 'There is a God' the concept 'God' is asserted absolutely and without a subject; so, too, in 'There are gods'." And then he adds: "The 'is' of the existential proposition *takes the place of the so-called copula* 'is'. In many but by no means all languages, the so-called copula 'is' is indispensable for the expression of judgement and performs the same function as does the personal endings of finite verbs. We see this clearly when we consider 'It dawns' alongside of 'It is dawn'.* Consequently 'is' is not a predicate." (Page 34; compare also the top of page 21.) Actually, however, if "*Es gibt einen Gott*" is to be regarded as subjectless, then so, too, is "*Es ist ein Gott* [There is a God]" as well as "*Es sind Götter* [There are gods]". Hence the general rule that Miklosich sets up is too restrictive. If existential propositions (and possibly analogous forms) are subjectless prepositions, then this fact would confirm what we have said above—namely, that there are no languages, and cannot be any languages, in which these most simple of propositions are entirely absent. Miklosich says that some languages have advantages over others in providing for subjectless propositions; but this is true only of certain subspecies of these propositions.

These are the criticisms I have thought it necessary to make. But if they are found to be justified, they will not prejudice the author's principal theses in the slightest; indeed, they will add to the significance of what he says. The second edition of this small but substantial work, unduly neglected when it originally appeared, corrects certain points of detail, enlarges upon many points, and with great conciseness refutes the objections of Benfey, Steinthal, and other writers. Let me express once again my hope that it will find that interest which is appropriate to the importance of the question and to the excellent treatment that Miklosich has given it.

* [Translators' note: Miklosich's own examples are not adaptable to English; they are "*Es sommert, es nachtet*" and "*Es ist Sommer, es ist Nacht*".]

APPENDIX

Drawn from Brentano's Letters and Manuscripts

I. Ethical Principles as A Priori
(From a letter to Oskar Kraus, March 24, 1904)

[Editor's note: On March 21st, 1904, I wrote to Brentano, making these points among others: "One thing has struck me in the course of my investigations. We call ourselves empiricists in ethics, but this is to be taken with a grain of salt. The concepts of *good* and *preferable* have their source in inner experience, in just the way in which the concept of *necessity* has its source in inner experience—and just as the concepts of *large* and *larger* have their source in so-called 'external experience'. But ethics is not based upon concepts; it is based upon certain *cognitions* (for example, the cognition that there can be no knowledge which, as such, is worthy of hate). These cognitions are acquired through consideration of the concepts that they presuppose. Hence they are 'analytic' or '*a priori*' in exactly the way in which the axioms of mathematics are 'analytic' or '*a priori*'. The only difference between the two cases is that the concepts of mathematics—those of geometry in particular—are 'ideal concepts' or fictions. Do you think that this is correct? And if not, why not?" The following is Brentano's reply.]

... A word about the question whether our point of view in ethics is to be called empirical. Obviously the answer depends upon the sense in which we take "empirical". There is no doubt but that we do get our ideas of good and of better from experience. But, as you rightly observe, the same is true of mathematics, and yet we do not on that account call mathematics an empirical science.

Now it is certain that the concept of *good* cannot be included in everything that is good; it is not included, for example, in the concept of knowledge. (Otherwise everything would include the concept of *good*, since everything contains some good.[1])

---

[1] [Editor's note: Brentano should be interpreted as referring here to beings that are psychologically active. Consider the man who is in excruciating pain: he is at least thinking, and he is aware of his own

III

"Knowledge is good" is not like the law of contradiction; the concepts, just by themselves, do not enable us to see that it is a true proposition. In this way it differs from the principles of mathematics; one *can* see, from the concepts alone, that two plus one is equal to three, for "two plus one" is the analytic definition of "three".

You note, however, that we also know, on the basis of concepts alone, that two plus one is *necessarily* equal to three, although the concept of *necessity* does not lie in the concept of two plus one. You are quite right. What happens in such cases is this: We combine three with two plus one by means of a negative copula, and then reject this combination apodictically. We are then led to concepts such as that of the *impossible* by reflecting upon the apodictic judgement. Thus there is an experience from which we derive such concepts as that of the *impossible*, and the object of this experience is the apodictic judgement.

It is in this way, then, that we arrive at the judgement, "It is necessarily true that two plus one is equal to three", despite the fact that the concept of "necessarily true" is not included in that of "two plus one". And this is quite different from the way in which we arrive at a generalization such as, "It is necessarily true that a physical body that is at rest will remain at rest unless it is disturbed by some other physical body, and that a physical body that is in motion will move in a straight line and with a uniform speed unless it is disturbed by some other physical body". In the case of the mathematical judgement, but not in the present case, the apodictic judgement, which provides the occasion for abstracting the concept of impossibility, arises out of the concepts alone. The ethical case is also unlike that of mathematics: the mere concept, "knowledge which is not good", does not provide the occasion for an apodictic rejection.

Thus still another experience is needed. The concept of knowledge must give rise to an act of love, and this love, just because it does arise in this way, is experienced as being correct. For a purely intellectual being, the thought that "two plus one is

---

existence and also of the fact that he is seeing or otherwise perceiving; to this extent, he is participating in what is good. Similarly for the man who is making a mistake and the man who is committing some criminal act.]

not equal to three" would be sufficient to give rise to its apodictic rejection; but (supposing, for the moment, that the concept of the good is given *a priori*)[2] the thought that "Knowledge is not good" would not give rise to apodictic rejection.

But the experience required is analogous to the one that we undergo upon contemplating, "It is impossible for two and one not to be equal to three". For the love that is experienced as being correct also arises out of concepts, and it is just because of this fact that the love is experienced as being correct. And so you are right in saying that this way of arriving at a generalization is quite different from what takes place when we make an induction. For where we have an induction in the strict and proper sense, as in the example above, we have only a probable generalization (in the most favourable case, one that is infinitely close to certainty). But in the ethical case, we have the absolute certainty of an apodictic judgement.

And so I think we should protest against calling this knowledge empirical—despite the fact that, in order to acquire the knowledge, it is necessary to feel and experience love. The knowledge that we have here is *a priori*. But when we say that a certain type of knowledge is *a priori*, we do *not* mean to imply that the concepts which it involves can be given without perception and apperception. What distinguishes the present type of *a priori* knowledge from the others is the fact that one must perceive and apperceive certain acts of *love* and not merely certain intellectual cognitions.

II. Decisions within the Sphere of the Emotions and the Formulation of the Supreme Moral Commandment
(From a letter to Oskar Kraus, September 9, 1908)

Actually much of what I say in the *Ursprung sittlicher Erkenntnis* should be supplemented and perhaps also corrected.

The acts of loving and hating which are experienced as being correct are comparable to those apodictic judgements or truths of reason which are conceptually illuminating and also experienced

[2] [Editor's note: The supposition is essential since, in this fictional case, there would be no emotional experience from which the concept could be derived.]

as being correct; I did not take special note of this fact until after the publication of the *Ursprung*. These truths of reason, or axioms, as distinguished from perceptions that are directly evident, are occasioned, so to speak, by the concepts they illuminate (or, more exactly, by the thinker in so far as he is thinking these concepts). The emotions that are experienced as being correct arise from concepts in much the same way. The point would be obvious to any reader of the *Ursprung*, but it is important, and in taking explicit note of it we have made a step forward which is not without significance.

A second observation that I have subsequently made concerns a distinction between two types of emotional activity comparable to the distinction that Leibniz speaks of in connection with the will of God. There is the *volonté conséquente*, which always involves a decision, and there is the *volonté antécédente*, which does not. Thus I may love two things which are mutually exclusive; they are incompatible with each other in the sense that they cannot both be pursued simultaneously. Thus I may love doing sums and writing poetry, but on any particular occasion I can make a decision in favour of only one.

All acts of *will*, in the strict sense, consist of decisions. It is not possible to will incompatible things. And there are emotional activities other than willing which also involve decisions; these are activities having nothing to do with any practical good or evil. Thus I can decide that I want the weather to be good tomorrow, or that I would like to have a certain person come to visit, even though I can do nothing to bring these things about.

It might be suggested that what we are concerned with in such cases is nothing more than a matter of preference; but this is not correct. On the contrary, a man may have a rational preference which conflicts with some passionate desire; the desire may win out, with the result that one decides in favour of the desire, despite the rational preference. (*"Scio meliora proboque, deteriora sequor."*)

It now seems to me that ethics is concerned with such decisions in the sphere of the emotions [*Gemütsentscheidungen*]. It tells us that we must decide in accord with love that is experienced as being correct whenever such love is in conflict with our passions or with love that is not experienced as being correct.

In requiring that we make our decisions in this way, ethics

also tells us how by reflecting we are to prepare ourselves for such decisions in cases where the correctly qualified preference is not immediately given. We are to take note of what things considered in isolation are to be loved or to be hated, of what things are compatible with each other and what things not, and of what, under given conditions, is possible or impossible.

It is also a part of ethics to tell us how a correctly qualified love may be helped to overcome the passions and the like, to tell us about the formation of our general character (*Habitus*), and to teach us to seek out conditions that are favourable and to avoid those that are not.

There are still other things that I have subsequently done in ethics—for example, in connection with the value of a temporal process in which there is an ascent [from evil to good] as contrasted with one in which there is a descent, and in connection with the law of compensation [*Vergeltungsgesetz*], concerning which Leibniz makes some valuable observations in his *Theodicy*.[1] These things, for the most part, are well known to you and I will not discuss them now. I will turn, then, to your questions.

(1) You say that the precept "Choose the best that is attainable" is not always binding. I would answer that, because the precept is put in positive terms, we should say of it what moralists have long since established with respect to every positive command—namely, that it does not require fulfillment at every moment. Even "Love God above all and your neighbour as yourself", if we take it in the positive sense, is no exception. Otherwise we would not be permitted to sleep, for one cannot love God or one's neighbours while sleeping. But on the other hand, such

[1] [Editor's note: Brentano had made a number of subsequent observations in connection with the table of goods and evils. Thus the letter mentions the *malum regressus* involved in descent from a higher to a lower good, and the *bonum progressionis* involved in the ascent from a lower to a higher degree of perfection. According to the "law of compensation", a co-ordination of sensuous and other evils to moral evil may be a good. Brentano also came to hold, as Marty has noted, that whereas a whole is false if any one of its parts is false, "a sum may be worthy of love *as a whole* even though it is made up of goods and evils that balance each other off". See "Franz Brentano" in Anton Marty's *Gesammelte Schriften*, Vol. I (Halle: Max Niemeyer, 1916), pp. 97–103.]

precepts as "You must never decide against what God requires of you," and "You must never put any kind of pleasure before the fulfillment of the commands of God and of your own conscience", are altogether without exception.

But the precept "Choose the best that is attainable" can also be taken negatively, as saying "Never choose anything less than the best that is attainable", and then it holds entirely without exception.

I think you might find it interesting to compare some good Catholic moralist, perhaps St. Thomas himself, with respect to this distinction between positive and negative commands. Perhaps the doubts which trouble you now would then disappear completely.

(2) You say that the supreme ethical duty is that of willing correctly. Willing, as you conceive it, is a broader concept than that of choosing, but you do speak of a will which is faced with a question. Isn't the question which is thus addressed to the will at least the one that Hamlet raised—"To be or not to be"? If so, the decisions of the will would be a matter of choosing, after all. But even for me, as you will gather from what is said above, *deciding*, in the sphere of the emotions, is a broader concept than that of *choosing*. Deciding goes beyond the sphere of the will itself, for it may include wishing, and my wishes may pertain to that which I cannot help to bring about or to prevent.

It should be noted that what I have said about the distinction between positive and negative commands also holds for the precept, "Will correctly". This is not a positive command, requiring that one always will correctly, for one cannot be perpetually engaged in willing.

III. The Relativity of Secondary Moral Laws[1]

Schönbühel bei Melk a. d. Donau,
September 2, 1893

To the Editor:

You ask whether I think that a person is ever justified in taking his own life. My respect for your paper compels me to reply, even though I cannot add anything to what has already been long known.

[1] [Editor's note: This brief letter, which Brentano wrote for the

116

If a man is still able to base his decisions upon considerations that pertain to good and evil, and the question is significant only to the extent that it pertains to such a man, then, without doubt, his life is something that is good. But it is not the highest good. Generally speaking, suicide is to be condemned. But there is one situation in which suicide is not only permissible, but is also an act of virtue—namely, when a good yet higher than one's own life is in jeopardy. Rebecca, in Walter Scott's "Ivanhoe", decides to throw herself into the abyss rather than to fall into the hands of the Templar; in so doing, she has the sympathy of the author and of any morally sensitive reader. And according to the most distinguished theologians, the Christian Church itself, though it forbids suicide in general, refuses to condemn the virgin who takes her life in order not to be dishonoured.

Like any other secondary moral rule, the rule forbidding suicide permits exceptions. The only rule having unconditional, universal validity is the basic moral law—the law telling us that there are no circumstances under which we may choose anything in preference to the highest good.

Here, too, what I say is in accord with the teachings not only of the most advanced science but also of that religion which for

editor of the *Deutsche Zeitung* in Vienna (September 6, 1893), is concerned with the relation that secondary or derivative moral laws bear to the one supreme moral law. Perhaps it would not be superfluous to anticipate an objection. I have often heard it said that there are, quite obviously, many unexceptionable moral laws; for example, "One must not commit murder" and "One must not lie" are universally binding and permit no exceptions. But this is to overlook the fact that such expressions as "murder", "steal", and "lie" are what Bentham called "dyslogistic". That is to say, they are expressions which already classify the deed in question as one that is wrong. A "murder" is a killing that is wrong; one tells a "lie" if one wrongly utters a falsehood. And so the real question becomes: is it in *all* circumstances wrong to kill, or to utter a falsehood, or to take over the property of another? And the answer is this: experience tells us that for the most part such acts are wrong and therefore that they are to be avoided as a general rule. But "One must not kill" is a secondary rule, since it allows for the possibility that some killings are justified. "One must not commit murder", on the other hand, is restricted in its application to those killings that are not justified, thus telling us only that unjustified killing is always wrong.]

117

centuries has been professed by the most advanced peoples—a religion that is ethically superior to all the others known to history. Christianity knows only *one* immediate supreme commandment, and it is this one commandment which gives validity to all the others. "Upon it depends the law and all the prophets."[2]

Under what circumstances, then, has a man the right to take his own life? It would be too much for me or any other moralist to try to enumerate them. Anyone with a good imagination could think of innumerable cases. But to make the general point clearer, I will add one example.

Suppose that a man has been entrusted with secret information and that the well-being of his countrymen depends upon his not divulging it. Suppose that he falls into the hands of the enemy; he knows that they will submit him to the most horrible of tortures in order to get the information and he is morally certain that he will not have the strength to withstand them. If such a man takes his life for the sole purpose of saving his country from ruin, I would not even think of condemning him morally. I would say instead that he deserves our admiration for his patriotism. And I suspect that there are very few who would disagree with me.

Let me add just one point in conclusion. Even if, generally speaking, suicide is morally blameworthy, it does not follow that the state should institute punishments for those who attempt it. If a man is prepared to take his own life, then he will hardly be deterred by the threat of any punishment that the state might inflict. After all, the state considers the death penalty to be the most extreme punishment that there is. . . .

IV. Punishment and its Justification

1 Why does the state punish people for breaking laws? Because only the threat of punishment assures, or makes probable, compliance.

2 Hence the reason for establishing punitive measures is the same as the reason for issuing penal laws.

[2] [Editor's note: Compare Brentano's *Die Lehre Jesu und ihre bleibende Bedeutung.*]

3 The most essential concern of the state is to safeguard the rights of property, life, honour, and the like; the protection of these goods is also the primary purpose of the criminal code.

4 And therefore this concern must also determine the means of punishment.

5 Given the purpose of punishment, two considerations should determine the severity of the measures to be used. These are: (1) the gravity of the wrong to be prevented; and (2) the probability that only the fear of very great punishment will be sufficient to deter people from breaking the law, and that a lesser punishment will be ineffectual.

6 But the calculations are not quite so simple. In determining its punitive laws, the state must also take into account the cases in which laws are broken *despite* the threat of punishment. If such cases did not occur, if it were possible to prevent transgressions universally and with certainty by means of draconic legislation, stipulating the most ghastly punishment for every violation, then this practice, which is condemned as inhuman, would be the one to follow. In fact, however, the consequences of criminal law are these: (1) in some cases, violation of the law is prevented; (2) in other cases, in which the law is broken despite the threat of punishment, punishment is inflicted; and (3) in still other cases, crimes are committed but concealed.

7 The second case demands particularly careful consideration.

8 The punishment adds still another ill to that of the crime itself. It places restrictions upon the person being punished and in many cases does him serious harm. The restraints lead to suffering; there is exile, imprisonment, degradation, mutilation. The more severe the punishment, the greater the injury. And the injury can be so great that the infliction of punishment is itself wrong even if it succeeds in securing general compliance. In such cases the state is transgressing against the moral law.

Furthermore, even if the state has as little desire as the individual to avenge the evil act, it certainly must take into account the degree of reprisal that is appropriate to the deed. The punishment should never be disproportionately severe. There are also proper limits to protection, not only for the individual but also for the state. If someone wants to steal my apple and I kill him because that is the only way I can stop him, I have far exceeded these bounds. The state would also exceed them if it were to threaten capital punishment in order to safeguard my possession of the apple.

The principle aim of the state is to protect property.[1] But the legal order itself is merely a secondary ethical principle; only the primary principle is valid without exception. Thus the state has a general duty to safeguard property, but in particular cases deference to the primary ethical law, which is called for at all times, may forbid the state to do what it is generally required to do. Then the moral law will set certain limits to the activity of the state, as indeed it always does, and may even curtail it completely.

9 Given these principles, it is possible to explain what many people have found incomprehensible. Many have despaired of finding the connection between the state's threats of punishment and the idea of protection. Why is it, they have wondered, that much milder punishments are allotted when greater temptations are present, even though these are the cases in which the law is most vulnerable to violations?

The answer is this: (1) a lesser degree of punishment is called for, and, as already noted, the proper boundaries may not be overstepped; (2) the people in question are relatively good, and the restraint and injury of such persons is less to be desired; and (3) the wrong produced by unbounded punishment would be the more regrettable, since the degree of temptation increases the number of infractions.

10 Consideration of the cases in which violation is concealed (see the third point at the end of paragraph 6) readily makes it clear that such concealment would become more common if unduly severe punishments were instituted. For in such cases, not only the guilty person, but other people, too, would be con-

[1] [Editor's note: "Property" is to be taken here in its broadest sense.]

cerned to prevent the authorities from knowing of the deed, and this concern would proceed from motives that are normally justified. And this, of course, would be detrimental to the aims of penal legislation in general.

11 Protection, then, is the proper motive for establishing a criminal code. And there is no glaring conflict, as some have thought, between this purpose and our actual practice.

12 One should not suppose, of course, that our practice is ideal or that it is guided by a clear knowledge of the reasons which ought to determine it. Nevertheless, these reasons unmistakably exert an influence. The fact that retribution ought to be taken into account has misled some into making revenge the essence of the penal law, something quite out of keeping with that sublime passage from the Holy Scriptures: "Vengeance is mine."

13 In instituting punishment, it is essential to take the following factors into consideration, among others. (a) The punishment should not be such that, though it is objectively the same for different offenders, it will be subjectively different.[2] (b) And the suffering which is the evil concomitant of punishment should be incurred so as to interfere as little as possible with the performance of good actions. Sometimes it is possible to inflict this suffering in such a way that either the offender himself or certain other persons will, in consequence, be able to do more good than they otherwise would have done. And this, quite obviously is the arrangement to be preferred, all other things being equal.

14 It is also important to determine the extent to which the severity of punishment should be a function of the probability that certain crimes will be concealed. Clearly threats are less effective when concealment is possible; the effectiveness is directly proportional to the probability of discovery. An increase in the severity may be permissible and advisable in these cases. But the severity should not exceed the bounds of suitable retribution. It would be a fiction, and one to be condemned as unjust, to view all offenders

[2] [Editor's note: Brentano probably means that the punishment should be suited to the particular circumstances of the offender.]

121

as though they were conjointly responsible for crimes that are individually committed.

15 Suppose that a thief has been punished and that the degree of punishment was suitable as retribution. Is it then permissible to go beyond this retribution and require him to make restitution? And may further injury be inflicted upon him to prevent him from stealing again? It can hardly be right thus to exceed the retribution that is called for. And what we have here is not *punishment*, in the strict sense of the term. People have sometimes spoken of *"legibus mere poenalibus"*. In such cases, there is no guilt and therefore no retribution is called for. But should there be such laws? Does not the very concept of such a law contain the confession of an unjustified imposition?

16 Other unjust demands are sometimes made. The maxim, *"Salus rei publicae suprema lex"*, is in itself immoral. It leads to unjust laws and therefore also to unjust punishment.

Self-preservation is not the highest principle of the state. Under certain circumstances the state is obligated to aim at its own dissolution. It should surrender without resistance, even in the face of unjust attacks, if defence is hopeless or requires too great a sacrifice on the part of its citizens. It must not be forgotten that the state is not itself the supreme end. The state is only a means to higher goods. And when these are sacrificed in order to preserve the state, then the proper order of things is reversed.

V. Epicurus and the War[1]

An article with the above title was recently published in the *Internationale Rundschau*. In stressing the fact that the craving for war cannot be condoned under any circumstances, even from the standpoint of extreme egoism, it has my complete approval.[2] The author is fully aware of the folly of viewing the state as an

[1] [Editor's note: This article first appeared in the Zurich *Internationale Rundschau*, January 15, 1916.]

[2] [Editor's note: Brentano was a decided pacifist and thought it madness to allow questions of international justice to be decided by the fortunes of war.]

entity over and above particular individuals, as though it were a higher being for whose welfare lesser creatures should sacrifice their lives and possessions. He knows how absurd it is to suppose that it is better for a whole people to be robbed of its happiness and to be subjected to unspeakable suffering than it is for the state to fail to maintain itself in full power or even to cease to extend its power. This species of madness, which is all too common at the present time, contains a most peculiar reversal of the proper order of means and end. Surely the state exists for man, not man for the state. The state exists only as a means; it is not good in itself. That patriotism which goes so far as to reverse this order cannot be admired as a virtue; we should rather condemn it as a moral error, similar to that of the miser who sacrifices his personal happiness to the collecting of riches as though this activity were something that is truly good, if not one of the higher goods.

The author is to be commended for having stressed once again a truth which so many fail to recognize in our time. But it is most regrettable that in condemning these excesses from the standpoint of the egoist, he accuses the proponents of theism of originating or encouraging them. He does not produce anything even vaguely resembling a proof of the latter claim, unless it be this: that any theory assuming the existence of a divine principle goes beyond the bounds of experience and is therefore pure nonsense or, as the author puts it, totally irrational. He finds it not surprising that those who can blunder into such absurdities are also capable of making a fetish of the state.

In referring contemptuously to *all* theistic thinkers, the author shows that he is not at home with the history of philosophy. If he were, he would know that in both ancient and modern times precisely the most important thinkers and those who were most acute have been theists: Anaxagoras, Plato, Aristotle, Descartes, Locke, Leibniz. In some ways, even Kant who is now so highly esteemed, should be counted as a theist, despite his view that the transcendent is incapable of investigation. And Albert Lange, the author of the *Geschichte des Materialismus*, was compelled to admit that we are indebted solely to spiritualists, and not to materialists, for the great discoveries in the exact sciences that were made in ancient times. Similarly, Romanes, the Darwinian psychologist, marvelled at the fact that almost all of the English investigators among his contemporaries who were especially noted for their mathematical acuity—for example, Maxwell, Lord Kelvin, and a great many of the better-known Cambridge professors—were convinced theists. In order to see that the same is true of great scientific thinkers in Germany, one need only mention Johannes Müller, Liebig, Schwann, Pflüger, and Helmholtz. The author's proof, which was bad enough to begin with, falls completely apart in the face of such facts as these.[3]

It is most regrettable, moreover, that in the practical interests of peace, one of its friends should make insulting attacks upon others, for this can only result in dispersing forces at a time it is most important to hold them together. Franklin, in trying to bring together all those who strive to do the good into one association, which he called the "Society of the Doers of Good", offered us an example of the kind of tolerance for which we are pleading; he took no offence at even the greatest differences of opinion. The intolerance of the present author becomes obvious when we consider that during our time almost no one has worked with greater zeal at restoring peace than Benedict XV, the head of the Catholic Church.

In spirit, Christianity has always been a religion of peace and it is so today, even if, time and again, the stupidity of mankind has led to wars that have been waged, supposedly, in the interests of religion. The folly of those who advocate an egoistic morality leads even more readily to war. Certainly the roots of our present ills lie in egoistical impulses and not in religious convictions. I could easily show that this is true. I could also show that if anyone is to be charged with having an irrational philosophy, it should be the followers of Epicurus and not those who are theists. Epicurus, perhaps more than any other philosopher, showed himself to be completely superficial. But for me to go further into these matters would be to fall into the kind of intolerance against which I have been protesting—an intolerance toward those who are one with me in loving peace.

[3] [Editor's note: Cf. Brentano, "Der Atheismus und die Wissenschaft", published anonymously in *Historisch-politische Blätter f. d. katholische Deutschland*, Vol. 2 (1873), pp. 852 and 916.]

VI. The Young Benjamin Franklin's Attack upon Ethics
(later emphatically repudiated but without insight
into the logical error involved)[1]

I

1 Morality, it is generally supposed, requires us to inform ourselves in as much detail as possible concerning the relative value of the things among which we must choose and then to give preference to what is better, and to do so *because* it is better. The conscientious man will proceed with care and often at considerable sacrifice to himself.

2 But all this seems absurd in the light of the most sublime of philosophical truths. There is a God and he is infinitely good, infinitely wise, and infinitely powerful. Nothing can happen unless it has been infallibly foreseen and arranged through divine providence and unless it is predetermined to bring about the best possible end in the most perfect way.

3 Consequently everything that does happen must be acknowledged as being without doubt—then and there, at the time at which it occurs—the best possible means for the best possible end.

4 But in that case what is the point of moral deliberation and self-sacrifice? Why shouldn't each man indulge himself as he pleases without any qualms of conscience at all? For whatever harm the indulgence may *seem* to threaten, this appearance will prove deceptive once the agent succeeds in bringing about what he has undertaken. For what has just been said of *every* event will also hold of his particular act: as a part of the divine world-plan it is precisely what is required at that time and place for bringing about the best that is possible. It is only our own limited perspective that prevents us from surveying the whole network of relations and giving an account of how and by what means each

[1] [Editor's note: Franklin speaks of this attack in his *Autobiography*. Brentano attempted to put the thought as precisely as possible and did not use Franklin's own words. This piece was written sometime before 1901.]

event occurs. Given that the agent has undertaken the act without any reflection and without sacrificing himself in any way, then it is only if he does *not* succeed, and to the extent that he does not succeed, that he may properly be said to have undertaken something which is not the best means to the best end.

5 What is the consequence of this? If what we set out to do without any probing of conscience is something that is *not* the best possible deed in just those circumstances, then it is something that we cannot possibly succeed in doing! Clearly *this* type of failure will do no harm at all to what is good or to what is best.

Whoever is unaware of this may have as many scruples as he likes and deny himself as often as he pleases. But whoever does know it—as we do, thanks to our philosophical deliberations— is released from all moral bonds, even if he does love what is good and what is to be preferred. Given this awareness, we would seem to be free of any type of moral reproach. Do what you wish and have no misgivings at all! That is the final word of the most sublime practical wisdom.

II

The young Benjamin Franklin, then, has given us an argument purporting to show that the belief in a God who is infinitely good, wise, and powerful, and in his predetermination of everything that occurs, is sufficient to produce moral paralysis in any consistent thinker.

To indicate briefly what is wrong with this argument, I will show (1) that the conclusion is false and (2) why the argument is not sound. Franklin saw the first point himself, but he confessed that the second always remained a mystery to him.

(1) It is easy to see that the conclusion is false. To the extent to which an agent in a given set of circumstances can foresee the results of his actions and then give preference to that which promises to bring about the greater amount of good, he will in fact produce a greater amount of good, generally speaking, than he would by acting merely upon impulse. This is just a point of good sound reason—which here, as elsewhere, is confirmed by the calculus of probability. (So far as the unforeseeable consequences of the two ways of acting are concerned, the probabilities are the same on both sides and therefore, according

to the law of large numbers, these consequences, generally speaking, would come out the same. Hence the difference with respect to the predictable consequences will tip the scale in favour of the act which proceeds from deliberation.) The result of such forethought and deliberation is most significant in the case of those agents who have the greatest amount of insight and who therefore are best able to foresee the results of their actions and to determine correctly the value of the various goods and evils involved and then to choose the most suitable means for bringing about what is good. But if Franklin's argument were sound, then the most perceptive among those who believe in God's predetermination would be led to choose and to act without any thought about the goodness or badness of what they do. In consequence these people would bring about less good than others and the result therefore would be as it should be—which is contrary to the claims of the argument.

(2) What, then, is wrong with Franklin's argument? The answer is this:

Some *preferences* may be said to have a moral character and others not.

The preference of one object over another is a preference that has *moral character* if the agent takes the one object to be *better* than the other.[2] His preference is moral if he favours what he believes to be better because he believes it to be better; his preference is immoral when he favours the opposite.

A preference is *without* moral relevance, on the other hand, when the agent believes that the objects in question are of equal value or when he finds himself unable to make any judgement about the preferability of the one or the other. And what has been said about preference in general also holds of what may be

[2] [Editor's note: Taking one object to be better than another is what is sometimes called making a judgement of value. More exactly, it is making a judgement of *preference*—arriving at a conviction which is based upon a preference that is experienced as being correct. The type of preference that is here under discussion, as Brentano goes on to observe, is a "preferential choosing and willing" which is based upon such a conviction. Those emotive acts which are experienced as being correct and which are presupposed by our judgements of value are not themselves acts of will; they are emotive acts that arise out of the concepts that are involved.]

called practical preference; that is to say, it also holds of acts of choice. For choosing is simply preferential willing.

(Not every act of preference is an act of choosing. The agent may also have a preference with respect to two incompatible things which he believes to be outside the sphere of his own influence. For instance, he may wish that the sun would shine and thus *prefer* the sun to rain, but there is no act of *choice* in such a case.)

Now what holds generally of acts of choice also holds of the choices that are made by those people who believe in divine providence and in God's unlimited power of predetermination.

What must we show, then, if we are to prove that the choices that such people make are without moral relevance? We must show one or the other of two things: either (a) that the people, if they are to be rational and consistent, must take the objects among which they choose to be of equal value; or (b) that in the situations involved it is impossible to form a reasonable judgement having any degree of certainty or probability.

But the doctrine of divine providence and predetermination does not imply either of these things.

It does not imply that the objects among which choices are to be made are all of equal value. To be sure, it follows from the doctrine that every event is a *part* of the best possible ordering of means to the best possible end, but not that all such parts are themselves of equal value. And indeed it is not the case that all such parts are all of equal value.[3] But Franklin is committed to saying that they are, since, according to him, the doctrine implies that each event is itself the best possible means to the best possible end. And this is quite wrong. A thing is a means only for whatever it is that the thing brings about.

If a thing is to be itself the means to the best possible end, then it must produce the best possible of all the effects that can be pro-

[3] [Editor's note: In a note on the manuscript, Brentano remarks that one must hold unequivocally to the proposition that every event is a *part* of the best possible means for the best possible end. From this it will follow that each event is ordered in the best possible way in relation to the best possible end. But, as Brentano goes on to say in the passage above, it does not follow that each individual event is *itself* the best possible means to the best possible end.]

The Vietnam Veterans Against the War/Winter Soldier Organization, "Veterans testimony on Vietnam: need for investigation," *Congressional Record* (April 6, 1971), E2825–E2936, trans. into Japanese by Kugai Saburo, *Vetonamu Kikanhei no Shogen* (Tokyo: Iwanami Shoten, 1973), pp. 103–9.

24 Reference should be made to the *Hankyoreh21* journalist Koh Kyung-Tae, who classified and analyzed the logic of the recorded testimony. See "The people who narrated the truth: massacres of civilians by the South Korean forces at the time of the Vietnamese conflict seen through the testimony of participating military personnel" (document for "Symposium Relating to the Vietnam War and South Korea's Sending of Troops" organized by Truth Commission on Massacres of Vietnamese Civilians, Seoul, October 2000).

25 A prime example is Ch'ae Myŏng-Shin et al., *The Vietnam War and the South Korean Forces* (Seoul: Vietnam War Buddies Association, 2002). Che Myung-Shin, the first commander of the South Korean forces dispatched to Vietnam, has been particularly active in providing comments to magazines and newspapers.

26 Ch'ae Myŏng-Shin et al., *The Vietnam War*, p. 35.

27 See Article 47, Mercenaries 2. A mercenary is any person who: (a) is specially recruited locally or abroad in order to fight in an armed conflict; (b) does, in fact, take a direct part in the hostilities; and (c) is motivated to take part in the hostilities essentially by the desire for private gain and, in fact, is promised, by or on behalf of a Party to the conflict, material compensation substantially in excess of that promised or paid to the combatants of similar ranks and functions of the armed forces of that Party; (d) is neither a national of a Party to the conflict nor a resident of territory controlled by a Party to the conflict; (e) is not a member of the armed forces of a Party to the conflict; and (f) has been sent, not on official duty as a member of armed forces dispatched by a State which is not a Party to the conflict.

28 In the 1970s, returned soldiers from Vietnam carried out sit-in protests against the Seoul to Pusan highway, which they said had been built with and symbolized the gobbling up of their blood and sweat.

29 This has been criticized as illogical from the very beginning, because the Vietnamese government had not been involved in the Korean War, nor had any of the other countries assisting and participating in the Vietnam War been directly attacked.

30 The proposal to send troops to Vietnam was of great significance to the Park Chung-Hee administration; it was a diplomatic card for gaining diplomatic trust and recognition from President John F. Kennedy. This much has already been made clear in the previously mentioned research by Choi Tong-Ju and others. See Ch'ae Myŏng-Shin et al., *The Vietnam War*, p. 40.

31 Symington Committee Hearings, p. 56.

32 Han Young-Won, *The Politics of South Korea's Military Establishment* (Seoul: Dae Wang Sa), p. 142.

33 The Korean National Defense Force was a constabulary whose sole purpose was to quell domestic uprisings. It was viewed as a police reserve by the Americans who feared domestic disturbances. Americans responsible for the constabulary saw tactical training in the "civil disorders and guerilla-like activities by Communist elements"; they were able to inculculate "the principles of village fighting" into actual operations. See Bruce Cumings, *The Origins of the Korean War* (Seoul: Yŏksapip'yongsa, 2002), p. 177.

34 *Dong-A Ilbo* (Seoul) (May 22, 1994).

35 *Diplomacy* (Seoul) 24/12 (1998), 14.

36 *Dong-A Ilbo*, 1998. *Maekyŏng* (Seoul), 1998.

37 Local English-language newspapers said it was the first time that a South Korean president had expressed regret for the role of South Korean troops during the

Vietnam War, but the Vietnamese Prime Minister Phan Van Khai reportedly said that Vietnam had not expected any apology or compensation. *International Herald Tribune* (Hong Kong), December 17, 1998.

38 In the meeting between President Kim Dae-Jung and the Vietnamese President Tran Du Luong, President Kim Dae-Jung reputedly put in a request for participation in $500 million worth of business ventures in return for $3 million in grant aid and an extra $42.5 million in funding for a vaccine plant. See Cho Hyun-Je, "The significance of President Kim's visit to Ho's mausoleum", *Maekyŏng* December 16, 1998.

39 Morita Yoshio, *Chŏsen Shusen no Kiroku (A Record of Korea at the End of the War)* (Tokyo: Gannando, 1964), pp. 297–301.

40 In his memorial to the Emperor dated February 14, 1945, Prince Konoye Fumimaro appealed frankly about the red threat: "Defeat, alas, will soon be inevitable. . . . Instead of this public adherence [*tatemae*] to the preservation of the national polity [*kokutai*], what I am most concerned about is not so much defeat, as a Communist revolution which might take place in the event of defeat. . . . If one argues from the premise that defeat is inevitable, then continuation of the war wherein there is no prospect of victory would only play into the hands of the Communists. Therefore, from the position of preserving the national polity, I am firmly of the opinion that we should seek ways concluding the war, ending it as quickly as possible." Konoye Fumimaro, *Konoye Nikki (The Konoye Diaries)* (Tokyo: Kyodo Tsushinsha, 1968), pp. 66–9.

41 Translation into English for Kim Dae-Jung is originally based on Korean, and for Shiina based on Japanese. It should be noted that neither case is cited from the official text.

42 Takasaki Soji, *Kensho Nikkan Kaidan (Examination of the Japan–South Korea Summit)* (Tokyo: Iwanami Shoten, 1996), pp. 297–301.

43 Meredith Woo Cumings, *Race to the Swift* (New York: Columbia University Press, 1991).

44 Michael Hardt and Antonio Negri, *Empire* (Cambridge, MA: Harvard University Press, 2000) p. 147.

45 Stories circulated in the 1960s of students being sent out to Vietnam if they had been arrested for demonstrating against the bilateral talks with Japan. See Nawauri Project, p. 39.

46 Hannah Arendt and Shimizu Hayao, *Kako to Mirai no Aida ni: II Bunka no Kiki (Between Past and Future: Cultural Dangers II)* (Tokyo: Godo-shuppan, 1970), p. 9.

47 Kim Dong-Hee refused to go to Vietnam, deserting from the army in 1965. He tried to seek asylum in Japan, but was arrested on Tsushima Island. Kim Hyung-Sung was a technical officer with the Marines. He too refused to go to Vietnam and fled to Japan, but ended up in an immigration detention center, where he committed suicide by self-immolation after the decision was made to deport him back to South Korea. Kim Jin-Su was an American of Korean extraction, also known as Kenneth Charles Briggs, who was a Private First Class in the US Army. In 1967, he entered the Cuban embassy in Tokyo and applied for asylum. Sekiya Shigeru and Sakamoto Yoshie, eds, *Tonari ni Dassohei ga ita Jidai: Jatekku, Aru Shimin Undo no Kiroku (The Era when Deserters Lived Next Door: The Record of One Civic Movement, Jatec)* (Tokyo: Shiso no Kagakusha, 1998), pp. 39–64. Also see Oda Makoto, Suzuki Michihiro, and Tsurumi Shunsuke, *Kokka to Guntai he no Hangyaku Dassohei no Shiso (A Traitor to the State and the Armed Forces: The Thoughts of Deserters)* (Tokyo: Tahei Shuppansha, 1971), pp. 77–80.

Part II

Toward a Northeast Asian approach to historical injustice?

7 The aesthetic construction of ethnic nationalism

War memorial museums in Korea and Japan

Hong Kal

Since 1990 both Japan and Korea have experienced commemoration booms, in which the number of private and public memorial museums and monuments has tripled. These institutions provide narratives of each nation's recent past and articulate the ideals of nation and citizenship. They compose tales to construct tradition, revise history, and reinterpret the past in order for the nation to remain relevant in public and private life. Like writing history, the museum collects and assembles fragments and carefully recontextualizes them into a particular narrative. Precisely because of its role in institutionalizing social norms, the museum becomes a crucial apparatus for the production of national identity. It shapes the manner in which the nation creates its past, imagines its boundaries, and constitutes its citizenship.

Central to the autobiography of the nation is the representation of wars and death, memories of which are considered essential in guaranteeing the immortality of the nation. Benedict Anderson has written that:

> Nations, however, have no clearly identifiable births, and their deaths, if they ever happen, are never natural. Because there is no originator, the nation's biography cannot be written evangelically, "down time," through a long procreative chain of begettings. The only alternative is to fashion it "up time" towards Peking Man, Java Man, King Arthur, wherever the lamp of archeology casts its fitful gleam.[1]

Since the nation has no fixed birth certificate, its biography can be written "up time" from its "originary present" toward its unlimited ancient past. The ancestral construction of the nation, according to Anderson, is marked by the narrative of death in reversed genealogy: "World War II begets World War I; out of Sedan comes Austerlitz; the ancestor of the Warsaw Uprising is the state of Israel."[2] The war memorial museum creates a precedent for securing such an inverted genealogical construction of the ancient past of the nation. It supplies a formal structure for the nation to fashion itself toward its ancestors who died to guarantee the continuity as well as the immortality of the nation.[3]

In Asia, the transformations of post-Cold War geopolitics have opened new possibilities for inter-Asian relations and inevitably led to a rigorous interrogation of the region's recent past. In the question of how to represent colonialism and catastrophic wars, war memorial museums have become one of the most controversial sites. Especially as the battles over the history within and between Korea and Japan have become more intense and divisive, war memorial museums demonstrate the tension between official and societal memories of the past, revealing conflicting, yet mutually constitutive, assumptions of postcolonial Korea, divided Korea, and postwar Japan. Can the forefathers be wrong when their wrongdoings secured "the goodness of the nation"? Can our heroes be killers? How should the enemy dead be represented? Can national war history be relational and plural when it is supposed to affirm the singularity of the nation?

In this chapter, I consider two war memorial museums: the War Memorial of Korea (hereafter WMK) and the Yushukan, a war memorial museum attached to the Yasukuni Shrine of Japan. Located in the center of each nation's capital city, both play symbolic and socially significant roles in the construction of nationalism in the two countries. In Korea, the WMK was built "to commemorate martyrs and their service to the nation" and thus to prepare citizens "to face a future national crisis."[4] Yet the WMK is also a site where the public resists the official representation of war and nation by criticizing the museum or consuming the space outside its original intention of patriotic nationalism. In Japan, located in the Shrine complex where conflicting memories meet, the Yushukan aims to nurture a sense of "lost" pride in being Japanese with a "glorious" history of war and thus poses a significant political question of how to represent Japan's recent past, colonialism, and wars.

Few apparatuses attempt the construction of nation as clearly as these war memorial museums, which while imported from the West have led a life of their own according to particular temporal and geographical conditions. I examine how they write biographies of the nation and invest the past with particular historical meaning. I focus on the important role of war dead in the creation of national immortality, and demonstrate that the source of this national ethos derives from the enactment of ethnic nationalisms in the two countries. I argue that the biographies of the nation written "up time" toward its ethnic "origins" are an attempt not only to create a linkage to the past, but also to produce an image of the future of the nation for today's generation, who are experiencing forces of globalization. In doing so, I pay particular attention to the spatial technologies of the museum in the discussion and analysis. Through the arrangement of objects, the layout of rooms, the sequence of collections, and the installation of exhibition devices, the museum offers carefully developed scenarios of the nation's war histories. These museum technologies claim the heritage of patriotism for their respective societies and equate that tradition with the nation. By walking through the museum, visitors are prompted to enact and internalize the values written into the exhibitionary script. The activity visitors engage in can be described as a *ritual* in which the programmed experience of the museum casts visitors in the role of an idealized citizen and heir of the national dead.[5]

My main purpose in this chapter is to examine ethnocentric nationalism in the two countries as represented in the war memorial museums. Clearly the WMK and the Yushukan are embedded in different forms of nationalism, for Korea and Japan have mutually antagonistic historical trajectories – one the colonized and the other the colonizer. The conflicting experience of colonialism has harnessed them with different burdens over how to deal with historical injustice. Even within national boundaries, a discourse of the nation and nationalism has evolved into various forms in adaptation to changing geopolitical and international contexts. For instance, in Japan, there was a shift in the dominant discourse of Japan from the multi-ethnic empire to the mono-ethnic nation.[6] However, as Harumi Befu has pointed out, what has remained in the discursive history of Japan is a sense of Japanese ethnic uniqueness and superiority, often enunciated as *Nihonjinron.*[7] Nevertheless I do not attempt to show that the war memorial museums are representative of a monolithic and official voice in society. While the WMK is a state-sponsored public museum, the Yushukan is ostensibly private. However, given that the Yushukan is attached to the prewar State Shinto Shrine, which is still strongly associated with the parallel image of the emperor, the state, and the nation,[8] the two museums are comparable in their political significance. They demonstrate the growing obsession with ethnocentric nationalism in contemporary Korea and Japan, which is partly a reaction to the changing domestic and regional political climate after the Cold War. My contention is that the question of reconciliation with historical injustice cannot be seriously dealt with without problematizing ethnocentric nationalism, which is defensive, exclusive, and thus constraining. The self-reflection of nationalism is indeed at the core of the issue of reconciliation within as well as between nations.

The War Memorial of Korea (WMK)

The WMK was opened on the site of the former Army Headquarters in downtown Seoul in 1994. Conceived in 1988 under the Roh Tae-woo regime, the WMK has survived the demise of the military authoritarian government and become a hallmark, ironically, of Kim Young-sam, who headed the first civilian regime in postcolonial Korea in over thirty years. Despite the public discomfort over the building's military legacy, the new president, Kim Young-sam, deploring Korean young people's lack of "national security consciousness," welcomed the WMK as a reminder to the Korean people of the ongoing threat posed by North Korea.[9]

Like other war memorial museums, the purpose of the WMK is to commemorate the war dead who sacrificed their lives for the defense of the nation. The museum is also devoted to teaching the patriotic spirit to younger generations who have no memory of war by providing them with historical grounds for safeguarding the country against threats.[10] However, there is something peculiar about the WMK. It not only constructs a narrative of the nation's patriotism but also, more problematically, creates an ancestral lineage of the patriotism; that is, a sacrifice of the forefathers to the children of the nation: the *Koreans*. Therefore, the museum becomes an apparatus that seeks to construct a national subject of Korea based on the idea of common bloodlines and shared ancestry. Ethnic nationalism, as Shin Gi-Wook has argued, stems from a sense of Korean ethnic homogeneity, which has been assumed as naturally originated from ancient times. This "ethnic nationalism," which posits the state, nation, and ethnicity as identical categories, is a major organizing principle of contemporary Korean society on both sides of the peninsula. Yet, as Shin has pointed out, its historicity, eternity, and naturalness have not been seriously questioned.[11] In this section, I analyze the architectural space and the visual environment of the museum, decoding a narrative construction of ethnic nationalism. In particular, I focus on how the museum constructs the "Korean ethnic nation" in terms of war, kinship, and familial sacrifice. I illuminate how this process of making "we, Koreans" is also connected to the construction of Korean "others," namely North Korea, Vietnam, and Japan.

The spatial order of the Memorial Hall: national ritual in the ancestral temple

The museum complex, like the palace, is designed to be different from the secular world outside. Located in the capital city, the museum is secluded from its surroundings by the building's overpowering symmetrical form (Figure 7.1). Like the series of gates one can find in the Gyeongbok Palace, the exterior of the museum is organized around the spatial sequence of the pathway, the steps, the moat, and the plaza, thus re-enacting the temporal ritual sequence and heightening a sense of solemnity as one enters the museum. Ascending another staircase, visitors are drawn to the museum building, which is constructed in classical Greco-Romanic architectural vocabularies that give the impression of a temple. Despite this Western façade, however, I would argue that the organization of space stems from the order of a Confucian temple.[12]

Upon entering the main gate, visitors start their pilgrimage by following a ritual of visit programmed by the museum along the processional central axis, from outdoors to the inner shrine at the north end of the museum. Inside the museum building, visitors ascend to the Central Hall, a round room with a skylight in its domed ceiling. The Central Hall opens onto a long corridor lined on both sides with half-body statues of heroic warriors. This corridor, representing the axial line of the museum, ends at the hemispherical domed Memorial Hall, the innermost "shrine" of the museum (Figure 7.2). Concealed behind the layers of space and located at the end

Figure 7.1 A view of the War Memorial of Korea.
Source: courtesy of the War Memorial of Korea.

point of the north–south axis, it recalls the place of the ancestral table in a temple. At the apex of the dome, a blue beam is projected straight down onto a bowl. With the concentrated light from the sky, the bowl resembles an altar where visitors can contemplate and perhaps communicate with the war dead. Consequently, visitors are encouraged to remember the dead. The bowl and the light are the focal point at which the spirit of the war dead meets with the living, enabling the latter to worship the "national spirit."

The movement of the visitor from the exterior to the interior of this innermost space is a journey back to the "origin." In her analysis of the WMK, Sheila Miyoshi Jager has aptly pointed out the search for tradition to construct the nation's political legitimacy.[13] Yet there is more to it than that. The logic of reversed genealogy is associated with the Confucian order of time, space, and origin. It is a scenario in which the patriotic present pays tribute to its ancestral past, where it was born and to where it should return. The journey to the innermost shrine is not only for the living, but also for the dead. Like the living, the spirit of the dead will return to, and become part of, the family of ancestors from whom they came. Both the dead and living find themselves returning to the ancestor from where they came and in whom they find meaning in their sacrificial life for the nation.

The WMK is an apparatus that seeks to produce a national subject based on ethnicity, encouraging visitors to recognize their shared origin and not to forget those to whom they owe their being. The museum suggests that as long as visitors identify themselves with the dead, they will recognize their

Figure 7.2 Memorial Hall.
Source: courtesy of the War Memorial of Korea.

sacrifice, as well as their blood relationship, and therefore be united in a national community. Visiting the museum and following the spatial order of the display enacts the ritual of paying tribute to the dead and the shared ancestral to whom "we" all belong. Like an ancestral temple, the museum represents the beginning of a lineage, reminding people of the historical existence of their ancestors and their duty to keep such a memory alive.

The War History Room: constructing the living war dead

The spatial sequence of the museum tells of the linkage of the national dead and the national living. The dead and the living mirror each other to ensure the continuation of the nation within which ethnic Koreans are embedded. The sequence of the exhibits from exterior to interior and from the secular to the sacred serves to awaken the national dead to interpolate the living, demanding the cooperation of all the war dead to perform as the ancestors of the living. As an apparatus for the production of ethnic nationalism, the museum claims to speak for the "Korean" war dead who did not know themselves to be such, for generation after generation. By bringing together wars engaged in the peninsula, the museum provides coherence for a larger historical context of a lineage of patriotic Korean ancestors. Speaking on behalf of the ancestors, the museum also speaks subtly to visitors about who they are in relation to the war heroes. The War History Room, for instance, narrates a history of Korea from the prehistoric age to the present. It stages weaponry technology and military tactics of each period. Yet they are exhibited in a standardized format that enables visitors to see them as similar to each other and therefore sharing the same heritage. No one would think about any particularity of each period except as an identical and collective heritage of Korea.

Visitors are also encouraged to notice the vast numbers of the war dead. In the left and right gallery wings of the main exhibition building, the names of the martyrs are inscribed on black memorial stones. The names are listed as uniformly as possible and organized in strictly regulated units. This standardized tombstone dislodges the war dead from their individuality, for no personal memories can be invested in a temple meant for collective identification. The visitors can only see the names as interchangeable with one another. In the attempt to nationalize the war dead, no other identities are allowed except that of ethnic Korean. It is in this ethnicity that official nationalism lives. By rescuing the dead from obscurity and giving them a national meaning, the museum creates for the state its lineage and ethnic identity. Once the Korean war dead have been enshrined for all to see, the state can claim legitimacy by linking itself to the descendents of ancient Korea and to the rightful bearers of a Korean ethnic nation.

Just as the museum represents the war dead as equivalent Koreans, regardless of their glorious or shameful lives, it also seeks to embrace visitors as collective Koreans. When the spirit of the dead is conjured up as the existence of Korean ethnic collectivity, the past dead and the present living become interchangeable with each other. The exhibition prepares the ground for the future war dead. Today's young pilgrims to the memorial are put in the position of future Korean fellows of the dead. It is perhaps more than a coincidence that the museum provides an auxiliary facility for wedding ceremonies in its Peace Hall. This brings together the idea of the normal nuclear family, the symbol of grateful and unconditional royalty, and the promise of the future reproduction of the national pure subject – as if only ethnic purity itself would guarantee the future of the nation.

The "contaminated" others: communist Vietnam and North Korea

Within the narrative of ethnic nationalism, the WMK presents the Korean War as one of the most critical threats to the Korean nation caused by North Korea. It offers a denunciation of the anti-Korean decadence of

North Korea led by the foreign communism. A major focus of the displays is the question of who is the rightful heir of the Korean nation. A return to the normal noncommunist state by the leadership of South Korea is then proclaimed as the necessary basis for the recuperation of true Korean nationhood. In this context, the major role of the US in the catastrophic war is dramatically downplayed.

The Korean War Room displays the victimization of South Koreans by the invasion of North Korean communist aggressors by mobilizing historical documents, pictures, films, and various kinds of wartime articles. This account reinforces the dominant ideology of the innocent South Korea versus the tainted North Korea. Yet the history of war is recast in such a way to prove the resilience, the idealism, and the fulfillment of Korean identity. The WMK also highlights Korea's participation in the Vietnam War as part of the US alliance to liberate the world from communism and to form a united front for freedom and democracy. What is remarkable in the demonstration of South Korea's involvement in Vietnam is the narrative of war and civilization, replicating the tone of not only US military occupation but also Japan's colonialism. Just as the massacre of Korean civilians by US soldiers was silenced, the brutality of Korean soldiers against Vietnamese during the war is nowhere to be found in the exhibition.

Both North Korea and Vietnam are objects of the patronizing mission of returning the communist regime to what is considered the normal state. Yet there is a fundamental difference in the museum's portrayal of Vietnamese and North Koreans. While the communist Vietnamese are portrayed as dangerous and inhumane others, the North Koreans are illustrated as communists yet brothers who have gone astray and pitifully left the family by adopting the foreign communism. Outside the museum there is a statue of brothers who wear two different military uniforms yet hold each other on the hemispheric pedestal (Figure 7.3). According to the catalogue, the statue depicts two brothers who met on the battlefield as enemies, but finally are reconciling with each other as a result of a "transcending ideology of brotherly love." The North stands in for a young Korean who, years down the road, after losing everything, will return to the embrace of the elder brother, the heir of the family's house. The statue also shows the association of the male youth with familial piety, national virility, and nondecay. The possibility of reconciliation is again framed within this code of the patriarchal family. In this way, the museum emphasizes South Korea as the only legitimate son who preserves the national spirit by continuing the unbroken patriotic military tradition.

Where has Japanese colonialism gone?

The representation of "Japanese colonialism" in the museum throws additional light on the political culture of postcolonial Korea. In her analysis of the WMK, Jager has quite correctly observed that the WMK curiously

Figure 7.3 The Statue of Brothers.
Source: courtesy of the War Memorial of Korea.

represents very few episodes in Japanese colonialism despite the fact that the modern Korean military owes much to Japan's rule. Jager suggests that this embarrassing period in Korean military history is suppressed by the museum's obsession with masculine patriotism.[14] Yet the question is still how we account for the invisible, yet significant, presence of Japanese colonialism. We can approach the invisible significance of the colonial past in at least three ways. The first relates to the WMK's position that at bottom Japanese colonialism makes no difference. The museum suggests that the Japanese occupation of Korea did not change the character of the Korean "military" tradition, but merely further proved its prowess. The museum represents Japanese colonialism as one of the major contributing elements to the strength of Korea, minimizing the sense of being a colonized victim. In this narrative, the world is absolutely divided between "we," Koreans, and "they," Japanese. The "we" are linked together across generations in a homogeneous moral bond against "they." Japan was counterpoised against Korea; this coupling represents two fundamentally antagonistic political forces and further sustains the coherency of the Korean nation.

Paradoxically, the peripheral position of Japan points to the centrality of colonialism in creating the exhibition culture in the WMK. The pervasive representation of military strength in the museum is connected to the experience of colonial Korea: the loss of manliness, the redemption of which has taken the repetitive form of retrieving masculinity.[15] In this sense, the WMK can be seen as a therapeutic apparatus for the state, which seeks to redeem the humiliating experience of the colonial past. Recuperating from this loss has taken the form of representing the brother (North Korea) and the neighbor (Vietnam) as weaker and in need of protection and reconciliation. In the museum's seamless story constructed through images of family, ethnicity, patriotism, and masculinity, ironically the marginal representation of Japanese colonialism plays a significant role in accomplishing the superiority of the Korean nation.

The WMK seeks to construct the nation's military patriotism based on the idea of a common bloodline and shared ancestry; that is, an ancestral lineage of the nation's patriotism. The process of making a national subject of Korea is closely associated with the construction of Korean others, namely North Korea, Vietnam, and Japan. I have shown how the WMK constructs legitimacy for the nation-state by adopting a sense of discontinuity with the colonial past and dissociation from the North Korean communist regime. I have also shown how the spatial technology of the museum constructs a narrative of ethnic nationalism. In the following section, I turn to the case of Japan to show the ways in which "ethnic nationalism" is being constructed in the Yushukan museum.

The Yushukan of Japan

Since its unconditional surrender in 1945 following the genocide of Hiroshima and Nagasaki, postwar Japan has subscribed to the belief in an utter disjuncture with its wartime past, what is popularly known as the "new beginning" of the nation.[16] This mission of making a new nation was carried out by constructing Japanese civilians as victims of the nuclear catastrophe, which was caused by the misguidance of the ruling military leaders. In particular, the atomic bomb peace museums have mounted a variety of initiatives to make postwar Japan a nation committed to peace. However, this postwar "peace culture" has recently been countered by the new war memorial museum, the Yushukan. As if returning to the past "great Japanese empire," the Yushukan seeks to revise national history by calling for pride in being Japanese, inheritors of a spirit of self-sacrifice for the emperor, the nation, and the state.

The Yushukan and the Yasukuni Shrine

The history of the Yushukan, a war memorial museum, tells of Japan's modern history. It was first built in 1882 in the Yasukuni Shrine complex in Tokyo in order to display articles left behind by the *kami* (deities) of the shrine from the time of the Meiji Restoration. It was expanded in 1908 to accommodate the increased collections after the Sino-Japanese War and the Russo-Japanese War and rebuilt in 1932 after the Great Kanto Earthquake. With the surrender of Japan in 1945, the museum was made inactive until it was restored in 1986, and finally reopened after renovation in 2002 with a new exhibition building. The Yasukuni Shrine is an unusual shrine. In 1869, the Meiji government built it in proximity to the imperial palace as a state Shinto shrine in order to preserve the divine souls (*kami*) of soldiers who fell in defense of the emperor, a project to construct a unified nation under the emperor.[17] To die for the emperor was to transcend physical annihilation, an act that was to be rewarded by being remembered as a glorious and noble death. The shrine demands neither mourning for death nor mere religious ritual but a glorification of self-sacrifice for the emperor and nation.[18] The authority of the shrine therefore lies not in its physical form, but in the practice of visiting. The act of visiting and offering thanks to the war dead became part of the definition and revelation of the purpose of their death: the survival of the nation. A visit to the shrine is therefore indispensable to the consolidation of national existence. Logically, then, a decrease in visitors to the shrine implies the diminishing authority of the nation. The constant appeals by Japanese leaders to visit the shrine can be attributed to anxiety about the decrease in popularity of the shrine among the populace.[19] It is within this context that after several years of renovation the Yushukan was reborn with a mission to nurture and renew a sense of pride in being Japanese, with the nation's "glorious" history of war.

The Yushukan, however, needs to be seen in part as a response to several historical conditions similar to those that generate ethnic nationalism in the WMK. The first factor concerns the place of Asia in Japan. The question of how to account for Japan's military past remains a critical issue in postcolonial Asia. In particular, as the post-Cold War era opens new possibilities for Asian political and economic integration, Japan's wartime conduct has become a serious issue in Japan and other Asian countries. This transformation has been accompanied by an equally strong reactionary nationalism in Japan. The reopening of the Yushukan stemmed from a rising new conservative nationalism that asks Japanese citizens to remember the nation's military past, which is no longer violent or shameful but glorious. The attempt to revive the war museum was concomitant with a campaign by a group of conservative nationalists in the 1990s to rewrite a "new history" that neither imposes a victim complex on Japan nor assigns all blame for the catastrophic wars on the Japanese military state.[20] Strongly opposed to any apology or compensation for Japanese war atrocities, the conservative nationalists claimed that the affirmation of wartime Japan is the ultimate way to achieve a full realization of Japanese identity, which was forcefully suppressed and abandoned under US hegemony.

The second factor involves the inheritance and bequest of national character and identity. In the early twenty-first century, Japan confronts a gap within its own space that is generational. It confronts a divide between those who share the memory of wartime and those who, having grown up or been born after the war, do not share that experience, except in a most mediated way. As the older generation is dying, some conservative nationalists feel the need to bequeath to the younger generation "heroic" memories of the war that have been forgotten. In one sense, there is an attempt in the museum to link the present to the past, a link that, according to the nationalists, has been disjointed by the culture of peace. Hence the restoration of the Yushukan museum implies a concept of generations in which the war dead are telling their children within the family of the nation that the future of Japan must be drawn from the history of their own struggle and identity. The third factor relates to the influx of more and more "Asian" peoples and cultures in Japan. The Yushukan serves as a reminder to (young) Japanese that they have "superior" ethnic values that should not be lost to the "lower" foreign cultures. Considering all these factors, there is, however, a real and painful paradox in the position of the museum. It offers the nation a political value, but finds the social life of many Japanese today increasingly out of its control.

In what follows, as in the analysis of the WMK, I explore meanings of the exhibition display in the Yushukan to shed light on some aspects of political culture in postwar Japan. Located in the shrine complex, where conflicting memories meet, the Yushukan museum offers a significant political answer to the question of how to represent Japan's recent past, colonialism, and wars in Asia. In a number of instances I make comparisons with the WMK, to highlight certain shared features of ethnic nationalism in the ways the museum features a biography of the war, the war dead, and the genealogy of the nation. The Yushukan not only represents the patriotism of the war dead, but also creates a historical narrative in which colonialism and wars are justified as part of Japan's mission as a liberator of Asia against Western imperial powers. In this sense, the museum is not only "looking back" by revising the past, but also "looking forward" by giving a history to the contemporary community based on the idea of Japanese "superiority."

Into the exhibition space: the spirit of the Samurai

The shrine is protected by a series of Tori gates that create a hierarchy of spatial transition and establish the authority of the Inner Shrine by separating it from the realm of mortal beings. It is no accident that the final

Figure 7.4 The new extension of Yushukan connected to the old building.

destination for visitors is the Inner Shrine, which is, however, unapproach-able and hidden from view. The arbitrary denial of entry and the partial revelation of the shrine grant visitors a glimpse of the world beyond, while suggesting that the ultimate truth is reserved for those privileged to enter: the war dead. The Yushukan, located to the west, next to the Inner Shrine, seeks to incorporate the Shinto deification of the war dead into its exhibition space by capturing the aura of sacrificial death.

The newly renovated Yushukan features the new extension, which has transparent glass walls and slightly tilted roofs (Figure 7.4). In stark contrast to the old Japanese imperial style of the main exhibition building, the new extension is modern and contemporary in its inspiration. As if to connect the past to the present, the new extension functions as an entrance lobby, creating a brighter, modern, welcoming atmosphere. As if to drum up the spirits of those who have lost faith in the spirit of the nation, the museum brochure declares that "we have selected items [from the old collec-tion] that shed new light on modern Japanese history," and the foremost concern of the new war museum is to re-establish the lost linkage between the individual and the national subject by way of encouraging love for our Japan.[21]

Upon entering the new lobby, a semi-open plaza with transparent glass walls, visitors first meet a Zero fighter aircraft, along with other artifacts used for the Asia Pacific War, standing like a sublime object on the sanitized floor with no trace of blood. This decaying object has been cleaned and elevated into a sanctified material. The care that has been put into polishing the aircraft signifies the living who care for the dead. Cleanliness is indeed next to godliness in Shinto. Once used by the war dead, the aircraft embodies their spirit. Preserved by the living, it becomes an inheritance that can be bequeathed to the future generations to remind them of those who sacrificed their lives for them.

Unlike the WMK, which is organized around a main axis, the Yushukan is designed to create circular movements in two stories of exhibition space starting from and returning to the lobby. The seamless procession-like flow of movement resembles a visit to a Shinto shrine, where the path snakes around rather than running in a straight line. The museum journey starts and ends in the hall of the fighter aircraft. The movement from one exhibition space to the next takes place through round doorways, which open onto different themes. From the entrance hall visitors ascend to the second floor, movement that resembles the crossing of a bridge constructed to divide the realm of the living from the domain of the dead. This movement from the profane to the sacred also leads visitors to the past, from where the nation started. Like the WMK that traces its origin back to its ancestor, the Yushukan presents visitors with the timeless spirit of warriors.

In the middle of the dim room named the "spirit of the samurai," a sword labeled "a marshal's saber" is enshrined in a monumental vertical glass display case with the inscription: "When the nation was in crisis, warriors were bestowed a sword from the Emperor. . . . Since the age of the gods, the sword reflects *the spirit of Japan*, who bears the souls of the warriors. The sword is a symbol of justice and peace."[22] As the military weapon turns into a sacred object, war is also given noble and transcendent meaning. This single object represents all attributes and absorbs all differences of the dead. The visitors are then surrounded by the spirit of sacrifice echoing from the scrolls hanging at the four corners of the hall. One of the scrolls writes, "In whatever way, *we* shall die beside the emperor, never turning back."[23] Who, then, are this "*we*"? This spirit is traced back to a thousand-year-long tradition, as inscribed on the other wall: "More than 2,600 years ago, an independent nation was formed on these islands. . . . Japan's warriors fought bravely, defending their homes, their villages, and the nation."[24]

The museum legitimizes war death as honorable and a righteous obligation for a life of the *Yamato* nation inhabited by *ethnic Japanese* for thousands of years. It therefore asks visitors to value its antiquity by paying tribute to all the war dead. The timeless war dead are condensed in the spirit of the warriors, which is also the spirit of Japan. The museum is, as it claims, precisely the place where people can *see* this spirit embodied in the sword. It urges people to witness and to assume loyalty and sacrifice for the nation. It provides the references necessary for the living to imagine themselves as a community stemming from the heroic sacrifices of their ancestors.

Liberating Asia

Like the WMK, the Yushukan shows an unbroken tradition of the sacrificial spirit by staging a history of modern Japan as a struggle that involves Japanese military prowess. For the Japanese war museum, however, the question is how to represent the aggressive and defeated wars. Without hesitation, it stages a seamless history of "glorious" warfare leading to the "Greater East Asian War." Yet, just before proceeding to the wars with China and Russia, the museum puts on display the rooftop of the (Ise) Shinto Shrine decorated with forked finials, as if to remind people of the significance of the spirit of Shinto renewal in the foundation of the Japanese modern state. This cross-reference between the ancient Shinto shrine and the modern nation-state conditions the audience to understand that war is not a mere human tragedy but a sacred mission for the integrity as well as the renewal of the nation.

The legitimation of the military effort extends far beyond the nation; it moves outward to realize "the peace of Asia." The museum portrays Japan as the nation that fought and sacrificed for the liberation of Asia from Western imperialism, emphasizing Japan's leading role in the formation of the pan-Asian world. Like the Yasukuni Shrine, the Yushukan also emphasizes the great sacrifice of Japan to maintain "the prosperity of all of Asia." For instance, the Sino-Japanese War and the Russo-Japanese War, waged in and around the Korean peninsula, are explained as unavoidable actions on the part of a Japan selflessly devoted to the collective well-being of Asia; Japan's annexation of Korea is portrayed as liberating Korea from China, based on agreement between the Korean and Japanese governments; and the invasion of China is seen as an effort by Japan to achieve pan-Asian peace. In this way, the Yushukan wittingly revises history so that Japan's invasion and aggression in Asia turns into a holy mission on behalf of Asia's liberation from Western imperialism, thus erasing Japanese atrocities committed in the name of pan-Asianism.

Ethnic nationalism in the Yushukan

While adopting the wartime rhetoric of pan-Asianism, however, the Yushukan seeks to renew the old concept of the "Greater Japanese Empire" as more akin to contemporary Japan. In the exhibition section dedicated to "mementos of war heroes enshrined at the Yasukuni Shrine," the wall is covered with individual photographs of those who died in the Asia Pacific War (Figure 7.5). On each photo, as small as the palm of a hand, is inscribed the name and age of the fallen soldier. Yet, despite this personal identification, the soldiers remain nameless. Stripped of all social and cultural significance, they are all immersed in the vast canvas of collective death, a single body of the nation. Yet this abstraction of individual death into a collective national whole also suggests the complexity embedded in the concepts of nation and ethnicity in Japan.

Figure 7.5 Photographs of war dead displayed in the Yushukan.

Eiji Oguma, tracing the genealogy of the discourse on the Japanese nation, has argued that the myth of Japan as a homogeneous and pure-blooded nation is to a great extent a postwar construction.[25] For instance, a broadly accepted belief in the prewar period that Japanese and Koreans shared a common ancestor changed with the collapse of the Japanese empire to the belief that Japanese and Koreans were fundamentally different in their culture and ethnicity. The emphasis on "one nation, one people" is not difficult to understand given that the prewar ideology of a multi-ethnic Japan mobilized to secure the Japanese empire was no longer needed, regardless of the fact that postwar Japan still consists of multiple ethnic groups. What is remarkable is the instability of the concept of Japan, which oscillates between the homogeneous nation and the mixed nation. However, as Harumi Befu has aptly pointed out, what has been maintained beneath the discursive shift of the nation in modern Japan is an idea of ethnic nationalism.

The Yushukan is a case in point. Although more than 21,000 Koreans and 27,800 Taiwanese out of 2,123,651 dead from the Asia Pacific War were reportedly included in the shrine, the museum erases any reference to the multi-ethnic nature of the war dead. The ethnic Koreans and Taiwanese were granted Japanese nationality, conscripted into the Imperial Army, and buried in the Shrine. In the museum, the ethnic others, who were Japanese but not quite Japanese, are asked to put on Japanese identity. They are recognized as Japanese only if they subsume their non-Japanese ethnic identities under the Japanese family system, in which the emperor is the central figure. In the museum, gone is the ambiguity embedded in the prewar concepts of nation and ethnicity, which often was expressed in the tensions between assimilation and segregation, and *naichi* (inner lands, homeland) and *gaichi* (outer lands, colonies). What we see in the museum is a history of Japan, "the land of Yamato" premised on ethnic uniqueness and superiority.

Conclusion: a crisis of ethnic nationalism in the era of globalization

I have shown so far the ways in which the war memorial museums aim to capture in the exhibition space the aura of sacrificial death that transcends the individual's physical annihilation. There is, however, something ironic in the practice of museumization, "a replica without aura" in Anderson's terms,[26] which in fact indicates a crisis of the ritual of making war death the prime material for the foundation of national identity. Indeed, the two museums discussed above have received not only welcoming but also critical receptions from the public. In concluding this chapter, let me consider some dissident voices regarding the war museums. In 1993, a year before the opening of the WMK, *Donga Ilbo*, a major daily newspaper in Korea, questioned the very need to build a war museum with such a belligerent appearance in the center of the city, criticizing the lack of accountability of the government in spending one million dollars for the museum project.[27] In response, the military monthly report *Military Journal* condemned the unfavorable media as ignorant and criticized them for seeking to manipulate public opinion.[28] However, in the past few years, which have brought significant changes in public perception, especially of North Korea, the museum's message of anticommunist and military patriotism has become problematic and dissociated from the everyday life of the public.[29]

Perhaps partly as a response to all these, the museum has made changes. For example, the annual commemoration of the Korean War on June 25 has focused more on cultural events, emphasizing unification and peace. As if revising the militaristic and masculine image represented in the "Statue of Brothers," in 2002 the museum added a new monument, "Peace Watch Statue," with two young *girls* holding two watches, one stopped at the moment of separation of the two Koreas and the other moving toward future unification. Yet despite the museum's effort to renew its image from that of war and masculinity to peace and innocence, the presence of the museum continues to elicit suspicion from the public. In 2003, a group of citizens proposed an alternative "peace" museum.[30]

Not unlike the WMK, the Yushukan has been unpopular since it opened in July 2002. Until May 2003, approximately 226,000 individuals had visited the museum, a small number compared with the atomic bomb peace museums in Hiroshima and Nagasaki, each of which has received more than one million visitors every year for more than two decades. The newspaper *Sankei* reported in 2002 that no schools are currently making field trips to the museum, nor does any school incorporate the museum's pedagogical apparatus into its curricula.[31] Many who visit the Yushukan find the museum disturbing. Resisting war memories as a glorious past, a war veteran said, "I did not want to recall stories of us stepping on dead bodies" and "there is nothing glorious at all about war."[32]

The museum's mission to re-establish the lost linkage between the national subject and the individual and to reinforce Japan as a nation-state can also be understood as a reaction to globalization in contemporary Japan. One of the phenomena of globalization apparent in the landscape of Japan today is the growing visibility of the postcolonial Asian. In the 1990s, along with the increasing number of migrant workers from surrounding Asian countries, popular interest in Asia, such as Asian pop music, film, travelogues, and so on, has dramatically proliferated. Despite the effort to forget the plight of people in Asia caused by Japanese imperialism, post-colonial Asia keeps haunting postwar Japan like a phantom. It threatens to disclose a cleavage in the putative wholeness of the citizenship project that conservative nationalists attempt to maintain in the face of globalizing forces in Japan. Not unlike the WMK, the Yushukan is the showcase for an ethnic-based reactionary nationalism that retreats to the military tradition, a symbol of loyalty to and sacrifice for the nation, at the moment when the idea of the nation based on ethnic homogeneity has been undermined by domestic and international transformations.

In a way, all the different visual and spatial communications employed by the WMK and the Yushukan stem from what can broadly be termed ethno-conservative nationalism, which invents an ethnic-based tradition of military prowess. The obsession with military ability relates to an amnesia over past colonialism and wars that both Korea and Japan have lived through. Both museums still find it difficult to integrate the dark past into their history. Each only tells a story that the nation-family wants to hear about its ancestors and does not tell other stories, such as those of military aggression at home and abroad and civilian collaboration with the wrong-doings. "We" do not have to talk about the embarrassing deeds in "our family." When the number of embarrassing deeds exceeds the space in the closet, the museum ends up telling only a few episodes that will uplift the patriotic members of the family. Out of this selective forgetting and remembering of the past, the seamless familial history of the ethnocentric nation and the idea of a "patriotic" national community has emerged.

The WMK can be seen as an enactment of manliness suppressed under Japanese colonialism. The Korean ethnic nationalism inscribed in the WMK can be seen as an enterprise for a mastery of cultural crisis and a subconscious, somewhat "postcolonial," project to assume coherency within the historical memories of colonialism, war, and the current phase of globalization. Hence, we see in the WMK a communal quest for a rooted identity expressed in the urge for ethnic unity, a role that can be most decisively played by the loud voice of military prowess. Nonetheless, in a period of dramatic transitions that witnessed the demise of the rule of military authorities, successful political democratization, the emergence of unification as a reality, the proliferation of transnational flows information, capital, people and culture, and the influx of foreign migrant workers, the presence of the WMK requires us to question whether a democratized and globalized Korea would further ethnicize or de-ethnicize the idea of nation and national membership.[33]

Like the WMK, the Yushukan calls for the recovery of a manly Japanese national identity by affirming the wartime past. The main target is the younger generation, which has been criticized for its disavowal of old values such as loyalty to the nation. For conservatives, it is urgent to rewrite history to nurture in young students a sense of pride in being Japanese and in the nation's military heritage. The urgent need to establish the morality of Japan's past by resurrecting the lost glory of the nation is closely associated with reaction to harsh criticisms of Japanese wartime atrocities from many fronts, not only from Asia and the West but also from its own public. Within this context, the Yushukan seeks to assume a significant role in securing the future of the nation by remembering the national past embedded in its singular history, ethnicity, and identity, and at the same time erasing the violence, fear, and anguish experienced during war by both "Japanese Japanese" and other "non-Japanese Japanese."

Juxtaposing Korea and Japan, we see interconnected discourses of ethnic nationalism. Comparing war memorial museums in Japan and Korea, I have suggested that despite their antagonistic discourses, they are engaged in similar strategies of representation: staging a ritual dedicated to the war dead as an embodiment of national identity. The dispute over the museums suggests a change in the social and political landscape of Korea and Japan. However, the public in both countries, although critical of militarism, still seems to take for granted the idea of ethnic nationalism, which often develops into xenophobic sentiment toward immigrant foreign workers. The unchallenged concept of nation and citizenship based on an ethnic collectivism poses a critical obstacle to the task of reconciling historical injustice between the nations as well as within them. Without critical self-reflection regarding the exclusive and aggressive nature of ethnic nationalism, it will be difficult to move ahead. In this chapter, instead of placing the two war memorial museums in the category of colonized versus colonizer or victim versus victimizer, I have paid attention to their similar ambition to exhibit the nation bounded by ethnic, not civic, sentiments. They urge citizens to be exclusively Koreans or Japanese and to unquestioningly identify themselves with the ethnic national community. Yet in a time when conventional gender and generational roles are weakening and the increasing cross-border interaction of information, capital, and people of different nationalities, cultures, and ethnicities is creating plural and heterogeneous identities, it is a struggle for them to drum up an imagined nationalistic purity.

Notes

This chapter developed from research funded by the Japan Foundation Dissertation Fellowship in 2001–2 and my dissertation "The presence of the past: exhibitions, memories, and national identities in colonial and postcolonial Korea and Japan" (PhD dissertation, State University of New York, Binghamton, 2003). I would like to thank the audience in the conference Rethinking Historical Injustice (2004), Park Soon-won, and two anonymous reviewers for their comments. I am also grateful to Yang Jae-oh for helping my research on the War Memorial of Korea.

1 Benedict Anderson, *Imagined Communities: Reflections on the Origin and Spread of Nationalism* (London: Verso, 1983), p. 205.
2 Anderson, *Imagined Communities*, 205.
3 My thinking about nationalism and the war dead in this section owes much to Benedict Anderson's "Replica, aura, and late nationalist imaginings" and "The goodness of nations," in *The Spectre of Comparisons: Nationalism, Southeast Asia, and the World* (London: Verso, 1998), pp. 46–57, 360–8.
4 See the WMK catalogue (English edition), *War Memorial of Korea*, p. 5.
5 See Carol Duncan, *Civilizing Rituals: Inside Public Art Museums* (London and New York: Routledge, 1995).
6 See Eiji Oguma, *A Genealogy of "Japanese" Self-Images*, trans. David Askew (Melbourne, Australia: Trans Pacific Press, 2002) and John Lie, *Multiethnic Japan* (Cambridge, MA: Harvard University Press, 2001).
7 See Harumi Befu, "Nationalism and *Nihonjinron*," in Befu, ed., *Cultural Nationalism in East Asia: Representation and Identity* (Berkeley, CA: Institute of East Asian Studies, 1993), pp. 107–35.
8 Indeed, the shrine still has a strong association with the state, as evidenced by the controversial visits of prime ministers and other government cabinet members to the shrine.
9 *Jŏnjaeng Kinyŏmgwan Kŏnlipsa* (*A History of the War Memorial of Korea*) (Seoul: The War Memorial Service, 1997), pp. 436–7.
10 *War Memorial of Korea*, 5.
11 See Shin Gi-Wook, "Nation, history and politics: South Korea," in Pai and Tangherlini, eds, *Nationalism and the Construction of Korean Identity* (Berkeley, CA: Institute of East Asian Studies, 1998), pp. 148–65.
12 For a description of early Confucian temples in ancient China, see Wu Hung, *Monumentality in Early Chinese Art and Architecture* (Stanford, CA: Stanford University Press, 1995), pp. 88–99.
13 Sheila Miyoshi Jager, "Monumental histories: manliness, the military, and the War Memorial," *Public Culture* 14/2 (2002), 387–409.
14 See Jager, "Monumental histories."
15 To fully grasp the insecurity of postcolonial Korea, we would need to have a sense of a Japanese version of orientalism in representing colonial Korea.
16 Carol Gluck, "The 'end' of the postwar: Japan at the turn of the millennium," *Public Culture* 10/1 (1997), 5.
17 Shintoism, often referred to as Japan's indigenous religion, centered on a reverence for deities (*kami*) that animistically inhabit nature. It was elevated to the state religion when the new Meiji government placed Shinto at the center of the nation's religious and social life. The Yasukuni Shrine embodied the political idea in Japan that the emperor is at the center of the religious and social life of the people. With Japan's surrender in 1945, the shrine was separated from the state.
18 Since the Second World War, under the sanction of the United States, Japan has represented itself as a liberal state. However, the national identity of Japan is still

constructed under the image of the emperor and Shintoism – a practice associated with prewar Japan. This discrepancy between the liberal culture of the state and the Shinto-invested national identity has made the visits of state officers to the Yasukuni Shrine a matter of controversy.

19 As a visible sign, its shrinking income from patrons and contributors tells us that the shrine is failing to secure the younger generation as a new patron to succeed the aging generation of contributors.

20 See Laura Hein and Mark Selden, "Learning citizenship from the past: textbook nationalism, global context, and social change," *Bulletin of Concerned Asian Scholars* 30/2 (1998), 3–15; and Gavan McCormack, "The Japanese movement to 'correct' history," *Bulletin of Concerned Asian Scholars* 30/2 (1998), 16–23.

21 See the Yushukan exhibition brochure.

22 From the display panel in the exhibition section entitled "Spirit of the Samurai" (emphasis added).

23 Ibid.

24 Ibid.

25 See Oguma, *A Genealogy of "Japanese" Self-Images.*

26 Anderson, "Replica, aura, and late nationalist imaginings," in *Spectre of Comparisons.*

27 *Donga Ilbo* (June 8, 1993).

28 See *Jŏnjaeng Kinyŏmgwan Kŏnlipsa*, pp. 432–3.

29 See *Donga Ilbo* (June 26, 2001). The number of visitors to the museum in 2000 was about one million.

30 *Hankyoreh* (September 24, 2003).

31 *Sankei* (August 5, 2002). Cited from Takashi Yoshida, "Sowing nationalism, reaping skepticism: the renovation of Yushukan War Museum," presented at the 2004 Association for Asian Studies.

32 Takuya Asakura, "WWII survivors fear return to warpath," *The Japan Times* (August 16, 2002).

33 Observing the growing visibility of migrant foreigners in the economic and social life of Korea, Katharine Moon aptly questions: "What is the meaning and content of the Korean nation if foreigners purport to claim Korea as their "second homeland"? Does Korea's pursuit of democracy and globalization require that it alter its definition of *nation*?" See Katharine Moon, "Strangers in the midst of globalization: migrant workers and Korean nationalism," in Samuel S. Kim, ed., *Korea's Globalization* (Cambridge: Cambridge University Press, 2000).

8 Difficult neighbors

Japan and North Korea

Gavan McCormack

North Korea: the grievance state

If there is one country in East Asia whose very existence and *raison d'être* is predicated on unresolved historical grievance it has to be North Korea, often described as a "guerrilla state" or a "partisan state" because the historical experiences of the anti-Japanese, antifascist partisans who fought against Japan in the 1930s, and the myths built upon them, are at its core; the regime's first leader was one on whose head the Japanese authorities had posted a large price, and his son and successor, seventy years on, still calls on the people to model themselves on the spirit of his father and the partisans of the 1930s. In Europe, the Franco-Prussian War and the First and Second World Wars and Cold War have long been consigned to history: studied in textbooks, commemorated in inclusive ceremonies, dramatized in film and literature and as much part of a long-gone era as the Punic or Napoleonic wars; not so in East Asia, where the wounds of imperialism, colonialism, war and Cold War remain fresh.

It is 110 years since the Korean queen was assassinated by Japanese troops in Seoul, and 100 years since a Japanese protectorate, later turned into colonial rule, was established over the peninsula. The Japanese colonial empire was liquidated over sixty years ago, but the country was then immediately divided by its occupiers. Negotiations between Japan and South Korea took thirteen years, from 1952 to 1965. However, normalization in 1965 included no apology and no provision for compensation. Instead Japan offered only "economic cooperation." It was not until 1995 that Japanese Prime Minister Murayama formally expressed regret and apology for the harm done by colonial rule. Even then, despite some warm exchanges, especially over the joint hosting of the soccer World Cup in 2002, and the pronouncement of 2005 as a year of Japanese–South Korean Friendship, the South Korean government in August 2004 established a special committee to investigate the "antinational activities" of Koreans who collaborated with Japan during the colonial era, and on March 1, 2005, the eighty-sixth anniversary of a peaceful Korean uprising against Japanese rule, South Korean president Roh Moo Hyun made it clear that he believed normalization had still been only partially achieved. "In order for the relations between the two countries to develop, the Japanese government and people need to make sincere efforts. . . . Japan must make the truth of the past known, and offer sincere apologies and if necessary, pay compensation. Only then can we be reconciled."[1] The wounds of Japanese colonialism are still only partially healed in South Korea.

Negotiations over normalization with North Korea took much longer to get started, in 1991, and have already taken longer, with little to suggest that the end might be near. Despite significant North Korean initiatives and concessions toward accomplishing the goal, the Japanese side has consistently drawn back. Today, as a result, it has diplomatic relations with virtually every country on earth save this, its near neighbor.

The simple justice of the North Korean claim has been obfuscated by the many issues arising from the prolonged abnormal relationship, including nuclear weapons, missiles, and abductions. Japan's long support for the US, both in the Korean War of 1950–3 and in the long-continuing subsequent confrontation, was for North Korea insult added to injury. Fear, insecurity, and isolation, drives the regime in P'yŏngyang to continue mobilizing its people relentlessly, even after well over half a century, and to seek to defend itself by development of the ultimate "deterrent," nuclear weapons. Needless to say, such nuclear and other programs threaten the peace and security of the region. The problems persist because the legacies of history have been left too long ignored and unresolved. Until they are addressed, normalization is accomplished, and North Korea's security is guaranteed in a "normalized" East Asian commonwealth or community, there can be no normalization for the region as a whole.

Whereas a half-century of unresolved colonial control is generally forgotten, North Korea is seen as inexplicably hostile and threatening, a black hole of absolute otherness, a mad, perverse, or ill place that threatens to suck the region as a whole into chaos for incomprehensible reasons. Over the past decade or so, an astonishing 600 books about it have been published, the overwhelming majority of them virulently hostile. North Korean stories flow steadily from Japan's newspapers and weekly and monthly magazines, and during 2002 and 2003 television was featuring up to three or four programs in a single day, and the flow continues, even if slightly abated. The Japanese appetite for stories of abductions and missiles, nuclear programs, hunger and refugees, and for the details of the private life of North Korea's leader, Kim Jŏng Il, his favored wines, menus and movies, his wives, mistresses and companions, seemed insatiable. A *manga* volume published in mid-2003, depicting Kim Jŏng Il as violent, bloodthirsty and depraved, sold half a million copies in its first three months,[2] almost certainly more than all books ever published about North Korea in all other languages put together.

North Korea is plainly a rogue state. Its prison camp gulags are notorious. It misgoverns its people, (probably) practices narcotic trading, counterfeiting and smuggling, says it has an active nuclear weapons program, and in the past was responsible for abductions and spy ships, and possibly for several major international terror incidents. It may indeed have committed almost every crime in the book and has few if any defenders. Many states commit crimes, however. What is unusual about North Korea is that in 2002 it admitted and apologized for at least some of its crimes, and in recent years it has repeatedly declared its desire to come in from the cold and become a part of the regional and international community.[3]

The discourse about "the North Korean problem" at both state and popular levels in Japan shows little understanding of this historical context, especially of the Japanese role in causing the problem in the first place. Despite the near collapse of its economy and widespread fatigue and hunger, and being frozen out of international trade and blocked from the World Bank and Asian Development Bank, North Korea maintains its "military first" posture. Its fears may be part paranoid, but are also part very real. It sees few options and is uniquely a "grievance state."

Whereas Europe entered upon a new era of peace and cooperation following the end of the Cold War, East Asia saw little movement in that direction. The blind eye Japan turned to North Korea over the Cold War decades helped to stabilize the regime on its anti-Japanese partisan state lines, and the continuing confrontation between North Korea and the United States maintained tension at a high pitch. A multiparty Japanese effort was, however, mounted in September 1990 by the veteran Liberal Democratic Party figure Kanemaru Shin, and a Three Party (Liberal Democratic Party, Japan Socialist Party, and Workers Party of Korea) declaration on normalization was adopted, expressing a Japanese apology and desire to compensate for the misery and misfortune caused by thirty-six years of Japanese colonialism and for the losses incurred during the forty-five years since then, and a readiness to open diplomatic relations.[4] Although this was a move in the right direction, the subsequent negotiations stalled. Japan's resistance to any compensation for post-1945 "losses" to North Korea, South Korean governments' negative attitude to Japanese approaches to North Korea (at that time and until the advent of the Kim Dae Jung administration in 1998), and suspicions over the North Korean nuclear program and, not least, US pressure, combined to block any progress. Nonaka Hiromu, a key Liberal Democratic Party power broker through the subsequent decade, writes in his memoirs of the "cautioning" from the US that followed the Kanemaru initiative.[5] In effect, the US continued to exercise an effective veto on any independent Japanese diplomatic initiative through the first post-Cold War decade, while the situation surrounding North Korea steadily worsened. Kanemaru himself was arrested on corruption charges in November 1992.

North Korea's Nodong missile test of 1993, its Taepodong satellite launch (indicating progress toward the development of long range missile technology) of 1998, and the various spyship encroachments into Japanese waters deepened Japanese fears. From 1997, Japan's National Police Authority declared its conviction that a number of cases of people who had disappeared from Japan in the late 1970s and early 1980s, hitherto treated as "missing persons" because of lack of evidence, would henceforth be treated as cases of probable abduction by North Korea. The problem of "Nihonjintsuma" – the approximately 1,830 women who accompanied Korean husbands repatriating to North Korea mostly in the 1950s and 1960s and in many cases suffered discrimination and oppression while being cut off from their homeland – also surfaced as small batches of them were allowed to make brief return visits late in the 1990s. Awareness of their plight served to deepen Japanese suspicion and distrust of North Korea.[6] The long continuing abnormal relationship also has domestic repercussions for Japan: widespread fear and hostility for North Korea translates into bullying and abuse of Koreans in Japan, especially children. One in five Korean schoolchildren in Japan report being subjected to various forms of abuse, from verbal to physical attack, sometimes involving their clothes being slashed with cutters while on the subway or on the street.[7]

Koizumi diplomacy: day trip to P'yŏngyang, 2002

While in many respects fawning uncritically on its powerful patron across the ocean and contemning its poor and recalcitrant neighbor, the Koizumi government that came to power in April 2001 nevertheless took a surprising stance on North Korea. In contrast to the Bush administration that began with the denunciation of North Korea as part of the "axis of evil" that plunged the region into crisis, Koizumi began with a sustained and serious search for detente. He seems to have been attracted by the prospect of settling the great, unresolved issue of the twentieth century by normalizing relations with North Korea. In due course, and alone among developed country leaders, he visited P'yŏngyang twice. His first visit, a one-day return trip in October 2002, held particularly dramatic promise of reconciliation. Its outcome was the signing of the "P'yŏngyang Declaration" on September 17, 2002 with North Korean leader Kim Jŏng Il.[8]

The Declaration was somewhat vague but was nevertheless a historic document: for the first time since the ignominious collapse of Japan's East Asian empire in 1945, Japan's prime minister committed the country publicly to a regional Northeast Asian future of peace and prosperity. However, the euphoria was short-lived. Within days, Japanese hostility was rekindled and surging to new heights, prominent figures calling for severing rather than normalizing the already tenuous relationship between the two countries, or even for making pre-emptive military strikes against North Korea.

For P'yŏngyang, the outstanding issue was to secure apologies and reparations for the crimes of Japanese colonialism; in other words to resolve its historic grievances and thus open the path to normalized relations with Japan, the region, and the world. For Tokyo, apart from the slightly nebulous prospect of a new Northeast Asian era, major immediate issues were the encroachment of North Korean spyships into Japanese waters and the suspicion that a dozen or so of its nationals in earlier decades had been abducted by North Korea. The two leaders did not sit down to eat or drink together, and on both sides the "apologies" themselves were strained, formulaic, and of doubtful sincerity. Koizumi expressed "deep remorse and heartfelt apology" for "the tremendous damage and suffering" inflicted on the people of Korea during the colonial era, while Kim Jŏng Il apologized for the abductions of thirteen Japanese, "eight dead, five surviving" – among them a schoolgirl, a beautician, a cook, three dating couples (whisked away from remote beaches) and several students touring Europe, between 1977 and 1982, and for the dispatch of spyships into Japanese waters. The abductees had, apparently, been taken to P'yŏngyang either to teach Japanese language courses to North Korean intelligence agents or so that their identities could be appropriated for North Korean agents operating in South Korea, Japan, or elsewhere. Insisting that he had no personal knowledge of all of this, Kim explained it in terms of "some elements of a special agency of state" having been "carried away by fanaticism and desire for glory." He also apologized for the incursions of so-called "mystery ships" into Japanese waters. A Special Forces unit had been engaged in its own exercises, he claimed lamely. "I had not imagined that it would go to such lengths and do such things. . . . The Special Forces are a relic of the past and I want to take steps to wind them up."[9]

The wording of the Declaration in respect of the colonial past was virtually identical to that used in the Japanese–South Korean talks in October 1998, and was acceptable to the Tokyo bureaucracy precisely because it carried no legal implications. In other words, unlike "apology" as conventionally understood in interpersonal relations, where sorrow for having caused harm or injury to another is naturally accompanied by the intent to "right" the wrong, this one specifically excluded any such intention to compensate; only economic cooperation would be considered. Furthermore, once issued and despite this serious qualification, the apology was quickly forgotten in Tokyo. The "harm" caused by Japan over thirty-five years of colonial rule was as nothing compared to the harm done to Japan in more recent decades.

For P'yŏngyang, despite the bitterness over having to abandon the claim for compensation for colonialism and war, the urgency of the need for economic reconstruction was compelling. Colonial era issues, if they would be settled at all, would have to be settled on Japanese terms, North Korea eating humble pie. It would have to abandon its long-held insistence that the Japanese colonial regime was an illegal imposition, maintained by military force, and yield instead to the Japanese view that it was properly constituted under international law. This was a bitter climbdown, the same as had been forced on South Korea as the price of its normalization with Japan in 1965.[10] While North Korea, in public at least, swallowed its pride, many in South Korea lamented the outcome as an opportunity lost for Korea as a whole to correct the historical record.[11]

In the way they reported the historic encounter, P'yŏngyang and Tokyo were equally cavalier. In P'yŏngyang, Koizumi was said to have come to "meet the beloved general and apologize and make amends for the past"; the talks were officially declared a triumph, and nothing was said of the abductions, the spyships, or Kim's apology.[12] Until some fruits began to flow from the agreement, however, such a face-saving formula was probably inevitable. Kim Jŏng Il had, after all, negotiated away a fundamental precept of the state: its anti-Japaneseness. Only a substantial *quid pro quo* could justify this to the country, and only a figure with Kim Jŏng Il's stature could even hope to accomplish such a profound adjustment to the national identity. In Tokyo, on the other hand, attention focused exclusively on the fact that the prime minister had forced an admission of guilt from a "disgraceful" state.[13] The question of whether Japan had evaded paying reparations to which P'yŏngyang had a moral or historical entitlement, or why the Japanese apology came fifty-seven years late, was ignored. Attention focused exclusively, and self-righteously, on the "stubborn" and "unreasonable" nature of the regime in the North.

Abduction and reconciliation

In October 2002 the five surviving abductees returned to Japan, in accordance with an understanding between the two governments that they would return first for one to two weeks, and then go back to P'yŏngyang to work out their long-term future in consultation with their families. However, the ink had scarcely dried on the document, and Koizumi had barely got back to his office from his trip, before it was decided in Tokyo to scrap the deal, and under no circumstances to allow the five abductees to go back to P'yŏngyang. The key initiative seems to have been taken by Abe Shinzo, who as Deputy Cabinet Secretary had been frozen out of the negotiations leading to Koizumi's P'yŏngyang visit. His position was that Tokyo should simply demand the unconditional handover of the families remaining in P'yŏngyang. He declared that North Korea lacked both food and oil, and therefore would be forced to yield to the Japanese demands before the winter was through.[14] He was wrong, however, trust plummeted, and the P'yŏngyang Declaration looked like being stillborn.

When a meeting to take forward the commitment to normalize was held as scheduled at Kuala Lumpur, Japan officially denied having ever made any such promise, called on the North Koreans to show more "sincerity," and told them that "although it concerned the life of human beings, Japan and North Korea seemed to place a different value on people's lives." The promise had been widely reported in the Japanese media at the time, without official contradiction, and the abductees themselves left P'yŏngyang with only a short stay in mind, carrying lists of gifts to bring on their return. The abductees themselves agree they were only persuaded by government pressure to change their stance.[15]

Furthermore, in the call for P'yŏngyang to show "sincerity," there was a breathtaking insensitivity, if not hypocrisy, on Tokyo's part because it not only rules out compensation to the former forced laborers, comfort women, and other victims of the colonial era, many of them abducted, but it had waited patiently for decades for P'yŏngyang to weaken its position to the point where it would abandon its claim for compensation for colonial wrongs.[16] The Japanese message to P'yŏngyang seemed to be precisely the opposite of what its delegate proclaimed in Kuala Lumpur: Korean and Japanese lives were of different value, a handful of Japanese lives weighing far more than hundreds of thousands, indeed millions, of Korean ones.

As the major representative within the government of anti-North Korean feeling, Abe was very popular, and his tough stance was a key factor in his appointment to the post of Secretary-General of the Liberal Democratic Party in October 2003. As antipathy for North Korea spread through Japanese society, Abe represented and articulated it at the highest level. Following the hard line he enunciated, Japan relied heavily on the application of economic pressure and the threat of sanctions. It continued to deny food aid to North Korea, suspended in 2000, turning a deaf ear to pleas from the World Food Program, even while funding a hugely expensive operation in the name of humanitarianism in distant Iraq. In February 2004 the World Food Program had to suspend the supplies on which 2.7 million people, mostly women and children, depended, because the offerings from donors had dried up.

As for the five returnees, the drama of their slow "recovery" of their Japaneseness was followed relentlessly by the national media. Television stations and print media gave the story blanket coverage. Their meetings with family or school friends, visits to hot spring resorts, every word they uttered and how much beer they did or did not drink, and what they sang for the karaoke were all scrutinized for inner meaning. The cohesion of the Japanese national family was celebrated by their return to the fold. The eventual casting off of their Kim Jŏng Il badges on December 19, 2002 and the announcement of their decision not to return to North Korea were greeted with tears of national relief. At last, it seemed, they were Japanese again; they were free.

The news of the deaths of the other eight abductees, however – "eight dead, five surviving" – and the inconsistent and implausible account P'yŏngyang gave of the circumstances of their deaths, provoked a wave of anger, fear, and frustration in Japan that made progress towards comprehensive resolution even more difficult. For a full twenty months, Koizumi was squeezed by domestic and foreign pressures that blocked any further progress on his initiative. The contest for control over North Korea policy pitted the prime minister against powerful sections of his party, with Koizumi, in effect, losing control of the normalization process to the uncompromising forces who opposed any deal with North Korea short of regime change.

Hostility to the P'yŏngyang regime and insistence on its overthrow became a popular cause, supported by major media groups and influential academics. Nishihara Masashi, an influential professor at the National Defense Academy, said "I believe that the proper strategy for our country is to seek regime change,"[17] and Satō Katsumi, Chairman of the National Association for the Rescue of Japanese Abducted by North Korea (Sukuukai) and head of the "Contemporary Korea Institute," insisted that North Korea was run by a terrorist, dictatorial fascist regime, and that there could be no way of dealing with it other than by demands to which it would have to submit unconditionally. The Koizumi government would be "blown away" if it softened its stance.[18]

Although P'yŏngyang was indubitably the party responsible for restoring, to the best of its ability, the human rights of the victims of its criminal acts in the 1970s and 1980s, its position on how to go about that restitution had its own logic and morality. It rested on three principles: its own admission of responsibility and promise of restitution, the P'yŏngyang agreement on the appropriate procedure (temporary return of the abductees followed by their return to P'yŏngyang to work out the long-term arrangements), and the subjective will of the families of the abductees themselves, now not children but (except in one case) adults, whose wishes could not just be ignored.

For Japan's first act in a new and supposedly equal and principled relationship to be the renunciation of its own promise did not augur well for the future. Furthermore, for Koreans, North, South, and overseas, *abduction* means primarily the Japanese seizure of tens, if not hundreds, of thousands of Korean men and women before and during the Second World War to work in Japan or elsewhere in the then Japanese empire under forced or near-forced conditions, including the so-called "comfort women." This is for them the context within which the obviously criminal abductions of thirteen Japanese citizens in the 1970s and 1980s have to be understood, and the hubbub in Japan in which the North Korean regime's abductions became quite literally the *crime of the century* and the Japanese the ultimate victims of Asian brutality therefore had a painful air of unreality. Already many in Seoul were filled with righteous anger at the Japanese triumph over North Korea in 2002 when P'yŏngyang agreed to a deal with Japan that required it first to set aside its long-held insistence on compensation, and accept "economic cooperation" instead. Japanese good faith is suspect throughout the Korean peninsula because of its calculating and in Confucian terms "insincere" behavior. In addition, even apart from the mass-scale Japanese abductions of the 1930s and 1940s, South Korea had been guilty of abduction of political opponents of its regime in the 1960s and 1970s,[19] and its 1973 abduction of then opposition leader Kim Dae Jung from his Tokyo hotel room was a gross infringement of human rights that Tokyo has since been at pains *not* to follow up or investigate thoroughly. It is not outrage over abduction, but selective outrage, that is the problem. North Korea's crimes were heinous, but not unique.

Diplomatically, the Koizumi–Kim meeting of 2002, like the Kanemaru initiatives a decade earlier, stirred the US into quick action. Washington first cautioned Japan through Deputy Secretary of State Armitage and Ambassador Howard Baker, and then within weeks of the agreement dispatched Assistant Secretary of State James Kelly to Tokyo to bring him back in line under Washington's direction. It relied on evidence of supposed North Korean uranium enrichment, a controversial and unconfirmed program of which it had known for years but done nothing about. Kelly insisted that P'yŏngyang had confessed this program to him during his October 2002 visit, while P'yŏngyang insists it did nothing of the kind.[20] China, Russia, and South Korea continue to doubt these US claims. The rift they opened, however, led to the collapse of the Agreed Framework that had governed the US–North Korean relationship since 1994, and soon afterwards the US National Security Strategy document declaring the pre-emptive attack doctrine was issued, further ratcheting up the pressure and leading P'yŏngyang, late in 2002, to resume its nuclear deterrent program. If P'yŏngyang did in fact make the admission attributed to it by Kelly, one would have to say it would seem an extraordinarily pointless, counter-productive, and uncharacteristic thing for it to have done, and it seems increasingly likely that in fact it did not.[21]

Return to P'yŏngyang, May 2004

On May 22, 2004, Koizumi made his second day-trip to P'yŏngyang, a dramatic attempt to break through the barriers of domestic and diplomatic opposition. His words on departure for P'yŏngyang about aiming at a recovery of mutual trust, so that the abnormal relationship between Japan and North Korea could be normalized and "hostility turned to friendship, confrontation to cooperation,"[22] pointed again to an agenda poles apart from Washington's, a mission to close the books on Japan's twentieth-century colonial empire, and thereby secure for Japan a central role in the emerging twenty-first-century Northeast Asian region. Later, asked his impression of his North Korean opposite number, Koizumi told the Diet that "I guess for many his image is that of a dictator, fearful and weird, but when you actually meet and talk with him he is mild-mannered and cheerful, quick to make jokes . . . quick-witted."[23]

In other words, having met and talked with him twice, he confirmed the view of Kim Dae Jung and Madeleine Albright, among others, that Kim Jŏng Il was a man to do business with. So keen was Kim to talk with George W. Bush that he suggested Koizumi provide the music so that they could sing together until their throats became sore.[24] The contrast with the US president's sentiment that he "loathed" Kim Jŏng Il and could not possibly deal directly with him was marked. Subsequently, Koizumi pledged to normalize the relationship within his remaining two years of office, if possible within a single year.[25]

In P'yŏngyang, this second visit was construed in effect as an apology for breach of the P'yŏngyang Declaration and a restatement of commitment to its principles. In response, the North Korean side agreed to consider the five returned abductees permanently rather than temporarily returned, to allow their children to leave the country with Koizumi (and Charles Jenkins and the two children of Jenkins and Soga Hitomi to met with Soga in a third country), and to reopen "sincere investigations" into the eight whose whereabouts were uncertain (but dead according to the 2002 P'yŏngyang explanation). Japan promised to reopen humanitarian aid (250,000 tons of grain and US$10 million worth of medical equipment), and to address the question of discrimination against Korean-in-Japan residents.

But, as in 2002, this visit soon turned sour. Two cases in particular focused attention, those of the Soga and Yokota families. The drama of Soga Hitomi, her American ex-deserter husband Charles Jenkins, and their two children proceeded to an apparently happy resolution following Koizumi's visit because Jenkins and the two children were dispatched from P'yŏngyang, arriving in Japan via a stopover in Jakarta. Following his court martial (over charges of desertion from his US army post in South Korea in 1965) and serving of a short sentence in military brig, the united family proceeded to settle in Soga's Sado Island hometown.

Mystery deepened, however, around the other case, that of Yokota Megumi, abducted as a thirteen-year-old schoolgirl on her way home from a badminton match in 1977, subsequently married, according to P'yŏngyang's account, to a North Korean man, and mother of a child.[26] She is then said to have died in 1993 (later changed to 1994). The identity of the child in North Korea was confirmed by a Japanese DNA test. However, Yokota Megumi's own purported remains, returned to Japan in November 2004, were pronounced, after DNA examination, to contain only material from two unrelated people.[27] The parents of Yokota Megumi became leaders of a powerful national movement, rejecting the prime minister's explanation of his P'yŏngyang visit and calling vociferously for stepped up pressure on North Korea. By early 2005, they disbelieved almost everything P'yŏngyang said and insisted that Megumi must still be alive. When they spoke, and they spoke often, the nation listened.

The nation, and most of the world, believed Japan and disbelieved North Korea. The Japanese government's rejection of the North Korean explanation of the Yokota remains appeared to rest on superior Japanese science and technology, and Japanese mass outrage and demand for punitive sanctions on North Korea on the assumption that the DNA analysis was definitive and scientifically beyond question. North Korean objections, on the other hand, were put down to bitterness over an attempted deception that had been exposed. In February 2005, however, the North Korean case gained support from an unexpected quarter. According to the account published in the February 5, 2005 issue of the world's most prestigious scientific journal, *Nature*, the analysis had been performed by a Professor

Yoshii Tomio of the medical department of Teikyo University. Yoshii, who had no previous experience in the analysis of cremated specimens, described his tests as inconclusive and remarked that such samples were very easily contaminated by anyone coming into contact with them. Such a finding was anything but definitive. Furthermore, the samples in question were used up in the process of the Teikyo University analysis, so no one could now ever know for sure what P'yŏngyang's package contained.

Others in the "eight dead" category were also shrouded in mystery. The stories P'yŏngyang stuck to by way of explanation of their deaths were unconvincing and in some cases contradictory. Amid mounting Japanese popular anger, frustration, and fear, the remaining Japanese humanitarian aid promised by Koizumi in May was frozen and the call for sanctions to be applied became almost overwhelming. The North Korean side, for its part, insisted that the remains provided were unquestionably those of Yokota Megumi, dismissed the Japanese protest, and in a January 17 statement by a Foreign Ministry spokesman asked Japan to show remorse and face the harm that its imperialist history had inflicted, adding that "the unfortunate incident of the abductions . . . would not amount to more than one thousandth of the misery and pain that Japan in the past inflicted on the Korean people."[28] As of early 2005, it was difficult to see how the impasse, broken twice by a prime ministerial initiative, could be broken a third time.

Koizumi, however, despite his annual visits to the Yasukuni shrine that outrage neighboring Asia, seems to have adopted normalization of relations with North Korea and thus closed the books on Japan's twentieth-century colonial empire, as his personal political mission.[29] Faithful to Bush in the Indian Ocean and Iraq, he has a different eye for Japan's immediate neighborhood.

Intimidation, conventional and nuclear

Of course Japan's "North Korea" problem is also real. Its fears over ongoing nuclear and missile developments, and its anger and frustration over the abductions and P'yŏngyang's devious and unconvincing explanation of the circumstances of the deaths, were natural. The problem in the Japanese response was the triumph of rage over reason, the sense of injured virtue and pure victimhood, the incomprehension of the Japanese responsibility for creating this situation in the first place and the failure to imagine how the world might look from a North Korean perspective.

Although Japan is singularly lacking in understanding, much less sympathy, for North Korea's plight, no country should understand it better, because it resembles nothing so much as the Japan of sixty-odd years ago, in the preservation of a beleaguered and dictatorial state regime being the major objective of state policy. For both regimes, the person of the central figure, emperor in the one and chairman of the National Defense Commission in the other, is crucial.

The shadow that North Korea casts over the Japanese popular imagination is disproportionate to the reality of the imbalance between the two countries. North Korea's GDP is about 1/200 of Japan's, or equal to that of the poorest of Japan's forty-odd prefectures, say Okinawa. The Japan that has dragged its feet for so long over normalization of relations with its former colonial dependency, and that today is so terrified by what it sees across the Sea of Japan, spends every year on military expenditure twice North Korea's GDP, has 200 F15 fighters, sixteen submarines (and builds one new one each year), and four Aegis destroyers (and two more on order), and budgeted in 2004 for two 13,500-ton aircraft carriers (coyly described as "helicopter carriers"). That is without taking into account items such as the two reconnaissance satellites it launched in March 2003 to spy on North Korea, and the fact that behind Japan stands the military colossus of the US. Were North Korea to launch spy satellites into the skies above Tokyo or Osaka (as does Japan over P'yŏngyang), a Japanese pre-emptive strike to get rid of them would be almost inevitable.

True, North Korea has a 1.1 million strong army, worthy – if sheer numbers count – of a superpower. However, some, perhaps many, units spend their time foraging and farming for subsistence rather than in war-related exercises or maneuvers, which are rarely if ever reported, equipment is mostly of 1950s vintage (the Iraq War of March 2003 showed the futility of even 1970s military equipment in contemporary conditions), and shortage of fuel is so severe that pilots can only practice flying their planes for a few hours per year. They would be about as much use in a war as a battalion of 1945 Japanese housewives armed with wooden rifles.

But the threat is said to reside in nuclear weapons and missiles (weapons of mass destruction) rather than conventional force. Undoubtedly, North Korea wants the US to think it has nuclear weapons. The CIA, which has spent a lot of time and money thinking about the problem, would have us believe that North Korea's scientists have accomplished the remarkable feat of producing nuclear weapons despite the decrepit state of the country's economy and without testing, something generally regarded as impossible. Through most of the 1990s it believed that North Korea had two or three such weapons but in 2004 revised that to estimate that it might have seven or eight "devices" of some kind.[30] No one outside North Korea knows the truth for certain, but at any rate North Korea certainly now has the raw material, plutonium, and since late 2002 has declared that it is working to reinforce its nuclear deterrent. As for a delivery system, it successfully launched a Nodong medium-range missile in 1993, and managed thereafter to turn it into a successful export item, but its three-stage rocket attempt to launch a Taepodong satellite in 1998, after streaking dramatically across Japanese skies, failed to achieve orbit and fell into the sea. North Korea's conventional artillery dug into the hills north of the Demilitarized Zone probably poses a quite serious threat to Seoul and other parts of South Korea, certainly more serious than any faced by Japan, yet South Korea, increasingly confident in its sunshine and engagement policies, faces it with equanimity.

When Japan berates North Korea over its putative nuclear and missile threat, it is blind to the fact that, through its cooperation in the alliance with the US, it itself has for half a century been part of the nuclear threat that P'yŏngyang has faced and to which it now responds by the attempt to build a nuclear deterrent. Japan's nominal avowal of the "Three Non-Nuclear Principles" is combined with encouragement for the US to maintain its nuclear umbrella over Japan, i.e. support for the nuclear threat extended over the Korean peninsula from Japan. Its regional and global posture is predicated on full support for the US, which possesses an arsenal of 7,500 nuclear weapons, most of them "strategic" and more powerful than the one that destroyed Hiroshima. In other words, nuclear victim country Japan bases its defense policy on (US) nuclear weapons.[31] In the UN, Japan supports nuclear privilege and opposes nuclear disarmament. In the years spanning the turn of the century, it cooperated enthusiastically in reorganizing its military ties with the US to facilitate the fighting of a second Korean War on the peninsula, transforming the alliance from one that was defensive, Japan-restricted, and in accordance with international law, to one that is offensive, global, and gives precedence to American demands over international law or the United Nations.[32] From a North Korean perspective, the Japanese "umbrella" is a pointed, aggressive instrument. Mohammed Elbaradei, Director-General of the International Atomic Energy Agency (IAEA), describes as hypocritical and unworkable Japan's position that "it is morally reprehensible for some counties [i.e. North Korea] to pursue weapons of mass destruction yet morally acceptable for others [i.e. the US] to rely on them for security."[33]

If North Korea has nuclear weapons, that is of course in defiance of the international will as expressed in the Non Proliferation Treaty (NPT) of 1968 and the North–South Non-Nuclear Agreement of December 1991. However, *if* any country has the right to develop a deterrent, which none has, then it would have to be North Korea, which has faced explicit nuclear threat longer than any country on earth, with the world showing not the slightest interest as long as it was just North Korea that faced that threat. Long before North Korea had taken its first steps on the nuclear path, US plans called for its nuclear annihilation, and gave serious consideration to the use of nuclear weapons against South as well as North Korea. Eager to reassure South Koreans that it would stop at nothing in their defense, the Carter administration in the late 1970s drew up plans to respond to any move by North Korean forces into South Korea by dropping nuclear bombs to within nine miles of Seoul's Post Office.[34] South Koreans were expected to see the nuclear mushroom over Seoul's suburbs as reassurance of the American determination to defend them at all costs.[35]

There can be no defense of nuclear weapons, but it is plain that the persistence in nuclear threat by a nuclear armed against a nonarmed state is more inexcusable than the attempted construction of defenses by a state under threat, and the International Court even refuses to hold such action illegal.[36] Furthermore, if North Korea's withdrawal from the NPT is serious, it is even more serious that the US (along with the other members of the nuclear club, Britain, France, China, and Russia) has been in breach of that treaty almost since the inception, ignoring its Article 6 obligation to take steps toward full disarmament. While Japan was vociferous in denouncing North Korea for its withdrawal from the NPT, it had nothing to say when the US withdrew from the Nuclear Test Ban Treaty, the Anti-Ballistic Missile Treaty, the Biological Weapons Convention, the International Criminal Court, and the Kyoto Convention on Climate Change, or when it adopted as "conventional" weapons cluster bombs, "daisy cutters," and depleted uranium-tipped shells, and declared its intention to develop a new generation of tactical nuclear weapons and to militarize and extend its control over the earth from outer space.

No one, even in the many intelligence agencies devoted to understanding North Korea, sees this small and debilitated state as gathering its forces for an invasion to conquer its neighbors. In other words, no one thinks of it as suicidal, although many caution that the combination of sense of victimhood, self-righteousness, and desperation can have devastating consequences. No other country has confronted the hostility of the world's greatest power for anything like the nearly six decades of North Korea, through the original act of division, the catastrophic war, and then fifty years of nuclear intimidation and economic sanctions.

North Korea as "axis"

There are two crucial senses in which North Korea constitutes an axis not of *evil* (as Washington would have it) but of *policy*, serving as a linchpin for both Japan and the US in holding together a comprehensive frame of state relations. Japan clings to its alliance with the US, sends troops and pays huge sums to subsidize the US occupation of Iraq, and supports the Bush regime in every possible way, at least in large part because of its fear of and hostility to North Korea. There is little or no indication that the Japanese public believed the war on Iraq in 2003 was justified or the subsequent prognosis good, but many were prepared to support Prime Minister Koizumi's explanation that the Japan had to support the US in Iraq because in a crunch with North Korea only the US, not the UN, would come to its aid.[37] In return for the Japanese troop commitment the US government specifically promised to support its position on the abductions. At the Texas tête-à-tête in May 2003 when the deal was done, a senior LDP official was quoted describing it this way: Japanese forces to Iraq in exchange for US support for the Japanese position on North Korean issues, especially the abduction issue.[38]

In other words, North Korea, long neglected and reviled by Japan, becomes the axis on which it makes major tactical and strategic decisions for its future and the future of the entire region, including the decision to send troops to Iraq. It constitutes an axis of domestic and foreign policy shift comparable to "Korea" in the late nineteenth century. Richard Armitage's prescription, for Japan to embrace the role of becoming the "Britain of East Asia," i.e. to develop the capacity to fight alongside US forces in matters deemed in Washington to be necessary for "collective security," would have little chance of adoption without North Korea.[39] The head of the LDP's Policy Research Council, Kyuma Fumio, describes the Japanese expression of support for the war in Iraq in these terms: "I think it [Japan] had no choice. After all it is like an American state."[40]

The US too is on the horns of a dilemma. Neoconservative moralists cannot tolerate the P'yŏngyang regime and are inclined to push it until regime change is accomplished; but the fact is that to eliminate that threat would also be to undermine the empire. The US has made clear that any attempt by Japan to pursue an independent foreign policy would be a matter of extreme seriousness. As the Rand Report put it in 2001, Japan must "continue to rely on US protection," because any attempt to substitute for that reliance an entente with China would "deal a fatal blow to US political and military influence in East Asia."[41] The thought that Japan might one day begin to "walk its own walk," intent on becoming the "Japan of the Far East" rather than the "Britain of the Far East," is a nightmare comparable to, if not worse than, 9/11. However, remove the "North Korean threat" and how does the US justify the continuing possession of a chain of bases, and the insistence on the adoption by both countries of hugely expensive MD systems? How, for that matter, does it persuade Japan and South Korea to maintain forces in Iraq? Even while seemingly aimed at regime change in P'yŏngyang, its post-Cold War vision requires Japan and South Korea to accept, in effect, a future world predicated on continuance of the "North Korean threat."

Conclusion

Japanese politicians and critics tend to make a large fuss over the possible Japanese payment in compensation (now disguised as "economic cooperation") for the forty-five years of colonial rule over Korea. The highest estimate of the sum involved is about 1.5 trillion yen (roughly US$12 billion) yen, a large sum to be sure, but far less than what the Japanese taxpayers have recently forked out to rescue just one of Japan's many floundering banks, and trivial by comparison with, for example, the sums spent in recent years to keep the dollar up and the yen down in global currency markets. North Korea has been experimenting for over a decade with efforts to get its economy going again through the adoption of market-based reforms. But economic reform is not really possible under conditions of continuing sanctions and without capital. A Japanese capital transfer on something like the envisioned scale could help significantly to set the country's reconstruction efforts under way, as the sum of $500 million did for South Korea in 1965. However, the national mood in the early twenty-first century is such that the Japanese "apologies" are likely to remain perfunctory.

Curiously, the hard line against North Korea seemed to be balanced, or matched in almost inverse proportion, by attitudes toward South Korea. From around the time of the World Cup soccer co-hosting of 2002 Japan's deep-seated prejudice against South Korea eased and slowly transmuted into its opposite, reaching in 2004 a positive frenzy of adulation over the movie star Bae Yong Jun ("Yon-Sama"), whose slight, smiling, bespectacled figure became the most popular Korean in the 1,300 years of contact between peninsula and archipelago. Yet warmth toward South Korea was more than matched by the coldness of antipathy toward the other half of the peninsula. When a time bomb was set at the residence of the Foreign Ministry official who in 2001–2 tried to negotiate a diplomatic settlement with P'yŏngyang, Tokyo's popular and powerful governor, Ishihara Shintarō, promptly declared his understanding: "He got what was coming to him." (Challenged, he said he had not meant to support terror, but added that Tanaka "deserved to die ten thousand deaths.")[42] With the support of 80 per cent of members of the National Diet and much of popular opinion, bills were passed into law during 2004 to allow the imposition of sanctions and the banning of North Korean ships from Japanese port entry unless Japanese demands are met.[43]

Believing South Korea and North Korea were fundamentally different, many in Japan were shocked, therefore, by the March 1, 2005 speech by South Korean president Roh Moo-Hyun about Japan's need to offer sincere apologies and compensation for its colonial era crimes. Roh specifically compared the Japanese anguish over the abductions to "the anger of our people who suffered thousands and tens of thousands as much pain over such issues as forced labor and comfort women," thus echoing almost precisely the words of the North Korean Foreign Ministry's statement issued six weeks earlier.[44] Forty years after Japan's "normalization" with Japan, President Roh pointed to the deep and unassuaged scars in the national memory of his country even as a special "Year of Friendship" with Japan was being celebrated. With North Korea, the process of normalization had scarcely begun.

Having pledged unconditional support to the US, Japan may be only slowly waking to the fact that the post-9/11 world order is not the order to which it was accustomed during the Cold War; it demands far more of it and offers far less. The US no longer just "protects" Japan but demands active, comprehensive, and subordinate cooperation in the establishment of US global hegemony. With the "war on terror" materializing as a state of permanent global martial law, and with the US government pursuing Israeli objectives (and its military explicitly adopting Israeli tactics) in the Middle East, Japan finds itself committed, indirectly but crucially, to an unfamiliar fundamentalism. Support for President Bush's America and adherence to the alliance comes to mean also commitment to the religious values of republican America, support for the torture, killings, and assassinations conducted by the Bush and Sharon regimes, and condoning of the evasions and breaches of international law and of the atrocities committed by the US against prisoners in Iraq. Japan's embrace of such a world order depends heavily on the perception of the North Korean threat.

North Korea looks a crazy and awful place, and in many respects it is. But it is both sinned against and sinning. Its plea for relief from steady nuclear intimidation should have been heeded long ago, and its plea for "normalization" (an end to sanctions, diplomatic and economic relations with the US and Japan, and security guarantees) as the price of abandonment of its nuclear program is not unreasonable. It surely should not have had to wait half a century for a normalized relationship with its former colonial ruler. For all sorts of reasons, not least fatigue after half a century of militarized confrontation with the United States, North Korea today seems extremely eager to normalize relations with both Japan and the US. Around it today the future of the region as a whole is contested.

Glimpses could be caught, in September 2002 and again in May 2004, of a radically different East Asia – of reconciliation, normalization, and economic cooperation. The processes of regional denuclearization and demilitarization, accelerated North–South Korean cooperation (leading ultimately to reunification), and a dismantling of the encrusted structures of the partisan state in North Korea depend now on nothing so much as the continuation of the normalization processes launched by Prime Minister Koizumi and Chairman Kim Jŏng Il. To achieve true normalization in twenty-first-century East Asia, Japan must solve the great question it failed to resolve in the nineteenth and twentieth centuries: a peaceful, cooperative, equal relationship between it and the states on the Korean peninsula. For that, setting aside the shrillness of tone, the justice of North Korea's message and of its claims for recognition and restitution has to be recognized. Whether Japan can bring itself to do that is the question.

Notes

1 "Roh tells Japan to sincerely apologize for sex-slave, forced labor misdeeds," *Japan Times* (March 2, 2005).
2 Lee U-jong and Lee Young-hwa, *Kim Jŏng-il nyūmon – Kita Chōsen shōgun sama no shinjitsu* (Seoul: Asuka shinsha, 2003).
3 Gavan McCormack, *Target North Korea: Pushing North Korea to the Brink of Nuclear Catastrophe* (New York: Nation Books, 2004); Gavan McCormack, "Remilitarizing Japan," *New Left Review* 29 (September/October 2004), 29–45.
4 Wada Haruki, "Jiyū minshutō to kita Chōsen," part 6 of "Kenshō – Nichō kankei," *Ronza* (August 2004), 783.
5 Nonaka Hiromu, *Rōhei wa shinazu* (Tokyo, 2004), p. 295.
6 Wada Haruki, "Kikoku undō wa nan datta no ka," part 4 of "Kenshō – Nichō kankei," *Ronza* (June 2004), 143.
7 Fujita Yutaka, "Zainichi Korian no kodomotachi ni taisuru iyaragase jittai chōsa," *Sekai* (October 2003), 248–54.

8 "Japan–DPRK P'yŏngyang Declaration" (www.mofa.go.jp/region/asia-paci n_korea/ pmv0209/p'yŏngyang.html).
9 Wada Haruki, "Can North Korea's perestroika succeed?," *Sekai* (November 2002) (http://japanfocus.org/005.html).
10 Korean Broadcasting Service, Sunday Special TV documentary, August 15, 2004. "Beru no naka no Kan–Nichi kyotei bunsho – Kan-Nichi ryokoku wa naze 40 nenkan mo chinmoku suru no ka?" (Korea–Japan Treaty documents kept secret – why have the two countries maintained silence for forty years?). My thanks to Mr Lee Yang-Soo for a copy of this program, with Japanese text translation.
11 *Hangyoreh Sinmoon* (September 18 and 24, 2002).
12 Ijuin Atsushi, *Kim Jŏng Il "kaikaku" no kyojitsu* (Tokyo: Nihon keizai shimbunsha, 2002), pp. 103, 109, 127.
13 *Mainichi shimbun* (October 14, 2002).
14 Gavan McCormack, *Target North Korea: Pushing North Korea to the Brink of Nuclear Catastrophe* (New York: Nation Books, 2004), p. 136. Wada Haruki and Gavan McCormack, "Forever stepping back: the strange record of 15 years of negotiation between Japan and North Korea," in John Feffer, ed., *The Future of US–Korea Relations: The Imbalance of Power* (London and New York: Routledge, 2006).
15 Chimura Yasushi and Chimura Fukie, "Chimura san fūfu no shuki," *Asahi shimbun* (October 15, 2003).
16 C. Sarah Soh (2003). "Japan's National/Asian Women's Fund for "Comfort Women," *Pacific Affairs* 76/2 (Summer 2003), 209–33.
17 *Japan Echo* (February 2004), 13–16.
18 Sato, speaking to a public meeting in Tokyo, April 18, 2004, my paraphrased translation.
19 Gavan McCormack and Mark Selden, eds, *Korea North and South: The Contemporary Crisis* (New York: Monthly Review Press, 1978), pp. 190–1.
20 Georgy Toloroya, "Overcoming the Korean crisis: short- and long-term implications from a Russian perspective," *Korean Journal of Unification Studies*, 12/2 (2003), 32.
21 Selig Harrison, "Did North Korea cheat?," *Foreign Affairs* (January/February 2005).
22 NHK TV, May 24, 2004.
23 *Asahi shimbun* (May 28, 2004).
24 *Asahi shimbun* (June 22, 2004).
25 *Asahi shimbun* (July 3, 2004).
26 Kim Hyegyong, born *c*.1987.
27 *Asahi shimbun* (December 9, 2004).
28 Wada and McCormack, "Forever stepping back."
29 Gavan McCormack, "Remilitarizing Japan," *New Left Review* 29 (September/ October 2004), 29–45.
30 Council on Foreign Relations, "North Korea's weapons program," New York, January 23, 2004 (www.cfr.org/pub6713).
31 "The GOJ [government of Japan] . . . cannot help but rely upon security policies which include nuclear deterrence." See discussion between Japanese NGO organizations and the arms control and disarmament specialists of the Ministry of Foreign Affairs, "The real thinking of Japan's Ministry of Foreign Affairs (MOFA)" (www.peacedepot.org/e-news/nd/japanup.html).
32 Asai Motofumi, "Busshu senryaku to yūji hōsei," *Gunji mondai shiryō* (February 2003), 8–15.
33 Brahma Chellaney, "Bush's blinkered nonproliferation policy," *Japan Times* (April 22, 2004).
34 Hans M. Kristensen, "Japan under the nuclear umbrella: US nuclear weapons and nuclear war planning in Japan during the Cold War," Nautilus Institute, July 1999 (www.nautilus.org/library/security/papers/japan.pdf).

35 Nautilus Institute, "Vulnerability of North Korean forces," Defense Nuclear Agency, Washington, April 1977 to March 1978, published under FOI, March 31, 2004 (www.nautilus.org/foia/NKVulnerability.html).
36 International Court of Justice, "Advisory opinion on the legality of the threat or use of nuclear weapons," July 9, 1996, para. 97.
37 *Asahi shimbun* (January 29, 2004).
38 *Asahi shimbun* (March 19, 2004).
39 Institute for National Strategic Studies, "The United States and Japan: advancing toward a mature partnership" (The Armitage Report), Washington, DC, National Defense University, October 11, 2000 (www.ndu.edu/ndu/sr_japan.html).
40 *Asahi shimbun* (February 19, 2003).
41 Zalmay Khalizdad et al., "The United States and Asia: toward a new US strategy and force posture," June 2001 (www.rand.org/publications/MR/MR1313).
42 McCormack, *Target North Korea*, p. 122.
43 *Asahi shimbun* (March 3, 2004).
44 *Japan Times* (March 2, 2005).

9   Dynamics of denial

Responses to past atrocities in Germany, Turkey, and Japan

John Torpey

We find ourselves in the midst of what the Nigerian writer Wole Soyinka has called a *"fin de millenaire* fever of atonement,"[1] an era in which expectations with regard to atonement for past wrongs have grown very large in many historical-political contexts. In view of the widespread contemporary expectation of apology for wrongful pasts, the reticence of some countries raises important questions. Why do some democratic countries – the only ones from which we can seriously expect an accounting for past wrongs – resist "coming to terms with the past" in particular cases? What is it about these countries, or the pasts in question, that keeps them from "coming clean"? Under what conditions might recalcitrants relax their guard and "come to terms with the past"? These are the questions that motivate the following inquiry. It goes without saying that all countries have dirty laundry to air and reasons not to air it, democracies included; my aim is to examine some significant cases in order to understand them more fully and perhaps to shed light on other cases as well.

In what follows, while I endeavor where necessary to reconstruct the historical events in question, the emphasis is on the contemporary political contestation over these past events. Eschewing the more usual comparison of the responses to their Second World War-era wrongdoing of Japan and Germany, I explore the reticence about coming to terms with past atrocities that is widely held to characterize contemporary Turkey and Japan. These two countries have been chosen because they fulfill three conditions: (a) they are, at least nominally, democratic in political form; (b) they face substantial demands to atone for past injustices; and (c) they are seen by significant publics as not doing enough to "come to terms" with their past. Further, I compare the alleged reluctance of the German government to come to terms with a different past than the one for its response to which it normally earns high marks, namely the Holocaust. Instead, the focus is on the alleged German reticence about atoning for atrocities committed in pre-First World War German Southwest Africa (present-day Namibia), where the Germans conducted what many regard as the first genocide of the twentieth century: the near-extermination of the Herero people of the region. The case of the Herero casts a somewhat different light on the widespread perception of German alacrity about "coming to terms with the past."

The similarity in these three cases lies in the perceived reluctance of each country to "come clean" about the relevant pasts, those of the genocide of the Herero under German colonial overlordship, the Turkish massacres of Armenians during the waning days of the Ottoman Empire, and the atrocities committed by the Japanese in the course of the Asia-Pacific War, respectively. At the same time, there are many obvious differences between the three cases that will require closer examination in the course of the inquiry. First, of course, the scale of the horrors ascribed to the Turks during the First World War is greater than that attributed to the Japanese in the much-cited case of "the rape of Nanking," particularly in proportional terms. The number of deaths caused by the Japanese in the Nanking episode, one of the chief events to which attention is called when "coming to terms with the past" is called for, is variously estimated by historians at between 100,000 and 400,000; the Japanese were, of course, responsible for many more deaths in the course of the colonization of Korea and the Asia-Pacific War as a whole.[2] Meanwhile, Ottoman forces may have killed somewhere between several hundred thousand and 1.5 million Armenians, equivalent to perhaps one-third to one-half of the Armenians living in the Ottoman Empire at the time of the massacres in 1915, although the matter is "complicated by the fact that no one knows how many Armenians lived in the Ottoman Empire on the eve of the genocide."[3] Appalling though this slaughter was, the proportional death toll ascribable to the German assault on the Herero in Southwest Africa is almost certainly the highest of the three groups, involving some 75 per cent of the presumed population of the Herero at the time. At a certain point, however, the numbers are so large that they may be said to be irrelevant to an appreciation of the wrongdoing in question; the matter is not one of comparative victimology, but of incontrovertible wrongs. In addition to these differences in scale, one might add that virtually no one who suffered the injustices for which amends have been sought in the cases of the Herero and the Armenians is likely still to be alive; this is not true of many who suffered abuse at the hands of the Japanese during the Second World War, although they, too, are dying off steadily.

The following discussion considers the particularities of the misdeeds in each case; the problematic application of the terms "genocide" and "holocaust" that derive from the experience in the now-paradigmatic case of Germany in the Second World War; the extent of domestic as opposed to external pressure for "coming to terms with the past" in each country; and the significance of mobilized diasporas and of foreign policy considerations in regard to these pasts.

Examining the relevant pasts

The atrocities for which reparations are sought in Namibia followed substantial revolts against German colonial dominance. In early 1904, two uprisings challenged German rule in Southwest Africa: one by the Herero in the northern and central parts of the territory, and another by the Nama in the south. After the battle at the Waterberg, in the northeast, in August 1904, the Herero fled by the thousands into the Kalahari desert, perishing of hunger and thirst in large numbers. They were uprooted and spread across the desert in flight from punitive German patrols. Those who did not reach Bechuanaland (present-day Botswana) either succumbed to the desert or were picked up by German patrols and thrown into concentration camps. In 1904, camps had been set up in the capital, Windhoek, in Okahandja to the north, and in the coastal town of Swakopmund, where conditions were often fatal.[4]

In the course of these operations, the Herero were extensively dispossessed of cattle and land. Indeed, "Germany terminated by conquest all Herero land rights in German South-West Africa, leaving the nation with no land at all" and laying the foundation of white control of farmland in the north-central and northeastern parts of Namibia.[5] The advantages accruing from this unjust transfer persist to the present day, as Europeans – especially Germans and Afrikaaners – and their descendants retain the dominant economic position in the country, despite the advent of majority rule in the political sphere.[6] Meanwhile, the Nama were targeted for destruction as well.[7] The combination of intentional killing of a specific population group and the expropriation of their lands bears more than a passing resemblance to the Turkish assault on the Armenian population in the midst of the First World War. Perhaps the most notable difference is that the German genocide was conducted against a distant overseas population, whereas the Armenians were inhabitants of the same soil as their attackers.

As liberal and national principles advanced in the nineteenth century, Europe's continental empires faced serious threats to their continued existence. In the Ottoman Empire, various lands on the geographical periphery had been falling away for some time. Armenia was a key problem here, as it brought the processes of political decline and territorial losses into the Anatolian heartlands of the empire. After the Russians conquered the Caucasus in the nineteenth century, a rising national consciousness emerged on the northeastern fringe of the Ottoman lands, posing a threat to Ottoman dominance. Ethnic, religious, and class antagonisms undermined a relationship that had long been regarded as one of robust loyalty toward the Ottomans on the part of the Armenians. A region in which Turks and Armenians had long been interspersed now became an object of heightened concern to the Committee of Union and Progress (CUP) government around the Young Turks that came into existence after the revolution of 1908.[8]

With the gradual loss of some of the conquered territories in the western portion of the empire, the bitterness among the Ottoman leadership toward newly separatist Armenians became intensified. This enmity and sense of panic fueled an intense reaction on the part of the Young Turk leadership. According to the Turkish historian Halil Berktay, "there was an intimate connection between the Ottoman psychosis of feeling hopeless and squeezed in, that their backs were to the wall, and the military dictatorship of the Committee of Union and Progress [CUP] on the one hand, and the implementation of measures against Armenians on the eastern front on the other."[9] Ultimately, those measures led to the deportation of many hundreds of thousands of Armenians and the deaths of somewhere between 800,000 and 1.5 million of them, as well as the death of significant (though by no means comparable) numbers of Turks and others. The attacks bore witness to the importance for those defending the waning empire of staving off the further loss of territory. These concerns would echo down through the years, influencing contemporary Turkish attitudes toward the demands of ethnic minorities and politicized religious groups to the present day.

The atrocities for which atonement on the part of the Japanese is sought were arguably less egregious than those perpetrated against the Armenians. These misdeeds include the "comfort women" system, the abusive medical experiments conducted on some three thousand victims by the notorious Unit 731 in Manchuria, the use of chemical weapons, and – perhaps above all – the rapine and pillage associated with the Nanjing Massacre. The comfort women system involved some 200,000 women from Korea, China, the Dutch East Indies, Malaysia, Burma, the Phillippines, and elsewhere who were forced or deceived into sexual service under the auspices of the Japanese Army. Not least because of Iris Chang's best-selling 1997 book[10] on the subject, the events that fall under this rubric – which involved a frenzy of killing and rape by the Japanese Imperial Army during 1937–8 – have generated tremendous attention on Japanese wrongdoing in recent years. In considerable part as a result of the concern provoked by Chang's book, we must consider more closely the question of the appropriate terms for characterizing the events in Nanjing and the others discussed above.

Of genocides and holocausts

The terms "genocide" and "holocaust" have been used by various commentators in connection with the atrocities in each of the three countries under consideration here. To the possible horror of the defenders of the uniqueness of "the" Holocaust, that term has come in recent years to be applied to all kinds of different killing campaigns: the "Herero Holocaust," the Nanjing Massacre ("The forgotten Holocaust of the Second World War"), the "American Holocaust" (against native Americans), the "red Holocaust" carried out by Stalin, etc. In other words, the uniqueness of *the* Holocaust has given way to a proliferation of "Holocausts" as the "canonical" one has assumed its place as the paradigmatic genocide against which all others are judged. Both the massacres of the Armenians and the Nanjing Massacre have been called "Holocausts" by some of those intent upon commemorating or seeking compensation for them, but no one, it seems, would argue that they were quite like the "canonical" Holocaust in the sense of a program aiming at the complete and utter extermination of the groups in question.

The parallel between the Herero Holocaust and the canonical one, by contrast, is stronger. The unrequited demands concerning the past that are raised by the Herero claimants have a particular frisson because the massacre of the Hereros has frequently been seen as a dress rehearsal for the Nazi assault on European Jewry.[11] According to the Herero Paramount Chief Kuaima Riruako, for example, "What Hitler did to the Jewish people . . . started with us here; Hitler was a continuation of what happened here."[12] In contrast to the case of the Jews, however, the Herero were slaughtered because they were actively opposing the encroachment of their German overlords; this was not the case with the Jews, of course, who were butchered simply for what they *were* rather than for anything specific that they had *done*.

So much for the "H-word"; but what about the "G-word"?[13] However brutal and inexcusable some of the actions of the Japanese during the Second World War were, few would argue that the country's policies were "genocidal" in the sense of the Holocaust. Japanese wartime policies appear to have been driven much more by considerations of military strategy and of long-term imperial domination than they were by any desire to exterminate those whom (to be sure) they regarded as their racial inferiors. As John Dower has argued, "despite the horrendous litany of atrocities exposed in the Tokyo proceedings . . . [there was no] real counterpart to the genocide planned and carried out by the Nazis." Indeed, following the views of the skeptical Indian judge in the Tokyo Tribunal, Dower casts doubt even on the idea that the Japanese leadership was guilty of the crime of undertaking an "aggressive war."[14]

Whether the CUP assault on the Armenians involved a "genocidal" impulse to kill all Armenians is a matter of intense contention. Taner Akçam, a leading Turkish historian of the Armenian massacres, has argued that evidence from the archives of the Ottoman Empire demonstrate "a genocidal intention on the part of the ruling party,"[15] but this is not necessarily the universal view. According to the historian Norman Naimark, "The evidence for intentionality, critical in any test of genocide using the 1948 UN definition, is . . . not as strong and unchallengeable as the historian would like." Despite this assessment, Naimark argues that "'genocide' seems the appropriate appellation" because of the evidence of government planning and organization of the assault on the Armenians.[16]

The scholarly consensus seems to be increasingly in favor of the notion that there was a "genocide," but that did not necessarily mean that all Armenians were slated for death. For example, many Armenians in the western portion of the empire, especially in Istanbul, survived the massacres apparently without substantial difficulty or concern. Some of those who remain today say that they see no contradiction between being Armenian and being Turkish: "there is no visible trace here of the anti-Turkish sentiment that burns in some Armenian hearts, and little desire to recall the horrors of the past."[17] It was not the policy of the Ottoman government to hunt down all Armenians, wherever they could be found, and to exterminate them. This preoccupation may have characterized the Nazis, but not the Young Turks. Clearly, execrable things happened, to a large extent at the behest of the Ottoman government of the Young Turks. If the appropriateness of the term "genocide" is not as compelling as one might be inclined to demand, it still appears rather more appropriate than in the case of the Japanese atrocities during the Second World War.

There seems less ambiguity about the appellation of "genocide" in the case of the Herero. A prominent historian of the Herero, Jan-Bart Gewald, writes unhesitatingly of the "deliberate policy of genocide which was practiced by the Imperial German army against the Herero."[18] The case for "genocide" derives in part from the fact that the Hereros were massacred and driven into the wilderness on the basis of a policy articulated by German Lieutenant General Lothar von Trotha in an address to his officers on a Namibian battlefield on October 2, 1904. Von Trotha there proclaimed, "The Herero people must . . . leave the land. . . . Within the German borders [of South-West Africa] every Herero, with or without a gun, with or without cattle, will be shot."[19] As a result of the Germans' persecution of the Herero, their numbers declined by around 80 per cent during the subsequent two years or so, falling from approximately 80,000 to around 15,000. Against this background, it is perhaps not surprising that no one seems to dispute that what was done to the Herero should be called "genocide."

In contrast, the focus of the contemporary struggle over the killings of Armenians revolves not around the question of whether or not terrible things happened, but precisely around the question of whether or not these killings should be officially "recognized" as a "genocide" – by the Turkish government as well as by other governments. Similarly, the pressures on the Japanese government have relatively little to do with denial of the *fact* of wartime misdeeds; the principal issues are how those actions are to be labeled and whether the degree of atonement for them has been adequate. We must therefore explore the nature of "denial" and the various forms it may take if we wish to understand more clearly the nature of the reticence in these cases about coming to terms with atrocious pasts.

States of denial and the denial of states

Having reviewed the historical "facts" involved in each of these cases, and some of the historiographical debates about the labels appropriate to each, let us now return to the question with which we began: why do the perpetrator governments or their successors (apparently) refuse to acknowledge their responsibility for the wrongs of the past? In what sense can it be said that they do so?

In his analysis of the "sociology of denial," Stanley Cohen identifies the following modes of denying wrongdoing: (a) outright denial ("it didn't happen"); (b) discrediting ("the accusers are biased, manipulated, or gullible");

(c) renaming ("yes, something did happen, but it was not genocide"); and
(d) justification (anyway, "it" was morally justified).[20] These categories are
useful for discussing the responses of Turkey and Japan to their respective
pasts. They contribute relatively little to making sense of coming to terms
with Germany's pre-First World War past, however. The German population seems barely aware of the atrocities of the colonial past, and lack of
knowledge leads not to denial but to lack of acknowledgment.[21]

In neither the Turkish nor the Japanese cases is there very much "outright
denial"; knowledge of the facts is, on the whole, too widespread, although
such knowledge is by no means universally disseminated. For example,
the Turkish government accepts that "tragic events occurred" at the time
in question.[22] Still, it appears that, outside of eastern Turkey, knowledge
about the massacres of 1915 may be very limited, in part because Turkish
school textbooks have generally been evasive about them and "stress that
Armenian militants were rebelling against the Ottoman Empire, and dis-
count or ignore the killing of hundreds of thousands of civilians after the
abortive revolt."[23] According to Taner Akçam, "there prevails in Turkey today
a grave ignorance about [the Armenian genocide], and that ignorance is
the intended result of a deliberate state policy." In consequence, "it would be
more accurate to accuse the Turkish people as a whole of disconnectedness
and indifference than with denialism."[24]

The second kind of denial identified by Cohen – discrediting the accusers
by charging that they are biased – is more frequently encountered in the
cases of Japan and Turkey. John Dower has noted that defenders of Japan's
honor often dismiss the criticisms of their country for being motivated by
racial prejudice.[25] Likewise, given the politics associated with Islam and with
Turkish efforts to gain membership of the European Union, it is not difficult
to imagine similar responses from the defenders of Turkish dignity. And,
indeed, might there not be something to this objection? The journalist Charles
Burress has argued persuasively that anti-Japanese prejudice is the basis of
much of the negative reporting about Japanese efforts to "come to terms
with the past."[26] Similarly, the involvement of many of the critics of how
satisfactorily Turkey and Japan have "come to terms with the past" with
various ethnic organizations may undermine their criticisms in the eyes of
some. Ethnic antagonism certainly plays a part in the contention around
"coming to terms with the past" in both the Turkish and the Japanese cases.

During the run-up to the ninetieth anniversary commemorations of the
Armenian genocide, the Turkish State Archive announced that it had compiled a list of more than 523,000 Turks supposedly killed by Armenians
between 1910 and 1922.[27] In other words, we have something here that is
very close to Cohen's notion of denial by "justification": that is, the killings
were justified because those killed were not innocent victims but legitimate
combatants. The problem, of course, is that these sorts of claims – especially
when articulated by the government – seem to be an attempt at self-
exculpation or of relativizing the Armenian claims out of existence.[28] This

strategy has often been invoked in the Japanese case as well.[29] Efforts are often made in both cases to suggest that the alleged wrongs of the past were justified in their time and place.

Perhaps the most appropriate characterization of the reticence about the past of the Turkish and Japanese political elites involves what Cohen calls "renaming." In the Turkish case, the situation seems to fit exactly his off-hand explication of the term: namely, "yes, something did happen, but it was not genocide." The problem here is that, as we have seen already, the term "genocide" is perhaps more open to dispute than first meets the eye. Even a concerned but dispassionate observer such as Norman Naimark can conclude, on the basis of the weight of evidence, that – for all their horrors – the term "genocide" is not unambiguously applicable to the Armenian massacres.

Notwithstanding this perceived ambiguity, in response to pressure by Armenian groups and their supporters the parliaments of a number of countries have entertained resolutions declaring the massacres a "genocide" or supporting a similar declaration by the Turkish government.[30] For its part, "Turkey has threatened to sever relations with countries over this single word."[31] Clearly, the question of the official recognition of the killings as a genocide is a major issue in Turkey's quest for membership of the European Union. In 2000, the European Parliament passed a resolution demanding Turkey's "public recognition of the genocide."[32] Turkey's prospects for admission to the European Union are hampered especially by French opposition, which in turn is not unrelated to the presence of a substantial Armenian diaspora population in France.[33]

Part of the reason for the ongoing reticence on the part of the Turkish government concerns the consequences that might flow from an official acknowledgment that the 1915 massacres constituted a "genocide." The recognition of ethnically based injustice at the very origins of the modern Turkish state could be seen as a weakness toward national minorities that might be exploited by others besides the Armenians, particularly the Kurds. Given post-Iraq war instability in the region and the persistent desire of the Kurds for a state of their own, the Armenian question is a delicate one. Still, all this concern about the integrity of the country may be predominantly a matter of elite rather than popular opinion; a recent survey found that 61 per cent of the Turkish population believe the time is ripe for a public airing of the "accusations of genocide," and Turkish scholars are increasingly discussing the subject in critical terms.[34] Against this background, and despite initial objections from high Turkish officials, a number of Turkish historians held the first-ever independent conference in Turkey on the history of the Armenian massacres in Istanbul in autumn 2005.

One major question regarding the struggle to have the massacres "recognized" as a genocide concerns whether or not this is intended as a step on the road to reparations. According to Stephen Kinzer, "Some Armenian nationalists say that if Turkey can be forced to concede that [what happened in 1915 was genocide], their next step might be to claim reparations or demand the return of land once owned by Armenians."[35] Yet a study by the International Center for Transitional Justice (ICTJ), which found that the events of 1915 did fulfill the definition of genocide, also stated that "no legal, fiscal or territorial claim arising out of the Events can be made against any individual or state under the [genocide] convention."[36] Needless to say, the threat of major reparations payments or the cession of lands is not likely to encourage the Turkish government to be forthcoming in this matter. The fear of possible material demands both undercuts the possible contrition of the Turkish government and potentially sullies the claim that what Armenians want is only official recognition of the atrocities that befell their ancestors.

In the end, it doesn't seem quite accurate to say that the Turkish government has "denied" the occurrence of the Armenian massacres, except in Cohen's qualified sense(s). It would be closer to the mark to say that it has conceded that many Armenians were killed, but that it has dismissed these killings as "justified" and rejected the label of "genocide" as an exaggeration motivated by anti-Turkish prejudice. It has therefore resisted the pressures, especially though by no means exclusively from the Armenian diaspora, to accede to the demand that it "recognize" the genocide of the Armenians in 1915.

All this raises the question of the extent to which it is desirable for governments to be involved in determining these matters at all. In contrast to the question of whether a genocide is in progress *now*, a finding that would compel action to forestall such an event *now*, it is less obvious that governments should be involved in resolving *historiographical* disputes over concepts and their significance. The remarks of Turkish historian Halil Berktay are relevant here: "Turkey takes many positions on this subject saying, 'it didn't happen,' or 'it happened but there was serious provocation.' The President of the Republic was correct when he said, 'The subject must be left to the historians.' There is something very simple the Turkish Republic can say today . . . this topic is open to discussion. Those who wish may discuss it as they desire. We have no official position."[37] Certainly this is not the only position to take on this matter; the proliferation of "truth commissions" in recent years suggests that some people prefer the stamp of authority that can be conferred on interpretations of the past by government-sponsored historical inquiries. But Berktay makes the important point that questions about the nature of past events may be better answered by historians with the expertise to assess complicated matters of causation, intentionality, and agency than by governments. Yet in recent years the past has become *politicized* to an extraordinary extent. Interpretations of the past are unavoidably "political," of course; the question is whether, to use a distinction advanced by Charles Maier, they ought to be "politicized" – "weapons forged for a current ideological contest."[38]

Such politicization often seems to be in play when the question of Japan's response to its Second World War misdeeds is at issue. It is often said that

Japan is unable to come to terms with its past – that it "can't say sorry," to borrow the words of Charles Burress. Again, this is not so much a matter of denying that certain events took place as it is of how they should be denoted, how they are to be conveyed to younger generations, and how the country should take responsibility for these past wrongs: in short, how they should be *acknowledged.*

In the case of the comfort women, the criticism of the government has been that it has not genuinely apologized and that it has not compensated the victims adequately. With regard to the first problem, according to a "Statement by President Tomiichi Murayama" of the Asian Women's Fund, "On August 4, 1993, the Chief Cabinet Secretary expressed the Japanese Government's sincere feelings of apology and remorse."[39] Here is where the accusations begin; advocates of the comfort women and other Second World War victims insist that the apology must come from the highest levels of the government, not from a lower-level official. They sometimes neglect to mention that in 1995, then Prime Minister Murayama expressed his "feelings of deep remorse" and his "heartfelt apology" for the suffering inflicted upon others by Japan during the Second World War, but without specifically mentioning the comfort women.

Next, the Asian Women's Fund itself was perceived as an inadequate response by many on the side of the comfort women, because it was not a specifically governmental undertaking showing official remorse for the comfort women system. Again according to its president, Tomiichi Murayama, the Asian Women's Fund engaged in "projects of atonement of the Japanese people" that would involve: "(i) atonement money financed by donations from the Japanese people; (ii) medical and welfare support projects financed by disbursements from the Japanese government; and (iii) a letter of apology from the Prime Minister of Japan, sent to each former comfort woman with these benefits."[40] Critics wanted the government to take all responsibility for the payments, not to leave this to the charitable impulses of the Japanese populace. This objection seems reasonable enough. The point, for the comfort women, is that the compensation they are due is a form of *reparations,* not a form of *welfare.* Similarly, many Herero reject as inappropriate the Germans' contributions of foreign aid to the state of Namibia generally because they are not specifically aimed at atoning for the Herero genocide.

In the case of making amends for the "rape of Nanking," the charge that the Japanese government is engaged in a process of denial is more complex. Beyond the matter of what to call the killings, there have been cases of denial by various Japanese intellectuals that anything like the massacres ever took place. Although the knowledge base concerning the overall numbers is once again rather shaky, there is little doubt that something awful took place in Nanjing during 1937–8. Indeed, General Matsui Iwane was sentenced to death by the Tokyo Tribunal on account of his " 'negative responsibility' . . . for having been derelict in preventing atrocities by troops under his command during the Nanking massacre."[41]

Part of what is shocking about denials of the events at Nanking flows from the comparison, now nearly axiomatic, of Japan with Germany. Whereas Holocaust denial is a crime in Germany, denial of the Nanjing massacres is entirely legal and not particularly uncommon in Japanese society. This situation does not help Japan to overcome its reputation as a country that "can't say sorry." Yet the Japanese government has recently done so – again. On April 22, 2005, at a meeting of international leaders in Jakarta, the Japanese prime minister, Junichiro Koizumi, "offered the most public apology in a decade over Japan's wartime aggression in Asia."[42] During the same period, however, Koizumi's insistence on visiting the Yasukuni shrine to the Japanese war dead has stoked considerable upset among Chinese and Koreans in the recent past. Koizumi is clearly playing to a variety of audiences, both foreign and domestic.

The events of the Asia-Pacific War play an important role in contemporary foreign affairs in East Asia. From the perspective of domestic Chinese politics, the government has tended to turn the tap of historical antagonism on and off in the interest of shoring up its own legitimacy and pursuing its political and economic aims *vis-à-vis* Japan. Thus, for example, in the interest of nurturing nationalist (and specifically anti-Japanese) sentiment as Communism recedes, "the Nanjing Museum now blows air sirens every December 13 at 10 a.m. to commemorate the start of the massacres of 1937–38."[43] Prime Minister Koizumi's 2005 apology in Jakarta was clearly in part a response to weeks of anti-Japanese protests in China that had been sparked by the adoption of new textbooks that were perceived in China as insufficiently contrite about the Second World War past. These demonstrations must have had the approval of the government, at least at first; after a certain time, however, the government seemed to be concerned that it had created a monster that threatened to outrun its grip.[44] The legacy of the comfort women, and of Japanese imperialism more broadly, also continues to roil relations between the Koreas and Japan.[45]

From the point of view of those outside China, as in the case of the Armenian massacres and their contribution to diasporic identity, the Nanjing Massacre has come to play a major role in overseas Chinese politics. Ian Buruma has observed that "the different Chinese dissidents from mainland China, from Taiwan, and Hong Kong, and other exiles in America do not have political goals in common that tie them together. . . . The one thing that does tie them together is a kind of emotional nationalism that has grown much stronger in recent years, and one of the great symbols of this new Chinese nationalism is the Nanking massacre."[46] Such symbols can provide a powerful stimulus, as we have seen in the case of the Armenian genocide and as Peter Novick has found with regard to the role of the Holocaust in American Jewish life.[47]

Another area in which Japan is perceived as failing to come to terms with the past is in the textbooks that are used to tell younger generations about the country's history. This is an almost perennial issue, especially in relations with Korea – twentieth-century Japan's first colony – and China. The usual charge is that the textbooks "gloss over wartime atrocities,"[48] but the bigger problem is that "in the absence of reconciliation – either domestic or international – both critics and supporters of the government look to the textbooks in search of a definitive statement on how the Japanese state views the nation's past."[49]

The textbook issue periodically inflames Japan's bilateral relations in East Asia, as could be seen again in the Chinese protests of March–April 2005. Yet in contrast to the situation in Turkey, it seems unlikely that the Japanese population in general could claim to be unaware of Japan's wartime atrocities. According to Charles Burress, "contrary to common perceptions, the basic theme in the [school] texts is that of Japan as an aggressor nation."[50] At the same time, a number of initiatives have been undertaken in recent years to try to advance the project of what I have elsewhere called "communicative history," whereby the various parties to a particular history collaborate in trying to develop a narrative satisfactory to all concerned.[51]

Money is once again an issue in the relative reticence of the Japanese with regard to the Second World War-related past. The comfort women have pressed for greater reparations than the government has come up with thus far. Moreover, there have been a number of lawsuits that seek compensation for the Japanese use of slave labor and for germ warfare experiments.[52] On the whole, litigants have not fared well in Japanese courts, and have therefore tried to use US courts to pursue their claims. These have not been terribly successful either; the reason courts typically give is that a decision in favor of slave laborers or prisoners of war would constitute inappropriate meddling in foreign affairs, particularly because the Japanese claim to have resolved all outstanding reparations demands in the San Francisco Peace Treaty of 1952 and its subsequent bilateral agreements.[53]

Just as we have seen in the Turkish case, there is reason to believe that the reticence about the past in Japan is to be found more among elites than among the general public. For example, a 1994 survey found that 80 per cent of Japanese polled "agreed that the government 'has not adequately compensated the people of countries Japan invaded or colonized'."[54] Political elites may therefore be out of step with their constituents; the problem in Japan, at least, is that the long-ruling Liberal Democratic Party – almost the only party in Japan throughout most of its postwar history – caters primarily to a conservative and hence more nationalistic constituency. In contrast to Turkey and its relationship to the EU, moreover, Japan is not facing the same pressures to meet extranational standards of contrition in order to gain access to coveted international institutions.

Meanwhile, using the standard of the Holocaust as their point of reference, the representatives of the Herero insist that the reason for the German refusal to make amends is simple racism. According to Professor Mburumba Kerina, a leading Herero figure and aide to Chief Riruako, the difference between their claims and those of the Jews is that "the Jews are white; we are black."[55] While this may or may not be correct, the massive weight of the Holocaust and other Second World War related claims has perhaps had a way of crushing other projects concerned with "coming to terms with the past" in Germany. In truth, however, there is another important source of opposition to the Hereros' claims: the SWAPO government of Namibia.[56]

The reason why the SWAPO government refuses to back the Hereros' claims, in this view, is that it is reluctant to antagonize the Germans, who are the country's chief source of foreign aid. Indeed, since independence in 1990, the German government has contributed some 500 million euros to the economic and social reconstruction of the country, which has only three million inhabitants.[57] In addition, SWAPO has been seen as resistant to explorations of the past in part because it has its own atrocities to reckon with, which are themselves the focus of reparations claims. As a result, the issue of reparations for those detained by SWAPO during the struggle "has monopolized human rights discussion" in post-independence Namibia, not least because of a "lack of cohesion among victim groups" and "a dearth of organizations that advocate for victims other than SWAPO ex-detainees."[58] The matter of reparations for the pre-First World War period have received more attention in the West, however, in part because of a renewed interest in the question of the extent to which the "Herero Holocaust" comprised a run-up to the one committed by the Germans against the Jews.

Clearly, as Foreign Minister Joschka Fischer expressed it, the German government feels a particular "responsibility for the colonial history."[59] Yet the Germans prefer not to portray these payments as resulting from pressure for reparations. The foreign assistance might nonetheless be viewed as "reparations" if either government wanted to call it so; the issue is in part purely terminological. Of course, foreign assistance to the Namibian government – even if represented as "reparations" – goes (at least nominally) to the whole country, whereas reparations specifically to the Herero would presumably benefit them (assuming they can be identified) more than the rest of the population. There thus appears to be in the Hereros' claims an element of identity politics, Namibian-style. The difficulties the Herero have faced *vis-à-vis* the German government indicate that it is a more complicated matter for a nonstate entity to bring reparations claims against a foreign government that is providing extensive financial assistance with a clear statement of "responsibility" for historical wrongdoing in the whole country.

In pursuing their claims, the Herero have been bolstered by the success of comparable efforts elsewhere. For example, the Herero frequently cite the precedent set by postwar German reparations to Jewish entities. In 1998, Mburumba Kerina had also pointed to another case he regarded as a parallel, though one that has not been notably successful in garnering reparations for its claimants. Upon hearing of the Japanese recognition of crimes against some of those whom they exploited as comfort women during the Second

World War, Professor Kerina – who like many Herero has a German grand-parent – said, "If the Japanese could pay for that, the Germans could [too]."[60] Yet the compensation for the "comfort women" and for Jews mistreated during the Second World War have involved reparations to those persons who had actually suffered the wrongs in question. It is not possible to make this claim with respect to the Hereros, whose historical distance from the injustices in question means that they have a more difficult case to make. One might say the same thing about the claims of the Armenians, yet their case seems rather more promising because of the power of the Armenian diaspora to attract attention to the century-old wrongdoing. Such power is not available to the tiny Herero group.

The claims of both the Herero and the Armenians raise the inevitable question: "how far back should we go?" Sidney Harring has noted that the Herero were effectively barred from making claims while they lived under South African rule (until 1990), and that postapartheid South Africa permits claims for restitution of native lands as far back as the Native Land Act of 1913 – a period roughly comparable to that in which the two groups suffered the wrongs for which they seek recompense.[61] Moreover, the State of Brandenburg in Germany recently concluded a treaty with the Vatican under the terms of which Brandenburg would pay the Church more than a million euros as "compensation for church property confiscated *during the time of the Reformation* as well as *at the beginning of the nineteenth century*."[62] An agreement such as this might seem to lift all "statutes of limitations" on how far back we can go. Ultimately, however, the question of "how far back we can go" is a political matter that cannot be determined in the abstract; it can only be answered on the basis of the strength of the demands mounted by the claimants and the willingness of the target of those demands to accede.

Conclusion

Let us sum up some of the findings and explore their likely implications. First, the intensified pressure on Turkey and Japan in recent years to come to terms with their past has led in each case to initiatives among intellectuals and historians to develop a better understanding of the history in question. This goal is not normally sufficient, however, for those groups that do much of the pressuring; their aims are more likely to be legal, material, or political than they are to be ("merely") scholarly. These groups, often ethnic organizations, politicize history in an effort to achieve their contemporary objectives. In each case, the more scholarly advances tend to have relatively little impact on a public debate that takes on a life of its own and that often has scant regard for the details of the historical record or the finer points of historical analysis. The result is often intransigence on the part of political decision-makers, who feel that they are being besieged by antagonists who are ill-disposed toward them in any case.

Apparent intransigence with regard to "coming to terms with the past" is sometimes modulated by a kind of renaming – that is, attention to the issues in question, though under a different rubric than that used by groups pressing for a reckoning with the past. For example, German Foreign Minister Joschka Fischer sought to circumlocute pressures for the Germans to pay "reparations" to the Herero, as we have seen, promising to continue as Namibia's leading donor of foreign assistance and avowing the German government's sense of responsibility for the colonial past.[63] Is this enough for the Germans to come to terms with this part of their past? Some Herero don't think so, but the money flows in from Berlin all the same. Yet, as in the case of the perceived Japanese failure to adequately *acknowledge* the wrongs done to those they sought to conquer and dominate in East Asia during the Asia-Pacific War, money without apology or contrition may not be enough. And the textbooks in all three of these countries – Germany, Japan, and Turkey – need to reflect the seamier aspects of their history. But no matter what happens in the writing of history, some groups will exploit the past for political advantage.

History and politics, it seems, are two different things. It is therefore worth pondering Halil Berktay's remarks on this matter. Berktay has vigorously criticized the Turkish government for drawing a "curtain of silence" around the Armenian massacres and getting its military allies to help in suppressing opposing views.[64] Asked in an interview how Turkey should handle demands that it declare the massacres a genocide, he said:

> [B]ringing up the issue renders the Turkish state and society more defensive on this topic and closed within themselves, and pushes them to become more rigid. Political polarization on this topic is so strong that even finding the courage to speak on this subject is a great problem. Of these two poles one is the politics of "having the genocide affirmed and recorded as public record," the other the politics of "denying the genocide." In this climate of polarization, which opens the way to intellectual terror, it becomes impossible to speak on common ground. I believe it is wrong for Turkey to apologize. . . . It is incredibly naive for any parliament to have the illusion that it has the right to make decisions about historical events that should be the subject of science. In truth the Turkish Republic also should quit discussing the Armenian question.[65]

This sort of view is often seen by advocates of "coming to terms with the past" as a regressive one, implying complicity in or even a repetition of the past in question.

That may well be in particular instances, but Berktay's position also has much to commend it – at least in some cases. It is a matter of professional obligation for historians uncompromisingly to seek the historical truth; there is no end, theoretically speaking, to their revisionism. Yet this commitment to revisionism "might well be subversive to the purpose of commemoration."[66]

Government declarations that some past event was "genocide" serve primarily political aims, not historiographical ones. It may be best to leave determinations of "genocide" to historians and stop making them the subject of political determinations.[67] Under the current circumstances of the intense politicization of certain histories, especially by diaspora ethnic groups for whom these pasts play an important role in fostering social cohesion, the reticence of the Turks and Japanese – to the extent that it is accurately characterized as such – is understandable, if not necessarily laudable. The advancement of understanding of each country's past (knowledge) and of accommodation of those who continue to feel burdened by these pasts (acknowledgment) will depend fundamentally on the progress of liberal forces in each country's political life. As Andrew Horvat has written, "Time may heal wounds between individuals; between countries, it seems only to magnify them – unless concerted action is taken to avert the vicious cycle of past conflicts leading to future conflicts."[68]

Notes

1 Wole Soyinka, "Reparations, truth, and reconciliation," in his *The Burden of Memory, the Muse of Forgiveness* (New York: Oxford University Press, 1999), p. 90.
2 For the estimates of those killed in the Nanjing Massacre, see Joshua Fogel, "Introduction: the Nanjing Massacre in history," in Fogel, ed., *The Nanjing Massacre in History and Historiography* (Berkeley, CA: University of California Press, 1999), p. 6 and Robert Darnton, "It happened one night," *New York Review of Books* 51/11 (June 24, 2004), 61.
3 Norman Naimark, *Fires of Hatred: Ethnic Cleansing in Twentieth-Century Europe* (Cambridge, MA: Harvard University Press, 2001), pp. 12, 40–1. The numerical estimates of deaths are quoted from Ronald Suny, "When genocide? Interpretations of the causes and timing of the Armenian deportations and massacres," paper for the workshop "Armenians and the End of the Ottoman Empire," University of Chicago, March 17–19, 2000.
4 Casper W. Erichsen, "A forgotten history," *Mail & Guardian* (Johannesburg) August 17, 2001.
5 Sidney Harring, "The legal claim for German reparations to the Herero nation," available at http://academic.udayton.edu/race/06hrights/GeoRegions/Africa/Nambia01.htm.
6 See "Opposition criticises Swapo's land appropriation plans," *SouthScan* 19/16 (August 6, 2004), 6.
7 See George M. Fredrickson, *Racism: A Short History* (Princeton, NJ: Princeton University Press, 2002), p. 112.
8 Bernard Lewis, *The Emergence of Modern Turkey*, 3rd edn (New York: Oxford University Press, 2002), p. 356, and Ronald Suny, "When genocide?"
9 "'A special organization killed Armenians': an interview with Halil Berktay," *Radikal*, Istanbul (June 30, 2000), translated by Marc David Baer.
10 Iris Chang, *The Rape of Nanking: The Forgotten Holocaust of World War II* (New York: Penguin, 1997).
11 See F. Bridgland, "Germany's genocide rehearsal," *The Scotsman* September 26, 2001, and T. Bensman, "Tribe demands Holocaust reparations: Germany's genocidal war against Namibia's Herero was rehearsal for World War II atrocities,"

The Salt Lake Tribune March 18, 1999; both cited in Jeremy Sarkin, "Holding multinational corporations accountable for human rights and humanitarian law violations committed during colonialism and apartheid," in Eva Brems, ed., *In Bedrijven en Mensenrechten* (Maklu, 2003), p. 31, n. 152 and p. 34, n. 164.

12 Interview with Herero Paramount Chief Kuaima Riruako, Windhoek, Namibia, January 3, 2003.

13 Mark Mazower, "The G-word," *London Review of Books* 23/3 (February 8, 2001).

14 John Dower, *Embracing Defeat: Japan in the Wake of World War II* (New York: W. W. Norton/The New Press, 1999), pp. 458, 463.

15 Quoted in Fatma Muge Gocek and Ronald Grigor Suny, "Turkish–Armenian dialogue on the Armenian deaths and massacres of 1915," *International Institute Journal* (University of Michigan), Summer 2002.

16 Naimark, *Fires of Hatred*, pp. 35–7; quotation on p. 37.

17 Stephen Kinzer, "Armenians among the Turks: a happier chapter," *New York Times* national edition (March 25, 1998), A4.

18 Jan-Bart Gewald, *Herero Heroes: A Socio-Political History of the Herero of Namibia, 1890–1923* (Athens, OH: Ohio University Press, 1999), p. 2.

19 Quoted in Gewald, *Herero Heroes*, pp. 172–3.

20 S. Cohen, *States of Denial: Knowing About Atrocities and Suffering* (Malden, MA: Blackwell, 2001), p. xi.

21 On this distinction, see Thomas Nagel, "Concealment and exposure," *Philosophy and Public Affairs* 27/1 (Winter 1998), 3–30, available online at: www.nyu.edu/gsas/dept/philo/faculty/nagel/papers/exposure.html.

22 Belinda Cooper, "Turks breach wall of silence on Armenians," *New York Times* national edition (March 6, 2004), 15.

23 Stephen Kinzer, "Turkish region recalls massacre of Armenians," *New York Times* national edition (May 10, 2000), A3.

24 Taner Akçam, "Is there any solution other than a dialogue?" in Akçam, *Dialogue Across an International Divide: Essays Towards a Turkish-Armenian Dialogue* (Cambridge, MA: Zoryan Institute, 2001), pp. 11, 20. See also Yigal Schleifer, "In Turkey, taboo lifts over past treatment of Armenians," *Christian Science Monitor* (March 17, 2005).

25 John Dower, "An aptitude for being unloved," in Omer Bartov et al., eds, *Crimes of War: Guilt and Denial in the Twentieth Century* (New York: The New Press, 2002), p. 227.

26 Charles Burress, "The American indictment: the Japan that can't say sorry," in Andrew Horvat and Gebhard Hielscher, eds, *Sharing the Burden of the Past: Legacies of War in Europe, America, and Asia* (Tokyo: The Asia Foundation/Friedrich Ebert Stiftung, 2003), pp. 126–8.

27 Sebnum Arsu, "Turkey says 523,000 were killed by Armenians between 1910 and 1922," nytimes.com (April 17, 2005).

28 See the transcript of "A conversation with historian Taner Akçam on Armenian genocide and Turkish statement," CBC Radio, February 6, 2005; see also the opinion piece by the Turkish ambassador to Washington, O. Faruk Logoğlu, "To reconcile Turks and Armenians," *Washington Times* (May 3, 2005).

29 See Dower, "An aptitude for being unloved," pp. 224–7.

30 See, for example, "Switzerland: lawmakers accept Armenian genocide," *New York Times* national edition (December 17, 2003), A8.

31 Cooper, "Turks breach wall of silence," p. 15.

32 "Turkey: new genocide charges," *New York Times* national edition (November 16, 2000), A10.

33 Emil Danielyan, "Armenia frustrated as ties with Turkey remain strained," *Eurasianet.org*, May 28, 2004, available at www.eurasianet.org/departments/insight/articles/eav052804.shtml.

34 Cooper, "Turks breach wall of silence," p. 15, and see especially the writings of Taner Akçam collected in *Dialogue Across an International Divide*.
35 Stephen Kinzer, "Turkish region recalls massacre of Armenians."
36 Quoted in Sahin Alpay, "Turkish–Armenian reconciliation," *Journal of Turkish Weekly* http://www.turkishweekly.net/comments.php?id=518; originally published in *Zaman* (March 19, 2005).
37 "'A special organization killed Armenians': an interview with Halil Berktay."
38 Charles Maier, *The Unmasterable Past: History, Holocaust, and German National Identity* (Cambridge, MA: Harvard University Press, 1997 [1988]), p. 32.
39 See www.awf.or.jp/english/statement_awf.html.
40 "Statement by Prime Minister Tomiichi Murayama, August 15, 1995," in Roy L. Brooks, ed., *When Sorry Isn't Enough: The Controversy over Apologies and Reparations for Human Injustice* (New York: New York University Press, 1999), p. 127.
41 Dower, *Embracing Defeat*, p. 459.
42 Raymond Bonner and Norimitsu Onishi, "Japan's chief apologizes for war misdeeds," nytimes.com (April 23, 2005).
43 Serge Schmemann, "The anniversary of World War II is an invitation to continue fighting," *New York Times* national edition (March 22, 2005), A22.
44 See Joseph Kahn, "State-run Chinese paper lashes anti-Japan protests as 'evil plot'," *New York Times* national edition (April 27, 2005), A5; Joseph Kahn, "Beijing finds anti-Japan propaganda a 2-edged sword," *New York Times* national edition (May 3, 2005), A3; and Jim Yardley, "Chinese police head off anti-Japan protests," *New York Times* national edition (May 5, 2005), A8.
45 See Schmemann, "The anniversary of World War II is an invitation to continue fighting," and Norimitsu Onishi, "Dispute over islets frays ties between Tokyo and Seoul," *New York Times* national edition (March 22, 2005), A3.
46 Ian Buruma, "Commentary," in Horvat and Hielscher, eds, *Sharing the Burden of the Past*, p. 139; see also Fogel, "Introduction: the Nanjing Massacre in history," pp. 3–4.
47 Peter Novick, *The Holocaust in American Life* (Boston, MA: Houghton Mifflin, 1999).
48 Howard W. French, "Japan rediscovers its Korean past," *New York Times* national edition (March 11, 2002), A3.
49 Andrew Horvat, "Moving forward into the past," in Horvat and Hielscher, eds, *Sharing the Burden of the Past*, p. 23.
50 Charles Burress, "The American indictment," p. 127; see also Julian Dierkes, "Teaching portrayals of the nation: postwar history education in Japan and the Germanys," PhD dissertation, Department of Sociology, Princeton University, 2003.
51 John Torpey, "Introduction: politics and the past," in John Torpey, ed., *Politics and the Past: On Repairing Historical Injustices* (Lanham, MD: Rowman & Littlefield, 2003), p. 6; see the discussion in Sakai Toshiki, "International exchange on textbooks in Japan: an interim report" and Chung Jae-Jong, "South Korea–Japan history reconciliation: a progress report," in Horvat and Hielscher, eds, *Sharing the Burden of the Past*, pp. 100–14.
52 See "Japanese court rejects wartime labourers' claims," *BBC World Service*, July 9, 2002; and "Japan: appeal of germ warfare ruling," *New York Times* national edition (September 4, 2002), A6.
53 See Laura Hein, "War compensation: claims against the Japanese government and Japanese corporations for war crimes," in Torpey, ed., *Politics and the Past*, pp. 132–3; see also Burress, "The American indictment," p. 123.
54 Dower, "An aptitude for being unloved," p. 241.
55 Author's interview with Professor Mburumba Kerina, Windhoek, Namibia, January 3, 2003.

56 See "Namibia: tensions revealed in Swapo," *SouthScan* 19/11 (May 28, 2004).

57 See "Opposition criticises Swapo's land appropriation plans."

58 See Warren Buford and Hugo van der Merwe, "Reparation in southern Africa," *Cahiers d'études africaines* 44/1–2 (2004), manuscript pp. 33–41. The quotations are from p. 40.

59 Quoted in Susanne Bittorf, "Fischer verspricht Namibia Hilfe," *Süddeutsche Zeitung*, October 30, 2003, 7.

60 See Donald G. McNeil Jr, "Its past on its sleeve, tribe seeks Bonn's apology," *New York Times* national edition (May 31, 1998), A3.

61 Harring, "The legal claim for German reparations to the Herero nation."

62 "Brandenburg schließt Vertrag mit dem Vatikan," *Süddeutsche Zeitung*, November 6, 2003, 8. My italics.

63 Quoted in Bittorf, "Fischer verspricht Namibia Hilfe."

64 Cooper, "Turks breach wall of silence," p. 15.

65 "'A special organization killed Armenians': an interview with Halil Berktay."

66 Daqing Yang, "The challenges of the Nanjing Massacre: reflections on historical inquiry," in Fogel, ed., *The Nanjing Massacre in History and Historiography*, p. 151.

67 See my review of Michael Mann's *The Dark Side of Democracy*, "Understanding ethnic cleansing," *Contexts* 4/3 (Summer 2005), 60–2.

68 Horvat, "Moving forward into the past," p. 24.

10 Pop culture, public memory, and Korean–Japanese relations

Chiho Sawada

Introduction

Cultural diplomacy – or, rather, pop culture diplomacy – is a hot topic in East Asia.[1] Indeed, a 2004 summit meeting between President Roh Moo Hyun of the Republic of Korea (ROK) and Prime Minister Koizumi Junichirō of Japan began with a conversation on pop culture and its edifying influences on relations between the two countries. Koizumi told Roh that the Korean television drama *Winter Sonata* (*Kyŏul yŏn'ga*) had gained a tremendous following in Japan, becoming "something of a social phenomenon" and sparking wider interest about Korea. Roh responded that Japanese pop culture is increasingly accepted in Korea amid ongoing lifting of import restrictions. To this, Koizumi noted his desire that liberalization policy be fully applied to Japanese animation (*anime*) products. They went on to declare that official efforts to resolve "issues of the past" and fashion a "future-oriented relationship" ultimately rely on a foundation of mutual understanding and shared values built through people-to-people interactions in cultural and economic realms.[2]

This brief exchange on a soap opera and *anime* captured issues of profound significance for the Asia-Pacific region; issues that also converge with key themes of the present book (which are articulated by the editors in the introductory chapter). First, Koizumi and Roh acknowledged in their exchange that the task of "squarely facing history" – facing, that is, injustices committed in times of colonialism, war, and dictatorship as well as present disputes about this dark past – is imperative for improving regional relations. Second, they recognized the limits of state power in addressing historical injustice and advancing reconciliation. In other words, state-to-state negotiation may be sufficient for restoring normalized relations between former antagonists, and thereby producing what has been called "thin" reconciliation; but diverse and sustained intersocietal interactions are crucial for arriving at "thick" reconciliation, which entails forgiveness, empathy, and shared visions of the past and future.[3] Third, the two leaders marked the present as a time of great opportunity for attaining thick reconciliation. One of them noted, for example, that whereas "the annual number of tourists between Japan and the ROK stood at 10,000 people" back in 1965 (when formal diplomatic ties were established), "the same number of people now travel between the two countries in a single day." They attributed such increasing interactions to not only the erosion of old (Cold War era) barriers to transnational trade and travel, but also the emergence of new facilitating factors, notably pop culture diplomacy.

Apropos of the above themes, this chapter explores connections between transnational flows of pop culture (which encompass stages of production, circulation, and consumption) and the monumental task of advancing thick reconciliation. Following this introductory section, I briefly survey factors that account for the rise of pop culture as a prominent component of Korean–Japanese relations, situating this phenomenon within a matrix of global, regional, and nation-specific developments. For heuristic purposes the first half of the survey emphasizes key state actions and the second private sector initiatives that have brought pop culture to the forefront of efforts to bring Japan and Korea closer together.[4] The next two sections problematize the contention that transnational flows of pop culture lead to mutual understanding about the past and shared goals in the present. In the remainder of this introduction, I touch on the concepts of popular memory and informal education as a prelude to subsequent sections in the chapter.

In the stimulating book *Silencing the Past: Power and the Production of History*, Michel-Rolph Trouillot points to disjunctures between academic historiography and the formation of collective or public memory.[5] He observes, in this connection, that the people-at-large most often access their communal senses of the past not by reading scholarly works but by partaking in "celebrations, site and museum visits, movies, national holidays."[6] Other thinkers such as Andreas Huyssen and Arjun Appadurai also acknowledge the importance of such forms of informal education in the shaping of collective historical consciousness. Among informal modes of history education, Huyssen and Appadurai place special emphasis on what the former calls "the new media" and the latter "electronic capitalism." Pointing to a global "memory boom," or a shift "from present futures to present pasts," Huyssen goes as far as to declare that we "cannot discuss personal, generational, or public memory separate from the enormous influence of the new media as carriers of all forms of memory."[7]

> [I]t is no longer possible, for instance, to think of the Holocaust or of any other historical traumas as a serious ethical and political issue apart from the multiple ways it is now linked to commodification and spectacularization in films, museums, docudramas, Internet sites, photography books, comics, fiction, even fairy tales (Roberto Benigni's *La vita è bella*) and pop songs.[8]

Similarly, Appadurai, in *Modernity at Large: Cultural Dimensions of Globalization*, argues that manifestations of "electronic capitalism" –

cinema and television in particular – are central to the formation of new collective identities and memories in an era marked by accelerating global flows of migrants, capital, information, and products.[9] Huyssen and Appadurai are by no means alone in their views. Recent years have witnessed growing scholarly interest in the historicizing potential of film, television, and other forms of electronic media.[10]

These observations apply to the Asia-Pacific. In many parts of this region, entertainment and leisure activities are increasingly entwined with the construction of popular memories (and collective identities) as state controls on cultural production are relaxed and "the new media" proliferate. Especially in affluent countries like Japan and South Korea, people are routinely exposed to "issues of the past" as they watch history-based television dramas and films, browse and chat on websites, and play computer games. Informal education in these forms is accessible and appealing since it entertains – and usually involves lower opportunity costs (in terms of time, effort, expense) than, say, attending a semester-long class, traveling to a historical site, or visiting a national museum. It is also freed from geographic or spatial constraints. One does not, for instance, need to be in Japan (or near its largest cities where the best museums are located) to interact with discourses on "Japanese" memories. Conversely, a person in Japan can access pop cultures from other communities near and far, fostering multicultural, transnational memories.

So it seems that President Roh, Prime Minister Koizumi, and other celebrants of pop culture diplomacy are not merely spouting vacuous rhetoric. This concept, when considered seriously, points to important new questions: notably, concerning the formidable power of informal – especially mass-mediated – educational processes in shaping public memory and potentially advancing regional reconciliation. By way of example, pop culture diplomacy complicates the widely held idea of the "textbook controversy" as central to resolving historical disputes between Japan and its Asian neighbors. I certainly would not disavow the importance of the textbook issue, particularly since it has inspired debates on a transnational level extending well beyond the classroom and into courts of law, newspapers and everyday conversations.[11] However, we should also consider the possibility that people in the Asia-Pacific more often engage public memory via mass-mediated entertainment than directly from history textbooks. Scholars have begun to take notice. Recent studies explore, for instance, how wars in modern Asia are remembered as well as forgotten in literature, film, and other popular art forms.[12] Several works even examine how the textbook controversy itself has been taken up in realms of pop culture such as comic books and Internet forums.[13] The present chapter seeks to build on this emerging literature exploring connections between popular culture and public memories of historical injustice in the Asia-Pacific; and it attempts to do so by focusing on the relatively uncharted topics of pop culture diplomacy and hybrid Korean–Japanese media products.

After surveying the rise of pop culture diplomacy, I offer close readings of the dramatic television series *Friends*[14] and the blockbuster movie *2009 Lost Memories*[15] – both the products of Japanese–Korean collaboration. Thinking about these texts allows us to address several problems in the way pop culture diplomacy is typically framed. To cite one problem, its prophets in political and journalistic circles usually speak too simplistically of "Korean" or "Japanese" pop culture, even as such categories are becoming increasingly unstable. Second, there is a troubling tendency both to avoid careful discussions of product content and to emphasize those products presumed to contain edifying lessons. Third, complex questions of media effects and audience reception have been largely ignored. This chapter illustrates the clear trend toward transnational linkages in the production, circulation, and consumption of pop culture. It also demonstrates the polysemy of pop culture. In other words, a single cultural text (or body of works) can contain a rich variety of symbols and meanings, often mixing politically progressive, neutral, and problematic elements. The chapter further discusses how pop texts not only are imbued with multiple messages at various stages of production but also take on new meanings as they are received and interpreted by viewers. All these complications lead to an overarching argument. The transnational flow of pop culture can impede as well as promote mutual understanding and shared values transcending ethnic nationalism.

Contextualizing pop culture diplomacy

In early 1993 then Director-General of UNESCO Federico Mayor observed that the potential for cultural exchange had grown substantially in the aftermath of the Cold War:

> [N]ew factors are working to bring different cultures into ever closer contact. Global upheavals have broken down old political barriers to movement. People can travel freely. Information can flow where it is needed. At the same time, tremendous advances in communications technology have created a planet-wide network capable of relaying information, sound and images from any one point on the globe to any other, instantaneously.[16]

He expressed the hope that cultural interactions facilitated by these "new factors" would, in turn, beckon a "multicultural springtime" of tolerance and reconciliation. As Mayor spoke, recent developments in the Asia-Pacific signaled that his optimistic vision may very well be realized. For instance, South Korea not only made significant steps toward democratic consolidation but also undertook *Nordpolitik* (policy toward countries to the north) diplomacy, whereby relations were normalized with erstwhile antagonists Russia (1990) and the People's Republic of China (1992), and an agreement was struck for South Korea and North Korea to jointly enter the United

Nations (1991). Granted, South Korea's efforts to improve relations with the North hit an impasse with the emergence of the first Korean nuclear crisis in 1993–4. South Korean cultural and educational exchanges with Russia and China would nonetheless grow dramatically throughout the 1990s, pushing a transition from "thin" to "thick" reconciliation.

State-led initiatives toward pop culture diplomacy between Korea and Japan

What about Korean–Japanese relations? South Korean President Kim Dae Jung staked his administration (1998–2002) on advancing democratic consolidation domestically and removing obstacles to reconciliation in the Asia-Pacific. His administration's record in terms of reducing political corruption and promoting economic justice was mixed at best. However, Kim gained worldwide renown for the "Sunshine Policy" of rapproachment with North Korea, which – despite its shifting fortunes – would garner him a Nobel Peace Prize. Less dramatic but no less significant was his role in improving bilateral relations with Japan.

In October 1998 President Kim visited Tokyo to confer with Japanese Prime Minister Obuchi Keizō, which resulted in a "Joint Declaration of Partnership towards the Twenty-first Century." Obuchi offered "deep remorse and heartfelt apology" on Japan's part for its colonial past in Korea, marking the first explicit apology by the Japanese government. Kim expressed appreciation for this acknowledgment of history, which he deemed a prerequisite for "a future-oriented relationship based on reconciliation . . . and cooperation."[17] Although this exchange was largely symbolic (skirting the knotty issue of colonial reparations), it has been heralded as an important step forward in Korean–Japanese reconciliation.

To provide "concrete form to this partnership," the Declaration enumerated priorities for future cooperation. This shortlist was not restricted to the cultural realm *per se*. Starting with recommendations for enhanced state-to-state consultation on security issues, it advocated new agreements on fishing rights, custom taxes, technology transfer, and other issues pertaining to cross-border commerce, travel, and communications. Significantly, however, the Declaration culminated in a call for people-to-people interactions based on cultural exchange as a necessary ingredient for thick reconciliation. That is, to realize "mutual understanding" between the peoples of the two countries and "raise to a higher dimension the cooperative relations . . . which have been built since the normalization of relations in 1965." This phrase might be read as an admission that "cooperative relations" since normalization had not extended to the people-at-large. In fact, scholars have noted that bilateral relations during the era of military rule in South Korea (1961–87/1992) were shaped "primarily through backroom deals between elites in late-night parlors in Seoul and Tokyo."[18]

According to the Joint Declaration, the state would maintain a key role in promoting cultural exchange and thick reconciliation; but its actions were to be carefully calibrated, enhancing those that facilitated inter-societal interactions and curtailing those that did not. Thus the two leaders advocated, on the one hand, greater state activism to support "exchanges among various groups and regions at various levels in the two societies – *inter alia*, [students], teachers, researchers, journalists, civic associations." On the other hand, they acknowledged that state-administered barriers to Korean–Japanese interactions must be rolled back. This entailed, for instance, easing visa requirements for Korean citizens wishing to visit Japan. It was also in this context that President Kim pledged that his country would begin lifting in several stages the half-century-old ban on importation of Japanese pop culture. Such steps, Obuchi and Kim concluded, would allow "peoples of both countries to share the spirit of this Joint Declaration and participate in joint efforts to build and develop a new partnership."

In tandem with the 1998 Joint Declaration and dismantling of Korean import bans on Japanese pop culture, the 2002 FIFA World Cup propelled pop culture diplomacy. The 2002 rendition of this huge international sports event was unusual in that it was co-hosted by two countries, South Korea and Japan. To build on the spirit of cooperation and unity symbolized by the joint hosting of the World Cup, in late 1999 the Japanese and Korean governments designated 2002 as "The Year of National Exchange" and began to sponsor a series of initiatives foregrounding pop culture, aimed especially at young audiences. Actresses Noriko Fujiwara (a former Miss Japan who regularly appears in TV dramas) and Kim Yun-jin (who starred in the Korean blockbuster film *Shiri*) were appointed goodwill ambassadors to promote the year of cultural exchange. Musical artists from the two countries were commissioned to compose an official theme song for the 2002 World Cup. The song – entitled "Let's Get Together Now" and sung in a mixture of Japanese, Korean, and English – offered the following message:

> Don't you think it's time we all let go of the fear inside
> Open up our minds, understand each other
> If we just decide to be as one, we'll set our spirits free
> Let this be a time, we can always keep within our hearts
> Far beyond today, till the end of time
> No longer a dream, peace and love becomes reality
> . . .
> Let's get together now.[19]

Aided by enthusiastic press coverage in both countries (that lavished attention on everything from the arrival of a Korean youth soccer team in Tokyo to the release of a Japanese film in Seoul), the message spread that cultural exchange promised a new future of peace and unity.

Pop culture diplomacy continued to unfold after the final match of the 2002 World Cup. On January 1, 2004 the Korean government implemented the fourth stage in the lifting of import bans on cultural products from Japan. Earlier stages in this process – enacted in October 1998, September

1999, and June 2000, respectively – sanctioned the importation of books and magazines, instrumental music, award-winning feature films, and a small number of animated programs. As Culture and Tourism Minister (and famed filmmaker) Lee Ch'ang-dong explained at a December 2003 press conference, the latest stage removes bans on game software as well as music with Japanese-language vocals, and permits broadcasting of selected television programs. Korea in the first months of 2004 thus hosted concerts by popular Japanese bands like TUBE (which was featured on the aforementioned "2002 FIFA World Cup Official Album") and a sumo-wrestling tournament that was also carried on television. Moreover, to commemorate the 2005 World Exposition in Aichi, Japan, the Japanese and Korean governments launched yet another "Year of National Exchange."

Societal agency in the pop diplomacy phenomenon

Culture Minister Lee's press conference elicited little controversy in Korea, whereas just a few years earlier there had been widespread concerns about "cultural imperialism" and the corrosive effects of Japanese pop culture on the Korean economy and society. Exploration of the underlying causes of this shift suggests that the state has often been a supporting rather than leading actor in processes of cultural exchange. Various overlapping factors account for reduced Korean anxieties about transnational cultural flows. One crucial factor is a growing awareness in Korea of how regulatory changes conform to social realities. Furtive importation of Japanese pop culture (by comics and *anime* aficionados in particular) had been going on for decades prior to the 1998 Joint Declaration and consequent policy changes. By 1998 satellite television, the Internet and broadband technology had made Japanese pop culture accessible at the click of a button, rendering futile attempts at blocking such access. Today Korean servers host thousands of websites dedicated to Japanese pop music ("J-pop"), *anime*, and so forth. It was only a matter of time before the people-at-large recognized that the official opening to Japanese pop culture was a belated effort by the state to assert a modicum of influence over transnational cultural flows. Second, entertainment and media companies have generally welcomed the regulatory changes. To be sure, some Korean business interests are lobbying to prolong import restrictions on Japanese *anime* and television programs to protect emerging domestic firms in these sectors from "excessive competition." Many companies nonetheless perceive the changes as a great opportunity: to combat online piracy (thereby maximizing profits from CD/DVD sales and fee-based file sharing), gain new sources of capital and content, and tap emerging markets. For instance, in November 2000, SM Entertainment of Korea and Avex Inc. of Japan signed a mutual licensing agreement whereby the former would market Avex's music CDs in Korea, and the latter market SM Entertainment's CDs in Japan. Then, in February 2004, Avex announced that it had agreed to invest nearly 2 billion wŏn in shares of SM Entertainment:

"to bolster the strategic relationship between our two companies in order to better compete in Southeast Asian (particularly Chinese) music markets."[20] A third important factor is the rising confidence among Koreans about the quality and appeal of domestically produced pop culture. Dire warnings about a Japanese cultural juggernaut and the weakness of Korean culture industries proved to be exaggerated. Japanese films, to cite a key example, captured only about 3 per cent of the Korean domestic market between 2001 and 2003. Meanwhile, the Korean film industry experienced a veritable renaissance, rolling back Hollywood dominance to regain a robust 40 per cent share of the local market.

Baleful images of Japanese cultural imperialism have been displaced to an extent by hopeful visions of a Korean cultural wave, crossing national and ethnic borders to win a following throughout Asia and beyond. The latter was born of numerous transformations in South Korea since the late 1980s. Among them, the following were perhaps most significant. Democratic consolidation has brought moderation of government censorship over cultural production. A shift from heavy industries toward the "new economy" and from capital scarcity to surplus promoted greater investments in information technologies and entertainment ventures. Although the major industrial conglomerates (*chaebŏl*) withdrew from investing in films during the 1997–8 financial crisis, venture capital firms like Mirae Esset and film distribution companies such as CJ Entertainment turned to financing big budget films and other pop culture productions. The general public, which was finally enjoying increased purchasing power and access to all sorts of products from abroad, demanded greater diversity of domestic pop culture. Thousands of people, many of them young and with modest means, eagerly bought up so-called "Netizen funds" and became film investors themselves. All of these changes allowed a new generation of creative spirits – less encumbered than their predecessors by censorship, funding shortages, or the imperative of expressing political dissent – to channel their energies in myriad directions. Building on indigenous influences as well as formats and content from overseas, this new generation has sought to fashion pop culture products that can compete with Hollywood and other global centers of cultural production. Whereas Korean films of the early 1980s consisted primarily of low budget "quota quickies," the end of the decade witnessed the emergence of a critical "new wave" cinema. By the late 1990s came blockbuster movies spanning a range of internationally popular genres such as the spy thriller, buddy film, romantic drama, and gangster comedy. Similar trends marked other entertainment sectors, with the appearance of highly polished Korean variations on the television soap opera, hip hop music, and so on. Thus was born a Korean-produced pop culture that is winning over audiences in Korea, the Asia-Pacific, and far beyond. By 1999 the imagery of a "Korean wave" (韓流, pronounced *Hallyu* in Korean) appeared in Chinese-language media, referencing the sudden craze for South Korean pop culture among residents of Hong Kong, Taiwan, Vietnam, and other parts of Southeast

Asia. The term was soon picked up by media sources throughout Asia, making it an integral part of everyday conversation.

Toward intersocietal cultural exchange and reconciliation?

Japan has not been able to escape the "Korean wave." Small ripples reached the islands by 2000, as evidenced by the successful theatrical release of the spy thriller *Shiri* and the popularity of musical acts such as S.E.S. and BoA (who is on the SM Entertainment label and promoted in Japan by Avex). *Hallyu* – pronounced *Kanryū* in Japanese – finally hit Japan at full force with the national broadcast of *Winter Sonata* on the NHK satellite channel in 2003, then on the basic NHK channel in 2004. "Fuyusona" (as the hit series is affectionately known in Japan) became undeniably "something of a social phenomenon." Bae Yong-joon, the actor who plays the lead male role in *Winter Sonata*, quickly gained a legion of adoring Japanese fans. By mid-2004 NHK's publishing arm had sold over a million copies combined of the DVD/VHS box set and spin-off novel. More significantly, the soap has inspired viewers to sample other manifestations of Korean culture. "Fuyusona" fans are reportedly subscribing to digital television services offering Korean programming, purchasing a variety of Korean novels and films, and, in not a few cases, visiting the peninsula.

Hallyu heightens the potential for genuine cultural exchange between the two countries. During the thirty-five years that Japan occupied Korea (1910–45), official policy was to assimilate, or Japanize, Koreans. Although it was sometimes acknowledged that Japan benefited in centuries past from cultural interactions with the peninsula, contemporary Korean cultural forms were denigrated as derivative and degenerate. Following Japan's defeat in the Second World War and the dissolution of empire, the Japanese media and public typically ignored Korean culture – except, it seemed, to point out instances when a South Korean pop song or television series had allegedly copied a Japanese model. This dismissive, indeed neo-colonialist, attitude may have appeared justifiable to some as long as South Korea maintained a ban on Japanese pop culture. (Of course, it should be noted again that the import ban was neither effectively nor consistently enforced. During the five decades prior to the 1998 Joint Declaration, in addition to furtive importation of Japanese comics, *anime*, fashion magazines, and so on, about 2,000 popular Japanese books deemed sufficiently "literary" were translated into Korean and legally sold.) Japan, in any case, no longer has a convenient excuse to ignore Korean cultural products. Korea's official "opening" to Japanese pop culture, bilateral promotional activities leading up to the 2002 FIFA World Cup, and private-sector initiatives (such as the Avex–SM Entertainment partnership) have combined to prod the Japanese people-at-large toward the *Hallyu* phenomenon. Having done so, many appear to be awed by what they have found – and pleasantly surprised at discovering their own long-suppressed capacity to appreciate Korean cultural forms.

Japan's rediscovery of Korea together with the latter's more receptive stance toward Japanese cultural products heralded the flowering of pop culture diplomacy. There are undeniable signs of growing transnational linkages through pop culture, involving state as well as societal initiatives, and extending across stages of production, distribution, *and* consumption of cultural products. Not only political leaders but also many media pundits and scholars are optimistic that such linkages will translate into shared visions of the past and present – and thereby ameliorate ethnic tensions. A journalist for *Japan Times*, to cite one example, expressed his hope that the impact of *Hallyu* in Japan would gradually reduce discrimination against Japanese residents of Korean descent: "now the Korean culture is hip, perhaps they will be appreciated for their difference."[21] A scholar at Kyoto University has sounded even more confident notes:

> culture can have tremendous significance in international relations. For example, the South Korean drama series *Kyŏul yŏn'ga* (Winter Sonata) became a major hit when it was broadcast in Japan . . . and it is now widely credited with helping many Japanese feel a sense of closeness to South Korea, which up to now has often been described as "near but far" – geographically close to Japan, but psychologically distant. Also, a survey of public opinion in South Korea has found that university students who are fans of Japanese pop music tend to be more lenient than non-fans on the issue of Japan's past colonization of the Korean Peninsula.[22]

Pop culture diplomacy, in other words, offers heady visions of transforming Japanese–Korean relations from "thin" to "thick" reconciliation. Unfortunately, the reality is not so simple; a point well illustrated by shifting from a broad discussion of context to critical analysis of the content of specific pop culture texts.

Textual analysis of television drama and film

Through textual analysis of the four-episode TV "mini series" *Friends* and the blockbuster film *2009 Lost Memories*, this section seeks insights on the extent to which commercial pop culture captures the complexities of historical injustice and persisting interethnic conflict. It also asks whether pop texts like *Friends* and *2009* contain messages that may help to promote reconciliation in a manner that transcends ethnic nationalism.

Before we turn to analysis, a few words are in order on the selection of the featured texts. I chose them, in short, because of their transnational character. Neither can be deemed purely "Korean" or "Japanese," with respect to production, content, and circulation. First, *Friends* and *2009 Lost Memories* are Korean–Japanese joint productions: an important new genre of pop culture text born of regulatory changes. Second, regarding content,

Korean–Japanese joint productions inevitably contain input from peoples of both countries, and works in this genre have tended to address contentious issues affecting bilateral relations. Third, the two hybrid texts have circulated widely, crossing many national borders. *Friends* was broadcast nationwide in both Japan and Korea in February 2002, then exported to Southeast Asia and beyond in DVD format.[23] *2009* had a successful theatrical run in Korea in 2002, ranking seventh in box office receipts among domestic releases. Though not faring quite as well in Japan, it was promoted at film festivals throughout the country. Moreover, *2009* has been a hot seller in DVD and VCD formats, reaching not only Korean and Japanese diasporic communities outside of East Asia but also many other ethnic communities globally. Its enduring appeal has, in fact, prompted theatrical re-releases in the United States and other national markets. For all these reasons, *Friends* and *2009 Lost Memories* present good case studies to test the proposition that pop culture comprises a key resource for helping societies to work through historical disputes and present tensions. In the remainder of this section, I provide brief descriptions of these contrasting texts – one promoting comforting visions of ethnic harmony and the other emphasizing insuperable conflict – then consider their potential and limitations with respect to helping to resolve contentious issues of the past and present.

Love conquers all?

Born of a partnership of TBS (Tokyo Broadcasting System) and MBC (Munhwa Broadcasting Company, Seoul), *Friends* proposes that Japanese and Korean peoples can get along after all. TBS offers the following synopsis of the drama:

> Left alone on a trip to Hong Kong, Tomoko finds herself the victim of a purse snatching. The police arrest the man she points out, but it turns out to be the wrong person: a young Korean man named Chi-hun. Despite his anger and humiliation he takes her out to dinner since she has lost all her money, and in return she agrees to model for his amateur film. What follows is a magical and romantic two days. Upon returning to their respective countries, Tomoko must return to her nine-to-five job and Chi-hun must resume studying to join the family business rather than pursuing his dream of becoming a film director.

All is not lost, however, as "the two begin to email each other and rekindle their relationship despite the distance and obstacles between them." The synopsis triumphantly concludes: "Marking the very first time in television history that a drama has been co-produced between Japan and South Korea, the story shows us that love has no borders."[24]

Framing Chi-hun's and Tomoko's union as Korean–Japanese relations writ small, *Friends* represents the bridging of cultural distance. Starting in the liminal, transnational spaces of Hong Kong (signified by shots of store signs in Japanese, Korean, Chinese, English) and the Internet, the protagonists gradually learn about each other and their respective countries. Tomoko (played by the popular Japanese "idol" Fukuda Kyōko) initially thinks Chi-hun (Korean heartthrob Wŏn Bin) is a Chinese resident of Hong Kong. When Chi-hun corrects her, she enthusiastically lists all the things she knows about Korea: "kimuchee, yakiniku, karubi, bibinba . . ." That is, not much beyond Japanese renditions of iconic Korean dishes. Chi-hun, in turn, presumes Tomoko embodies the unflattering stereotype of young Japanese women as spoiled consumers, flitting about traveling and shopping. In Hong Kong they meet by chance and find little in common – other than an undercurrent of sexual attraction and the fact they share a Chinese character (智, meaning "knowledge") in their given names. But mutual understanding gradually develops through the aforementioned e-mail exchanges (which are facilitated by a friend of Chi-hun's who has studied Japanese language). Tomoko and Chi-hun reveal to each other their hopes and fears. Both, it turns out, are struggling to negotiate an almost universal rite of passage: to find a place in the world while balancing individual desires, family expectations, and social norms. Inspired, Tomoko decides to take night classes to learn the Korean language, and eventually lands a job with a travel agency in Seoul catering to Japanese tourists. She also encourages Chi-hun to chase his dreams, which leads first to an apprenticeship as a production assistant in Seoul, and later an internship in northern Japan. Although a series of obstacles conspire to separate them, the two "friends" never give up hope.

Ethnicity trumps friendship?

2009 Lost Memories borrows a compelling, counterfactual scenario from a novel by the South Korean writer Pok Kŏ-il: what if Imperial Japan had fought alongside the Allied Powers in the Second World War and Korea remained its colony?[25] A bricolage of familiar cinematic genres – history-based epic, futuristic sci-fi flick, buddy film – *2009* begins with Korea's national hero An Chung-gŭn's attempt, in 1909, to gun down the Japanese statesman Itō Hirobumi. In reality An mortally wounded Itō (who headed Japan's "protectorate" regime in Korea, 1905–9); but in the film a descendant of a colonial governor travels back in time to foil the assassination. This intervention disrupts the flow of "history" and triggers a series of distortions, which are pithily presented in the film's second shot: Japan's victory in the Second World War, emergence as a nuclear power, and continued appropriation and effacement of all things Korean. After this arresting opening sequence, the film cuts to a shot of Seoul in the year 2009, depicted as the third city, behind Tokyo and Osaka, of the "Great Empire of Japan." A century of Japanese rule has reduced the Korean resistance to a small, beleaguered underground movement, which calls itself a "Liberation Army" but is dismissed by officials and the Japanese-controlled media as "terrorists" or "lawless Gooks." The group carries out an attack on a Japanese exhibition of ancient Korean artifacts to reclaim a "Lunar Stone" that can unlock a portal through time and allow them to put history right. Enter the Japan Bureau of Investigation (JBI), which is charged with stopping the underground separatist movement.

The narrative is driven by competing relationships, which parallel as well as cut across the battle between Japanese colonizers and the Korean Liberation Army. Viewers are first introduced to the quasi-brotherly bond linking two JBI officers, "Sakamoto Masayuki" (played by Korean mega-star Chang Tong-gŏn) and "Saigō Shōjirō" (Japanese actor Nakamura Tōru). Sakamoto and Saigō are not only partners on the job but also best friends, having supported each other through university and the JBI Academy. Though they are united by friendship and occupational prerogative, a fault line runs through this relationship: Saigō belongs to the ruling ethnic group, whereas Sakamoto is ethnically Korean. Sakamoto does his utmost to deny this source of tension. He appears to epitomize the assimilated colonial subject, who has mastered the Japanese language, adopted a Japanese name, prefers sushi over kimch'i, and voluntarily demonstrates his loyalty to empire by leading efforts to crush Korean separatists. But trouble lurks beneath the surface. We soon learn that Sakamoto's assimilationist zeal is symptomatic of his ambivalent struggle against the memory of his father, rumored to have been a corrupt official who accepted bribes from Korean "terrorists." Ashamed of both his ethnic and family background, he tries to forget by throwing himself into his work – to no avail. What he consciously denies seeps into dreams (e.g. Sakamoto is haunted by fragmented images of the Lunar Stone and a mysterious Korean woman who, viewers later learn, is one of the resistance leaders), which pull him to his destiny.

As the story unfolds, tensions between these relationships (and in Sakamoto's psyche) become untenable. Fearing that Sakomoto is close to deciphering the secrets behind Japan's manipulation of history, his bosses at the JBI move to stop him by framing him for murder. Saigō, albeit reluctantly, aids the conspiracy when he learns that his family's welfare is at stake. On the run, Sakamoto is drawn to the underground. Once there, he not only encounters the woman from his dreams but also discovers the glorious history of the Korean nation (which has been suppressed by Japanese-controlled media and education), his father's true role as secret agent for the resistance, and, ultimately, his ethnic identity. Thus enlightened, Sakamoto chooses ethnicity over friendship, turning guns ablaze against former colleagues – including his best friend Saigō.

Toward mutual understanding and shared values?

Friends and *2009 Lost Memories* were launched in no small part by desires to cash in on new opportunities afforded by the aforementioned regulatory changes and the hype surrounding the joint hosting of the 2002 World Cup.

Many in the entertainment industry have seized on joint ventures, seeking lower production costs, new creative synergies, and larger markets. For Japanese filmmakers, shifting location shots to Korea and other parts of Asia makes good business sense given the high costs and onerous regulatory restrictions that accompany shooting in Japan. Korean filmmakers welcome added sources of funding and a new pool of stars to enhance the regional exportability of their films. Performers, both Korean and Japanese, are attracted by prospects for expanding their fan bases beyond the borders of their own countries. Overall, industry insiders throughout Asia are angling to increase profits by sharing production skills, formats, and content, while pooling promotional and distribution power.

These less-than-altruistic motivations notwithstanding, the people behind the two works appear to have embraced the spirit of the 1998 Joint Declaration: that is, to nurture a new Korean–Japanese partnership, founded on mutual understanding and shared values. Kijima Seiichirō, executive producer of *Friends*, has spoken of "the possibilities and responsibilities" of the televised drama:

> There is still a great gap between Korea and Japan. However, if we *understand our differences*, we will realize that the passion for drama-making is [the] same for both countries. We hope that you will see in this drama *the possibilities and responsibilities of the TV media*, and the dreams and delight it creates. [Emphasis added][26]

Members of the joint writing team for *Friends* reportedly labored for many months on the script in an effort to bring serious issues affecting regional relations into the story line. In fact, the drama references, *inter alia*: persisting discrimination facing residents in Japan of Korean ancestry; the comparatively tight visa restrictions Japan maintains against visitors from Korea; and tensions on the peninsula that subject Korean males to compulsory military training. It was these elements that prompted Wŏn Bin to say, "I accepted the role when it was offered to me because I saw great significance in it."[27]

Similar good intentions were involved in the making of *2009 Lost Memories*. Its co-producer Kim Yun-yŏng has claimed, for example, that the joint production team attempted to set to screen Korean historical concerns in a manner that engages young Japanese audiences.[28] Imamura Shōhei, one of Japan's most renowned directors whose films have consistently evinced anti-establishment views and critiqued prewar Japanese militarism, found the screenplay of *2009* compelling enough to serve as consultant and make a cameo appearance. Actor Nakamura Tōru (who gained fame in *GenX Cops* and *Tokyo Raiders*) has been attracted, in recent years, to roles in works that consider serious aspects of Japanese–Korean and Sino–Japanese inter-actions. Amid the entertaining action sequences and special effects, *2009* indeed introduces real Korean grievances against Japan regarding "issues of the past." The exhibition attack and Lunar Stone theme reference the contentious issue of reparations: in this case, repatriating Korean cultural treasures removed to Japan during the colonial period (1910–45). Sakamoto poignantly represents the tragedy of colonial era assimilation policies that forced Koreans to suppress their ethnicity while denying them genuine inclusion.[29] Read against the grain, the character is also innovative, portraying Korean members of the colonial police force in sympathetic ways and thereby injecting an element of complexity into the still highly controversial issue of colonial collaboration. And, of course, the time travel/alternate history theme both references colonial era experiences and indicts renewed postcolonial attempts among reactionary elements in Japan to promote history textbooks that whitewash the country's imperial past in Asia.

Numerous factors nonetheless undermine the progressive potential of these two pop culture texts. Let us consider *Friends* first. Though many important issues are introduced, they are not developed or treated in a nuanced manner. The issue of discrimination against "ethnic Koreans in Japan" (J: *zainichi Chōsenjin*, K: *chaeil kyop'o*) is brought into the story by way of a third-generation "zainichi" character named Kaneda Midori (played by Toda Naho) that Tomoko befriends at night school. Yet this promising thread is quickly dropped.[30] *Friends* can also be criticized for reifying ethnic and gender stereotypes. Korean cultural patterns are simplistically contrasted to those of Japan. For example, Korean families are depicted as "traditional" *qua* patriarchal; Japanese families are presumably the polar opposite, characterized by weak family life. Predictably it is Chi-hun who exercises agency by achieving acclaim as a director, which gives him the confidence to challenge his father's authority and reclaim Tomoko, the *object* of his affections. (Meanwhile Tomoko, having given up a bid at an overseas career and returned to her old life, pines away for her man.) To put matters another way, Chi-hun masters cinematic language and controls visual representation; Tomoko is the object of the gaze.[31] All these shortcomings – lack of depth, reliance on dichotomous stereotypes, problematic gender construction – arguably characterize popular movies and television dramas in general, which are, first and foremost, vehicles for entertaining *and* selling. *Friends* projects a fantasy world where complex issues of the past and the present are reduced to the ups-and-downs of an imagined relationship between two media-generated "idols"; a world in which our eyes are guided by a camera that lingers on not only their tight embrace but also boutique windows and fashionable accessories (e.g. a baseball cap with the New York Yankees logo). In other words, to the extent that *Friends* promotes shared values transcending ethnic fault lines, it may most effectively reinforce desires for consumption-oriented, corporate-driven visions of modernity. Some thinkers, notably Arjun Appadurai, suggest that even modernity of this sort can be liberating. He discerns spaces for transnational agency in the interstices of "electronic capitalism" and hyper-consumption, spaces for imagining myriad "diasporic public spheres" rather than only dominant "imagined communities" of nation-states. But other theorists who hew closer to the Frankfurt School of cultural interpretation may wonder whether the world depicted in *Friends* is actually an "open-air prison."[32]

The promising threads found in *2009* are intertwined with hyper-masculinist and ethnic nationalist excess. By the second half of the film, the critique of Japanese militarism and imperialism is muted, becoming a syncopated accompaniment to a dominant theme celebrating "Greater Korea." Sakamoto, upon meeting the spiritual leader of the resistance, is told that the Lunar Stone and the portal it unlocks, a giant stele, were originally located in Manchuria because that territory was and shall be again a part of Korea. (Such claims hardly help to resolve present-day conflicts between Korea and China over the cultural heritage of Manchuria.) He also learns that the Japanese resorted to historical distortion not only to wash away the humiliation of defeat in the Second World War but also in a desperate attempt to prevent the emergence of a reunified Korea that will rightly be the "new light of Asia." Irredentist ethnic nationalism is not disavowed; instead one strain is invoked as more legitimate than another version.

2009 exploits cinematic techniques – notably, cross cutting and non-diegetic music – to drive home this problematic message to mind-numbing and ear-splitting effect. Consider the agonizingly drawn out sequence (just after Sakamoto learns the truth about his father and fatherland) when the JBI attacks the rebels' underground base. Sakamoto reaches out to try to protect a young boy who runs toward him trailed by a hail of bullets. This action is repeatedly intercut with a parallel action occurring above ground. Saigō, enjoying a festival with his family, holds out his arms to catch his little daughter who scampers toward him as fireworks dance in the background. The boy stumbles, shot in the back just before reaching Sakamoto; the girl lands happily in her father's arms. The message is unmistakable. Japanese–Korean relations form a zero-sum situation: the luxury and levity enjoyed by ethnic Japanese derive from oppressing Koreans, and, when push-comes-to-shove, mercilessly killing them.

As if this ethnic nationalist narrative were not already clear enough, the filmmakers have amplified it by a melodramatic score, excessive use of slow motion, and yet another layer on the theme of hallowed paternity. As the boy stumbles he drops a box that had been clutched against his bosom, causing cherished belongings to spill forth – including a photograph of his father. At this moment, multiple paternal narratives converge. Sakamoto, to his dismay, realizes that he himself had cut down the boy's father, who was the leader of the exhibit attack. With his authentic (read: ethnic) self finally awakened, he stands up (literally and metaphorically) and seizes a hefty machine gun. Emerging from his collaborationist nightmare, Sakamoto vows to atone for his past sins by turning guns ablaze on the Japanese and vindicating all the fathers who had died for the Korean nation.

Mixed motivations and mixed messages

The very attributes that make film and television highly effective media for shaping public memory also complicate their potential for promoting interethnic understanding and resolving "issues of the past." As vehicles for entertainment and profit, didactic appeals to universal harmony – as expressed in the 2002 World Cup theme song "Let's Get Together Now" – are often overshadowed by other elements (action, sex, fantasy, violence, chauvinism) that appeal to less noble instincts and desires. Furthermore, by seeking to facilitate historical reconciliation between Japan and Korea as well as achieve commercial success, the makers of *Friends* and *2009 Lost Memories* produced pop texts that project mixed messages. Both begin strong with respect to the first objective, but commercial imperatives and genre limitations undermine their progressive potential. *Friends*, as explained above, touches on important issues of ethnic discrimination and cultural difference. But framing Japanese–Korean relations as a charming love story – and adhering to conventions of romantic comedy (i.e. a variation on *You've Got Mail*) and the television family drama *qua* product-placement vehicle – works to derail exploration of historical and structural factors inhibiting interethnic reconciliation. *2009*, as a "history-based film," outdoes *Friends* in projecting instances of historical injustice and lingering ethnic animosities on screen. Yet *2009* is also hampered by reliance on generic formulae: most notably, the crowd-pleasing story of the heroic underdog beating a well armed band of bad guys. As *2009* unfolds, it grapples less and less with complex issues such as cultural assimilation, gives way to gunplay and special effects, and begins to resemble the many other Korean-produced films, television dramas, and other pop media that have tended to essentialize Japan as evil incarnate.[33] Ultimately, it might be accused of deviating entirely from the humanistic spirit and encouraging rather cavalier attitudes toward suffering in that the atomic bombings of Hiroshima and Nagasaki are uncritically framed as imperatives for restoring justice and the Korean nation.

One might be tempted to dismiss such critiques, saying that *2009* is "just a movie" and *Friends* "only a TV show." Doing so may not be prudent, however, as movies and television can cloak politicized, tendentious historical views by wrapping them up as innocuous entertainment; something not to be taken too seriously, while subtly naturalizing such interpretations in the minds of viewers as matter-of-fact historical knowledge. Fortunately, audience members are not mere dupes. Cultural texts like *Friends* and *2009 Lost Memories* not only are imbued with multiple messages at various stages of production but also take on new meanings as they are received and interpreted by viewers. In the final section, I turn briefly to issues of media effects and audience reception, which further complicate the pop culture diplomacy thesis.

Media effects, audience reception, critical interventions?

In late 2004, a news segment on KBS (Korea Broadcasting System) decried that "computer games imported from Japan and China have been found to present distorted explanations of Korean history." The segment proceeded to suggest state action to curtail such phenomena: "The government takes extra care about the issue of Japan's distortion of history in textbooks and China's move to limit access to ancient Korean historic sites in northeast China. But the government has failed to show any response to the problem of computer games."[34] This suggestion, however well intentioned, is misguided. The paradigm of state regulation to root out "distorted" history and enforce "correct" history is difficult to apply to pop culture. (Although it is reasonable to expect that compilers of official textbooks be mindful of personal and ethnic-cultural biases in their works – despite the elusiveness of what Peter Novick has called "That Noble Dream" of historical objectivity – creators of historical fiction are usually not bound by such an obligation.) Instead of a demand that art and entertainment conform to strict content requirements and represent historical narratives only as government-commissioned bodies deem appropriate, a more fruitful approach might be to not only study the polysemous content of pop culture but also explore how individuals and social groups engage with cultural texts. This brings us to another layer of complications: questions of *media effects* and *audience reception*.

Acknowledging the polysemy of pop culture discourages the adoption of any simple notion of direct media effects. Sometimes called the "hypodermic needle model" or "bullet theory," the concept of direct effects posits the media (meaning, *inter alia*, common forms of mass media, those controlling media production and distribution, specific media texts) shooting their potent effects directly into weak unsuspecting audiences.[35] If, for example, *Hallyu* pop products circulating through Asia contain multiple and even contradictory meanings, we must at the very least ask which of the messages leave impressions on audiences. Asking such a question may lead, in turn, away from a view of audiences as passive receptacles and toward a more nuanced approach that seeks to understand how people selectively consume *and* interpret the many meanings embedded in pop culture.

In contrast to the hypodermic needle model, theories of "minimal or limited effects" hold that "we selectively expose ourselves to media messages that are most familiar to us, and . . . retain messages that confirm values and attitudes we already hold."[36] Korean consumption of Japanese pop culture demonstrates in some ways such minimal effects. Although formal studies (especially in English) on the spread of Japanese pop culture to other Asian countries often emphasize putatively favorable qualities to explain its appeal, my conversations in Korea and with Korean exchange students in the United States reveal a more complex picture.[37] To be sure, Korean aficionados of Japanese pop culture not uncommonly admit to seeing their favorite idols or products as a synecdoche for desirable attributes presumably characterizing Japanese culture and society as a whole – for instance, diversity (relative to Korea) and technical sophistication. Yet compliments of this sort are typically accompanied by another opinion. Unbeknownst perhaps to Prime Minister Koizumi and other champions of pop culture diplomacy, South Korea's "opening" to cultural imports from its island neighbor has done little to diminish stereotyping of Japanese society as excessively permissive and its pop culture as fetishizing violence and deviant sexuality. Many Koreans are acutely attuned to a subset of pop phenomena in Japan (*i.e. Toruko* baths, *hentai anime*, *ko gyaru*) that confirm an image of decadence. This stereotype is so prevalent in Korea that as the fourth-stage opening to Japanese pop culture approached, officials there were forced to announce that a strict ban would remain in place against products from the Japanese adult entertainment industry.[38]

The above examples also point to other ways of understanding media effects: variants of the familiar "uses and gratifications model" and more recent cultural studies approaches that, in a sense, turn the question of media effects on its head. These approaches do not as much ask what mass media do to us as explore "how people make meanings, understand reality, and order experience through their use of cultural symbols in print and visual media."[39] On the side of studies foregrounding positive reasons for the wide appeal of Japanese pop culture, scholars like Aoyagi Hiroshi speak of the emotional power of its signature "cute" (*kawaii*) style and further hypothesize that consumers use it to create a unifying regional consciousness. Aoyagi suggests, for instance, that Japanese pop idols (as representatives of the first Asian country to experience industrialization) serve to help young people in South Korea, Taiwan, Hong Kong, and mainland China to "mak[e] sense of the changing social and workplace conditions that accompany economic growth and 'modernization' in Asia."[40] On the other hand, selective attention by Koreans to somewhat unorthodox manifestations of Japanese pop culture can be interpreted as more than vicarious enjoyment of the exotic and passive reinforcement of existing stereotypes about a morally bankrupt Japan. It may also represent efforts to map out (ethnic-nationalist) claims of enduring difference (and superiority), rather than growing similarity or unity. In other words, this rhetorical distancing maneuver might be read as an active, albeit defensive, response to the specter of neocolonial assimilation to a Japan-centered modernity and the reality of increasing regional integration in cultural production, distribution, and consumption.

These complications about media effects and audience reception also apply to Japanese consumption of cultural products from various Asian countries. Although celebrants of pop culture diplomacy invoke the promise of a "multicultural springtime" bringing interethnic tolerance, shared values, and historical reconciliation, more pessimistic observers like Iwabuchi Kōichi point to persisting cultural stereotyping and ethnic-nationalist inflections in Japanese reception of other Asian pop cultures.

> As [regional] economic development stirred Japanese media and industry attention and broadened Japanese interest in Asian popular culture in the 1990s . . . a reflexive posture [to engage Asia on equal terms] was gradually swallowed up by Japan's historically constituted conception of a culturally and racially similar, but always "backward" Asia.[41]

That many Asian nations are "modernizing" is not denied. But the majority of Japanese people, according to Iwabuchi, "refus[e] to accept that [Japan] shares the same temporality as other Asian nations." This refusal inhibits, he says, a conscious or emotional sense of "coevalness" with other groups that might be expected to emerge from partaking in a common set of cultural products. Ironically, it also functions to strengthen a narcissistic impulse while looking outward to other societies. Regarding Japan's "Asia boom" of the 1990s that began with a focus on cultures to "the south" (Okinawa, Hong Kong, Singapore), Iwabuchi emphasizes that people have tended to "nostalgically see Asia as embody[ing] a social vigor and optimism for the future that Japan allegedly is losing or has lost."[42] This stream of critique can be applied to the more recent "Korean wave" in Japan. Part and parcel of the craze for Korean pop culture is the championing of supposedly essential Korean qualities ("Korean purity," "Korean vitality") – a discourse that feeds a nostalgic and narcissistic fixation on what post-bubble "postmodern" Japan has supposedly lost. Japanese fans of Korean pop who claim a new appreciation for Korea are to an extent gazing at an imagined version of "Korea," and possibly hoping that this imaginary will serve as a magical mirror to reflect and restore their former selves.

Conclusion

The full effects of the "Korean wave" in Japan and Korea's official opening to Japanese pop culture remain to be seen – and carefully analyzed, as both are recent phenomena that continue to unfold. At this point we must proceed with the hypothesis that while pop culture and public memory are undeniably linked – as Trouillot, Huyssen, Appadurai, and many thinkers have emphasized – transnational flows of pop culture do not necessarily lead straightaway to conscious and conscientious reflections on history. A glowing report on *Hallyu* compiled by the Ministry of Culture and Tourism of the Republic of Korea is revealing. In a sample of just over 2,000 people in Hong Kong, Taiwan, and China surveyed about their "desired purpose of visiting Korea," more than two-fifths chose "visit[ing] TV drama/movie locations" as their number one priority. But fewer than one in ten respondents mentioned "want[ing] to know more about Korea," such as its culture and history.[43] In another study, after interviewing numerous Japanese fans of Hong Kong pop culture, the lead researcher could claim no more than that transnational cultural consumption had encouraged *"at least some* [to become] more critically aware of Japan's modern experiences and imperialist history."[44] These examples offer only rough indicators of the frequency at which transnational flows of pop culture prompt an individual or a community to reflect on questions of historical injustice and reconciliation. (Note: space constraints do not allow for the presentation of my preliminary findings on the reception of *Friends* and *2009*.) They illustrate, nevertheless, that the former does not perforce lead to the latter.

Furthermore, whereas evidence abounds of increasing interactions between Japanese and Korean societies facilitated by pop culture, we must acknowledge uncertainty as to whether such interactions are serving more to break down or reinforce ethnic nationalism. The lack of systematic study on such questions represents a serious oversight, especially considering that as economic liberalism and "electronic capitalism" spread their ambit across the Asia-Pacific, the forms of informal history education discussed in this chapter grow correspondingly. Many governments in the region, moreover, are racing to bolster cultural diplomatic efforts, not only within the Asia-Pacific but also other key places in the world – notably the Middle East. For instance, before the Japanese government dispatched Self-Defense Forces to Iraq in 2003, it provided Japanese TV dramas with Arabic subtitles to local television stations throughout the country. Recently, Prime Minister Koizumi has sponsored an advisory panel (drawing primarily on figures from the arts and academe, including experts on Asian and Islamic cultures) to formulate plans for reinvigorating Japan's cultural diplomacy. Similar initiatives are being formulated in South Korea, China, and the United States.[45] Amidst this frenetic activity are troubling signs extending beyond government circles. In discussions of pop culture diplomacy, notions of "soft power" and unilateral benefits deriving from cultural export are increasingly inflected, rather than multilateral cultural exchange and genuine dialogue.[46] The "Korean wave" has also triggered nativist reactions in Japan and China, which deploy virulently ethnic-nationalist comics and web pages.[47]

Rather than retreat in the face of these uncertainties, it is my hope that more and more scholars, from a variety of disciplinary and ethnic backgrounds, will grapple with open questions on the relationships between pop culture, public memory, and interethnic relations. In this connection, I turn again to Trouillot, who counsels that historical lessons people acquire through movies, holiday celebrations, and other sources of informal education can be "sustained, modified, or challenged by scholars," particularly if the latter "become increasingly quick at modifying their targets and refining their tools for investigation."[48] By acknowledging pop culture as a site of important historical and political dynamics, and by acting as public intellectuals who engage discourses on pop culture reaching far beyond the academy, scholars can indeed intervene in complex processes of informal education. And intervene,

I hope, in a manner that enhances the edifying potential of pop culture in the global quest for peace and reconciliation.

Notes

1 "Cultural diplomacy" comprises key components or instruments of what is called, in the United States, "public diplomacy." Public diplomacy most commonly "refers to government-sponsored programs intended to inform or influence public opinion in other countries; its chief instruments are publications, motion pictures, cultural exchanges, radio and television" (US Department of State, *Dictionary of International Relations Terms*, 1987). Yet public diplomacy also encompasses "private activities – from popular culture to fashion to sports to news to the Internet – that inevitably, if not purposefully, have an impact on foreign policy and national security as well as on trade, tourism and other national interests." (http://uscpublicdiplomacy.com) I use the term "pop culture diplomacy" to signify cultural diplomacy relying centrally on pop culture. Generally speaking, "pop culture" can be understood to include books and magazines (novels, comics, self-help manuals), murals, poster art, movies, television programs, music, computer/Internet games, and the like, which are "popular and enjoyed by ordinary people" (Freesearch Dictionary).
2 Ministry of Foreign Affairs of Japan, "Japan–Korea Summit Meeting" (in Korea), July 21–22, 2004, summary transcript of July 21 session (www.mofa.go.jp).
3 On "thin" and "thick" reconciliation, see David Crocker, "Reckoning with past wrongs: a normative framework," *Ethics and International Affairs* 13 (1999), 43–64.
4 In this chapter, unless otherwise stated, "Korea" refers to South Korea (the Republic of Korea).
5 Michel-Rolph Trouillot, *Silencing the Past: Power and the Production of History* (Boston, MA: Beacon Press, 1995).
6 Trouillot, *Silencing the Past*, p. 20.
7 Andreas Huyssen, "Present pasts: media, politics, amnesia," *Public Culture* 12/1 (2000), 21–38.
8 Huyssen, "Present pasts," p. 29.
9 Arjun Appadurai, *Modernity at Large: Cultural Dimensions of Globalization* (Minneapolis, MN: University of Minneapolis Press, 1996).
10 See, for example, Marcia Landy, ed., *The Historical Film: History and Memory in Media* (New Brunswick, NJ: Rutgers University Press, 2001).
11 Laura Elizabeth Hein and Mark Selden, eds, *Censoring History: Citizenship and Memory in Japan, Germany, and the United States* (Armonk, NY: East Gate Book, 2000).
12 See, for instance, T. Fujitani, Geoffrey M. White, and Lisa Yoneyama, eds, *Perilous Memories: The Asia-Pacific War(s)* (Durham, NC: Duke University Press, 2001).
13 Tessa Morris-Suzuki and Peter Rimmer, "Virtual memories: Japanese history and debates in *manga* and cyberspace," *Asian Studies Review* 26/2 (June 2002), 147–64.
14 Envisioned as a transnational text, *Friends* was released under that same title in Korea (though also transcribed as 프렌즈 in Korean han'gŭl script), Japan (フレンズ in katakana), the United States, and other national markets.
15 *2009 Lost Memories* has also been released under a single title in multiple national markets.
16 Federico Mayor, *The Multi-Cultural Planet*, edited by Ervin Laszlo (London: Oneworld Publications, 1993), p. ix.

17 For a transcript of the joint statement, see, for instance, the Ministry of Foreign Affairs of Japan, "Joint declaration: a new partnership towards the twenty-first century," October 8, 1998 (www.mofa.go.jp).

18 Victor D. Cha, "Hypotheses on history and hate in Asia: Japan and the Korean peninsula," in Yoichi Funabashi, ed., with foreword by Ezra Vogel, *Reconciliation in the Asia-Pacific* (Washington, DC: US Institute of Peace Press, 2003), pp. 37–59.

19 Vocals for "Let's Get Together Now" were provided by Brown Eyes, CHEMISTRY, Lena Park, and Sowelu. Lyrics were written by Sawamoto Yoshimitsu, Matsuo Kiyoshi, Lena Park and Kim Hyung-suk, and the music composed by Kim Hyung-suk and Kawaguchi Daisuke. See *2002 FIFA World Cup Official Album: Songs of Korea/Japan* (Tokyo: Sony Music Asia, 2000).

20 AVEX, Inc. press release (February 4, 2004).

21 Philip Brasor, "Korean wave may help erode discrimination," *The Japan Times* (June 27, 2004).

22 Shiraishi Takashi, *Japan Echo* 31/6 (December 2004); see his "Introduction" to the special section on cultural diplomacy.

23 The drama performed well in both countries. But it was more successful in Japan, attracting a 15 per cent share of the television audience.

24 See TBS online catalogue (www.tbs.co.jp).

25 Pok Kŏ-il, *Pimyŏng ŭl chajasŏ* [In search of an epitaph] (1987). The book created a sensation for its provocative scenario – which is retained in the film *2009 Lost Memories*. But Pok's novel also evinced a belief in science and a critical spirit (manifested at times as black humor) to address historical and contemporary problems. In this connection, he took issue with the way his novel was adapted for the screen and sued to have his name removed from the film credits.

26 TBS online catalogue.

27 TBS online catalogue.

28 For example, the screenplay was tested on college students in Japan, who were asked to read it and offer their opinions.

29 Sakamoto embodies bitter memories of Japanese colonial policies that promoted distorted forms of inclusion, denying Koreans equal opportunity in most arenas of public life while channeling them to join the police force. See Carter Eckert, Ki-baik Lee et al., *Korea Old and New* (Cambridge, MA: Harvard University Press, 1990), pp. 259–60.

30 "Kaneda" (金田) is a common Japanized version of the familiar Korean surname "Kim" (金). This example of "name change" recalls painful memories of forced assimilation during the last decade of the Japanese empire.

31 On gendered aspects of cinematic representation, see Laura Mulvey, *Visual and Other Pleasures* (London: Palgrave Macmillan, 1989).

32 Appadurai, *Modernity at Large*. For a sampling of works by an iconic figure of the Frankfurt School, see Theodore W. Adorno, *The Culture Industry: Selected Essays on Mass Culture*, edited with an introduction by J. M. Bernstein (London: Routledge, 1991).

33 Examples include the television series *Yain sidae* and the lyric opera *Myŏngsŏng hwanghu*.

34 The transcript of the news segment, which was aired on October 1, 2004, can be found on the KBS News website (http://news.kbs.co.kr).

35 Richard Campbell, *Media and Culture: An Introduction to Mass Communication* (New York: St Martin's Press, 1998), p. 420.

36 Campbell, *Media and Culture*, p. 421.

37 Informal interviews conducted at the University of Texas at Austin in 2002–3 and Stanford University in 2003–4.

38 *Korea Herald* (December 30, 2003).

39 Campbell, *Media and Culture*, p. 426.
40 Aoyagi Hiroshi, "Pop idols and the Asian identity," in Timothy J. Craig, ed., *Japan Pop! Inside the World of Japanese Popular Culture* (New York: M. E. Sharpe, 2000), pp. 309–26, quote on p. 323.
41 Iwabuchi Kōichi, *Recentering Globalization: Popular Culture and Japanese Transnationalism* (Durham, NC: Duke University Press, 2002), p. 158.
42 Iwabuchi, *Recentering Globalization*, p. 158.
43 "Survey report outline on actual conditions of Hallyu (Korean fever) tourism" (Korean National Tourism Organization, ROK Ministry of Culture and Tourism, 2004). The survey was conducted by KNTO overseas branches in Beijing, Hong Kong and Taibei, during a period between September 20, 2003 and October 14, 2003. It yielded 2,004 "valid samples" with the following breakdown: Beijing (399), Shanghai (402), Guangzhou (207), Hong Kong (398), and Taiwan (398).
44 Iwabuchi, *Recentering Globalization*, p. 179.
45 Advisory Committee on Cultural Diplomacy, "Cultural diplomacy: the linchpin of public diplomacy" (US Department of State, September 2005); "Culture minister on China's foreign exchange," *People's Daily Online* (December 21, 2004).
46 "Is 'hallyu' a one-way street?," *Korea Times* (April 21, 2005); Maeda Mikihiro, review of *Soft Power*, by Joseph S. Nye (Public Affairs, 2004), in GLOCOM Platform of the Japanese Institute of Global Communications (www.glocom.org, posted April 16, 2004).
47 "Pan Hallyu," *JoongAng ilbo* (October 20, 2005); "Controversial comic puts bitter touch on Korean craving," *Mainichi Daily News* (August 10, 2005); Tony McNicol, "Political tensions in East Asia mirrored online," *Japan Media Review* (June 6, 2005).
48 Trouillot, *Silencing the Past*, p. 20.

11 A strong state, weak civil society, and Cold War geopolitics

Why Japan lags behind Europe in confronting a negative past

Andrew Horvat

Introduction

In the wake of the sixtieth anniversary of the end of the Second World War, Europe and East Asia present stark contrasts in the handling of negative historical legacies. Whereas Europe has achieved regional integration in part thanks to concerted efforts to confront the horrors of the Second World War, in East Asia today history remains a contested area both domestically and diplomatically for all countries in the region, particularly for Japan.

The purpose of this chapter is to contrast the active and constructive roles of NGOs as transnational nonstate actors (TNAs) in Europe with the very limited activities of counterpart civil society organizations in Japan in dealing with the negative legacies of the past. As a guide to the patterns of activity of TNAs, I rely on the work of Lily Gardner Feldman, who has focused specifically on the roles of TNAs in post-Second World War Germany's foreign policy of reconciliation.[1] I attempt to show that the lack of progress in resolving pending historical problems in the region stems not from any alleged "collective amnesia" on the part of the Japanese public but from legal and financial constraints on civil society in Japan that have been in effect throughout the twentieth century and have been particularly strong in the period after the Second World War. Such constraints – together with the geopolitics of the Cold War – have made it difficult for ordinary Japanese to express, through institutions available to citizens of Germany and other European nations, feelings of remorse toward victims of their nation's past acts of aggression.[2]

Although the focus of this chapter is to compare Europe with East Asia, there is much in the East Asian historical condundrum that should be of interest to the US foreign policy community. American leaders were the chief architects of the 1951 San Francisco Peace Treaty at which claims against Japan stemming from the Second World War were hastily settled and from which the People's Republic of China, the two Koreas, and the former Soviet Union were excluded. Today, Asia is home to more than a quarter of the world's population and an even greater proportion of global GDP. China has nuclear weapons and all other East Asian governments have the ability to possess them should they feel the need to do so. Nationalism is on the rise throughout the region. Therefore, encouraging East Asian nations to move beyond mutual recrimination stemming from an unresolved past and to learn from the formulas of reconciliation adopted through more than half a century of negotiations by governments and civil society groups in Europe ought to be a high priority foreign policy issue for the US as well as for any nation with an interest in peace in the region.

But there is another, more positive reason why Americans and citizens of other third countries might wish to take an interest in historical reconciliation in Northeast Asia: they are in a position to do something about it. As this chapter shows, Japan's civil society organizations are too weak to be able to nurture on their own the TNAs needed to achieve European-style, people-to-people reconciliation on historical issues. The independently run, well funded, and professionally managed foundations of the United States and Europe have both the experience and resources needed to initiate programs in this area and to function as TNAs.[3]

Transnational nonstate actors: the European experience

In her analysis of the German government's attempts to improve relations with France, Poland, Israel, and the Czech Republic after the Second World War, Gardner Feldman creates four categories of TNA–state relations: TNAs can act as catalysts, complements, conduits, or competitors. Gardner Feldman writes: "As catalyst or competitor, it is the TNA that dictates the terms of reference, with the German government performing in a more reactive mode. When TNAs are complements the government sets the overall tone. The role of catalyst or competitor involves relations of tension with the government, whereas activity as complement or conduit by TNAs suggests harmonious relations."[4]

Gardner Feldman offers many examples of faith-based catalytic activities such as the outreach by the French Protestant church to German POWs in the immediate post-Second World War period, the missives of the German Evangelical church to Poland in the 1960s, the exchange of letters between German and Polish Catholic bishops, similar attempts between German and Czech Catholic leaders, and the formation of the Societies of Christian–Jewish Cooperation promoting ties between Germany and Israel.

With regard to TNAs as complements, Gardner Feldman focuses on the various school book commissions whose aim was to "decontaminate"[5] school history textbooks by removing from them one-sided nationalistic versions of the past. Also in the complement category are TNAs, mostly NGOs, engaged in the promotion of exchanges including "youth associations, sports clubs, language centers, training centers, trade unions, schools, universities and town twinning organizations."[6]

To explain the role of conduits, Gardner Feldman homes in on the activities of the German political foundations: the Friedrich Ebert Stiftung (Social Democratic Party), the Konrad Adenauer Stiftung (Christian Democratic Party), and the Friedrich Neumann Stiftung (Free Democratic Party). Although all of these foundations are supported from the public purse, they function independently of the state. All three have offices outside Germany and engage actively with the publics and opinion leaders of former enemy countries, holding symposiums, administering scholarships, and generally promoting activities stressing shared values of democracy, free markets, and human rights.[7]

As for competition, Gardner Feldman provides examples of organizations opposed to the German government's policies of reconciliation. In the case of Israel, competition from TNAs refers to the clandestine activities of former Nazi scientists who tried to help Egypt develop nuclear weapons in the 1950s, and the recent public questioning of Germany's Middle East policies by a younger generation of Germans sympathetic to the Palestinian cause. In the case of Poland and the Czech Republic, German governments have faced internal opposition to rapprochement from large groups of expellees, ethnic Germans forced to flee from these two countries after Nazi Germany's defeat in 1945.

Are there Asian TNAs?

The above descriptions raise certain obvious questions. Are there TNAs active in reconciliation between Japan and South Korea or Japan and China? If such TNAs exist, do they function as catalysts, conduits, complements, or competitors to the Japanese government? If TNAs do not exist, or if they exist but in far smaller numbers, what might be the reason for such a state of affairs? What other factors, such as regional geopolitics, could account for differences in approaches to historical problems in the two areas? Finally, if functioning TNAs are not in evidence, what other opportunities exist for Japanese and third-country policy-makers to promote reconciliation?

First of all, the role of religious organizations as TNAs in Northeast Asia is extremely limited. The last time Koreans and Japanese shared a faith that transcended national boundaries was in the fourteenth century when Buddhism was practiced widely in both Japan and the Korean peninsula. The legacy of good relations of those days consists of about 100 Korean Buddhist paintings now in the possession of a number of Japanese temples.[8] Although today some 40 per cent of South Korea's 47 million citizens say they are Christians, in the case of Japan, less than 1 per cent of the population has adopted the foreign faith. Moreover, although Christians in both Japan and Korea are represented heavily among groups supporting the *ianfu* (so-called "comfort women," Korean, Chinese, Filipina, Indonesian, Dutch, and other victims of Japan's wartime practice of coerced military prostitution), the kind of large-scale faith-based activities common in Europe in connection with historical issues are unknown in Northeast Asia. (Since Christians were persecuted in the PRC during the first decades of communism and religion in general remains under government supervision, transnational activity by Christian churches between Japan and China is, for the time being, inconceivable.)

We can also eliminate from the patterns the conduit roles played by Germany's three political foundations.[9] No such organizations exist in Japan, South Korea, or the PRC. In the case of Japan, most transnational activity in international relations is in the hands of either government-supported organizations or a handful of large foundations that according to law must report to "competent governmental agencies." As explained below, the overwhelming strength of the state in comparison to civil society has inhibited the development of Japanese NGOs and therefore has made it extremely difficult for all but a handful of civil society organizations to function as TNAs.

One of very few Japanese NGOs that can be described as having a significant track record as an active TNA in historical issues is Peaceboat, which organizes cruises to all parts of the world holding on-board seminars aimed at achieving better understanding of the viewpoints of Japan's neighbors. Peaceboat supports its activities through fees it collects from cruise participants.[10] Founded in 1982 when attempts to remove from Japanese history textbooks references to aggression on the Asian mainland triggered anti-Japanese demonstrations in Seoul and an official protest from Beijing, Peaceboat has grown into a mainstream, national organization with broad-based support throughout the country. Posters advertising its cruises to such trouble-spots as North Korea, the Middle East, and Cuba can be seen on the walls of restaurants, coffee shops, language schools and colleges even in remote communities. The fact that individual Japanese spend as much as $10,000 each to take part in the cruises indicates a willingness to invest both time and money in getting to know the often negative views of one's neighbors.[11] In taking on the task of holding shipboard conferences in ports of both Koreas, Taiwan, the PRC and Russia – countries with which Japan has historical and territorial disputes – Peaceboat has the potential of acting as a catalyst for future government action. One of its former leaders has recently been re-elected to the Japanese parliament. Its shipboard lecturers represent a broad cross-section of Japanese society, from leading public intellectuals to television cooking instructors.

VAWW (Violence Against Women in War – Network Japan), a feminist NGO, is a more typical small-scale organization, unusual only in that it functions actively as a TNA. Organizer of a mock trial in December 2000 that found the late Emperor Hirohito guilty of war crimes, VAWW acts as a competitor to the Japanese government. Nicola Piper states, "VAWW-NET Japan is one of the few Japanese groups active on behalf of gendered violence generally, and the 'comfort women' issue in particular, which has strong transnational links. The original, and possibly still the main impetus for concrete lobbying at the international level, however, seems to come from Korean groups." Although a comparison of the Japanese and South Korean civil society sectors is beyond the scope of this chapter, Piper is correct in highlighting the far greater level of activity on the part of South Korean NGOs, especially on the issue of the former comfort women.[12]

Contrasting geopolitics: America's Faustian bargain

Without a doubt, the geopolitical environment of post-Second World War Europe created conditions in which historical reconciliation could be seen as being in the national interest of each state. In the case of East Asia, the Cold War demarcation line – known back in the 1950s as the "bamboo curtain" – placed Japan and the People's Republic of China in opposing camps, thus making it impossible to carry on constructive dialogues about the past. In the case of Korea, division and war, followed by decades of poverty, conspired to delay coming to terms with a complicated relationship with Japan. As for Japan, the Cold War created domestic ideological divisions, which would make it certain that Japan would lack the domestic consensus[13] on historical issues necessary to engage former victims and enemies in constructive dialogue.

Contrasting geopolitics meant that in Europe de-Nazification of Germany became absolutely necessary for the harmonious functioning of NATO. In Japan, however, the Cold War required the mobilization of Japan's prewar elite – including the rehabilitation of officials who had overseen aggressive expansion and colonial exploitation – in order to turn Japan into a prosperous ally in the war against communism. But obtaining the help of Japan's prewar elite forced the US into a Faustian bargain: the Western alliance would get an efficient, prosperous Japan with an anticommunist government, but dealing with Japan's negative historical legacy would have to be shelved. The Japanese left, which had originally welcomed US victory over Japan as paving the way for democracy through the purging of prewar leaders, felt betrayed when Washington reached out to, among others, Nobusuke Kishi, a member of the wartime cabinet of Hideki Tojo, and helped him become prime minister in 1957.

One can understand that given the context of the Cold War, mobilizing Japan in the effort to contain communism had to have been a top priority for American foreign policy in the early 1950s, but the consequent failure of the Japanese to come to terms with negative aspects of the past would forever politicize reconciliation, providing both domestic and foreign critics of Japan with ammunition with which to embarrass the government and its leaders. It is for this reason that Japan has never been able to adopt high school history textbooks that deal with Japan's record of aggression on the Asian mainland in a manner that has satisfied Chinese, Korean, and domestic Japanese constituencies of either the left or the right. For example, news reports of a move in 1982 by the Japanese Ministry of Education to replace the word *shinryaku* (aggression) with *shinkō* (advance) to describe Japan's march into Korea and later China was enough to trigger massive demonstrations in Seoul and a protest from Beijing. To this day, Japanese nationalists accuse the domestic left of having instigated the crisis by urging Chinese leaders to express official displeasure about the change. Although there is little evidence that China (or Korea) needed to be incited to protest, the fact that one hears such accusations within Japan even today is indication of the ill will historical issues can generate domestically.

Although it is true that the Ministry of Education has shown a tendency to gloss over negative aspects of the country's recent history, since the early 1980s most high school history textbooks have mentioned sensitive issues.[14] Although there was backtracking in 2005, the problem at present is not so much the textbooks themselves but the fact that in the absence of reconciliation – either domestic or international – both critics and supporters of the government look to the textbooks in search of a definitive official statement on how the Japanese state views the nation's past. For this reason, every textbook is scrutinized by opposing camps in search of what they believe are changes in the official position on issues such as the Rape of Nanking, the "comfort women," or colonial rule of Korea, which all inevitably lead to accusations of having either whitewashed the past or kowtowed to Beijing and Seoul.

The AWF debacle: comfort women conundrum

The Japanese government-inspired program to compensate surviving *ianfu* offers a textbook case of the obstacles posed by the combination of strong state, weak civil society, and a divisive political environment on historical issues. Confronted in 1992 with irrefutable evidence of official complicity in the coercion of tens of thousands of Asian and some European women to provide sexual services for Japanese troops during the war, the Japanese government came under pressure from two sides: on the one hand from the left to accept legal responsibility, show sincere contrition, and provide condolence money; and on the other, from the right, to stick to the official position that all pending claims have been fully settled by the San Francisco Peace Treaty and subsequent international agreements.

Unused to collaborating with nonstate actors and confident that officials are best suited to handling international crises, bureaucrats took the lead and encouraged a group of scholars and prominent individuals to act as advisors to a foundation set up with the support of the Foreign Ministry. Despite its noble purpose – to apologize and pay compensation to former *ianfu* from countries occupied by Japan – both prior to its creation and thereafter, the Asian Women's Fund (AWF, in Japanese Josei no tame no Ajia heiwa kokumin kikin, or literally Japanese Citizens' Asian Peace Fund for Women) became a reviled symbol to leftists and nationalists alike.

Funding for AWF came mostly from the Japanese government but also, significantly, from voluntary contributions made by private individuals, who felt sympathy for the aging *ianfu*.

Although the reasons for combining public and private funding were largely legalistic, the AWF did break new ground in being the first Japanese organization that sought to deal with a controversial historical problem as a public–private partnership. Set up in 1995 under Prime Minister Tomiichi Murayama, a former socialist, AWF sailed into controversy the following year, when Ryūtaro Hashimoto, a political conservative who replaced Murayama, reportedly resisted signing individual letters of apology to surviving comfort women. Hashimoto was also said to have opposed the idea of using funds directly from the national budget to make compensation payments on the grounds that doing so would undermine Japan's official position that all claims against Japan had been settled. Although Hashimoto did eventually sign the letters of apology, the news of his hesitation severely undermined the mission of the fund.[15]

Because, at Japanese government insistence, the comfort women could receive direct payments only from donations given by private citizens, critics could argue that the government was using AWF as a smokescreen to sidestep its moral responsibility and avoid making official payments of compensation. Korean and Taiwanese NGOs put pressure on the *ianfu* to refuse both the financial compensation from the AWF and the letter of apology from the Japanese prime minister on the grounds that neither represented a sincere act of the state. In their move to oppose the AWF's attempts to compensate the *ianfu*, the Korean and Taiwanese NGOs were supported by counterpart organizations active in gender rights issues in Japan. What followed was a sad sight: seven former Korean comfort women faced severe public criticism for having accepted funds from the AWF. As a result of this public condemnation, the AWF made all subsequent payments in private, refusing to divulge the names of recipients.[16] In the end, the AWF was able to compensate no more than 285 former comfort women.[17]

AWF versus the German Future Fund

What the AWF debacle illustrates is that Japanese NGOs working in the history field bear such strong animosity to their own government that even when political leaders do take steps to compensate survivors the pursuit of a political struggle against the state appears to the NGOs to be more attractive than compromise on behalf of long-suffering, elderly victims. It would seem that reconciliation is not part of the vocabulary of the Japanese (or Korean) NGOs that have supported former comfort women in their struggles against the Japanese government.[18]

The inability of the AWF to carry out its goals is truly sad because despite its flaws, it bears a remarkable structural resemblance to the German Future Fund, which by contrast has been a success.[19] Both funds were set up to address unresolved historical issues, initially reluctantly by two former aggressor states.[20] In the case of the German fund, the need was to provide compensation for the approximately one million surviving victims of Nazi forced labor mostly from former communist countries, who because of the division of Europe during the Cold War could not be parties to previous compensation schemes. Both the Japanese and the German governments chose a formula in which both government and private funds were mobilized. In both Germany and Japan, conservative forces resisted the compensation schemes and in both countries industry was most reluctant to contribute to the funds.

But by 2000, just two years after law suits were brought against German companies in US courts by survivors of Nazi forced labor, the fund "Remembrance, Responsibility and the Future" was set up and fully functioning. By making contributions to the fund tax deductible, Chancellor Gerhard Schroeder was able to get nearly 3,000 German companies to take part. Other than paying out about $7.5 billion in compensation to nearly a million survivors, the Fund also undertakes programs such as arranging for traveling photographic exhibitions on Nazi forced labor, the disbursement of scholarships to needy students, and recently even a German speech contest for Polish children in Gdansk (formerly Danzig) where the first shots of the Second World War were fired.

By way of contrast, the AWF finished compensating individual former comfort women in 2002 and will wind up all activities in 2007. (No plans exist to commemorate the sufferings of the comfort women or to offer scholarships to needy women in the lands where the comfort women were conscripted, and no Japanese language speech contests are to be sponsored in neighboring countries.) The AWF debacle highlights the inadequacy of Japanese institutions – governmental and NGO – to give voice to the desire of the majority of Japanese to see victims of past aggression properly compensated.[21]

Downside effects of Japan's state-centered society

Perhaps the most important difference in dealing with history between Europe and Northeast Asia is the relative weakness of Japanese civil society organizations of any kind. It is crucial to stress the middle initial of TNA, i.e. the nonstate aspect. Until very recently, in all three countries in the region, Japan, South Korea, and the PRC, the coming together of ordinary citizens for the kinds of activities that might benefit historical reconciliation with neighboring countries has been strictly controlled by the state. For this reason, TNA activity in any of the four categories cited by Gardner Feldman can be expected to take place on a far smaller scale between Japan and South Korea than, for example, between Germany and France, even though the former two neighbors have a combined population well in excess of the latter two. In Japan, until the coming into effect of a new Nonprofit Organization (NPO) Law in 1999, advocacy groups, environmental organizations, in fact all but large-scale corporate foundations had virtually no hope of obtaining legal status. Without legal status NGOs could not rent offices, lease telephone lines, open bank accounts (needed to receive donations), or hire employees.

Although Article 34 of the Japanese Civil Code, the law defining the activities of NGOs and NPOs, has been in force virtually unchanged between 1896 and the present day, the definition of permitted activities for private nonprofit groups was actually narrowed in the 1970s and would not be broadened for almost thirty years – not until after the 1995 Kobe Earthquake when an embarrassed central government was forced to admit that it needed to harness the energies of ordinary citizens to cope with emergencies. The bursting of the Japanese economic bubble in the early 1990s and the sudden aging of the Japanese workforce a decade later put new strains on social services, alerting policy-makers to the need to promote the growth of the nonprofit sector. Until that time, Article 34 limited nonstate or nonprofit activity to so-called *kōeki hōjin*, literally "public benefit juridical persons," commonly translated as "public benefit corporations" or "foundations." An international survey of the nonprofit sectors of some forty countries described the challenges facing Japanese wishing to take part in civil society activities in the latter part of the twentieth century in the following words:

> In order to establish a *kōeki hōjin*, approval by the "competent governmental agency" is required. . . . [I]t is a very difficult and time-consuming process, except when the government itself takes the lead in establishing a *kōeki hōjin*. Moreover, approval is also subject to the discretion of the officer in charge of the application case, and no clearly stated and standardized criteria for incorporation exist. One of the major obstacles to creating a *kōeki hōjin* is the substantial amount of financial assets required by the public authorities prior to the actual establishment of the organization. The actual amount may vary from case to case, but it is very difficult for groups of citizens to accumulate assets of 300 million yen (US$2.3 million) or more, as required by the Ministry of Foreign Affairs.[22]

An example of the negative impact that an overwhelmingly state-centered political system can have on transnational civil society activity in reconciliation is the refusal in 1997 by the Japanese committee of UNESCO to accept an invitation from its South Korean counterpart to initiate a dialogue on the teaching of history in high schools. In proposing the textbook talks, South Korea was following the precedent of UNESCO mediation between West Germany and Poland on history issues begun in 1972 and concluded successfully four years later. The reason for the Japanese refusal was simple: Japan's UNESCO committee is a part of the Japanese Ministry of Education. Officials charged with representing UNESCO one year may be transferred to the department that oversees high school history textbooks the following year. In a state-centered society, such as Japan's, there is little room for nonstate actors.[23]

Although the new NPO Law permits NGOs to obtain legal status through a much simplified reporting procedure, it still takes as long as three months to obtain approval. Moreover, tax exempt status has to be applied for separately; it is granted only rarely and often after long months of negotiations with officials. Since tax exempt status is reviewed annually, the whole procedure must be repeated every year. No wonder thousands of Japanese NGOs have opted not to obtain legal status even under the new much more liberal NPO Law.

"Sky clear" for demonstrations

This kind of legal environment – both past and present – has had far reaching negative consequences for the development of large-scale mainstream civil society organizations in Japan and has kept all but the most zealous activists out of such sectors as human rights, advocacy, and other related activities common to the NGO communities of other industrially developed democratic societies. Without legal status, Japanese NGOs have been unable to provide either salaries or fringe benefits for staff. To work full time for organizations devoted to causes such as historical justice, or human rights of foreign workers, still requires sacrifices that an average individual can hardly afford. (One Japanese NGO leader I know postponed marriage until he was forty because he could not earn enough to support a family.) In the 1970s and 1980s, most Japanese NGOs had no permanent offices. If they did have an office, it would be rented in the name of its most prominent member, someone who paid the equivalent of the $1,000 needed until recently to obtain a single telephone line and who also lent his or her name to the organization's bank account, who obtained donations from wealthy individuals and who paid the meager salaries of one or possibly two part-time employees. Perhaps a dozen other members worked as pure volunteers. Too heavy reliance on a single "charismatic leader" has turned many Japanese NGOs into undemocratic units where members are so dependent on the disproportionately large contribution of one person that free and open discussion of policy issues becomes difficult and the NGO becomes ideologically rigid. Such a one-man, top-down organizational structure is hardly ideal when trying to work toward historical reconciliation, a goal that requires a willingness to listen to opinions at odds with one's own.

The small size and poor financial condition of all but officially approved or government-supported large-scale NPOs has meant that the environment needed to nurture the growth of nonstate actors in general – to say nothing of those that can function across borders – has not been present in Japan. Although Korean NGOs have flourished since the transition from military-dominated authoritarian governments to civilian rule in 1993,[24] Japan–South Korea cultural and educational exchanges have been managed almost entirely by government-funded organizations, such as the Japan–Korea Cultural Foundation. The absence of grassroots NGOs is at least in part responsible for the trickle of activity even by TNAs acting in a complementary mode to the government. The much talked about Korea boom in Japan is not the result of the work of TNAs but a government-engineered PR campaign begun when NHK, Japan's government-affiliated TV network, broadcast *Fuyu no sonata* (*Winter Sonata*), a South Korean soap opera, in the spring of 2003. The joint hosting in 2002 of the FIFA World Cup soccer games was also a government-inspired project, as was the "Year of Japan–Korea Citizens Exchanges" in the same year. The schedules of events, for example, of both that year and the Japan Korea Friendship Year in 2005 can be accessed via a website managed directly by the Japanese Foreign Ministry. In other words, Japanese TNA activity in international relations independent of central authority is limited.

Despite heavy government support, the number of sister city relationships between Japan and South Korea as of present writing stands at a mere eighty-eight. Between France and Germany there are approximately 2,200 twinnings of cities. According to the most recent figures, in one year Franco-German exchanges managed by labor unions, student groups, or purely local organizations involved 200,000 people in 7,000 separate events – or almost twenty functions per day.[25] In 2005, the officially designated "Year of Japan–Korea Friendship," no more than a few hundred events took place in the two countries; one event in February consisted of a visit by Prime Minister Junichiro Koizumi in the company of the Korean ambassador to the Sapporo Snow Festival, where Japanese Self Defense Force soldiers had carved in ice a replica of an eighteenth-century Korean fortress. The event called for zero TNA (or even local NGO) participation and consisted primarily of an opportunity for the Japanese prime minister to appear on the NHK evening news to state, "Yesterday it snowed but today the sky is clear."

Within a few days, however, there would be anti-Japanese demonstrations in Seoul to protest the declaration by Shimane Prefecture of Takeshima Day, to mark the one hundredth anniversary of the annexation by Japan of the islands Koreans call Dokto and that South Korea has occupied for more than half a century. The reason for the provocative act by the Shimane prefectural legislature (other than the fact that Takeshima/Dokto had once been part of its territory) had to do with a long-smoldering fisheries dispute. Japanese fishermen have accused South Korea of shutting them out of the rich fishing grounds near the islands. The declaration of Takeshima Day would spark an international incident: jet fighters of the South Korean Air Force would scramble to intercept a business jet belonging to the *Asahi* newspaper sent up to take photos of the disputed islands in the Sea of Japan.[26]

The legally and financially hostile environment for small-scale NGOs has had other deleterious consequences for historical reconciliation. Japan today has an unusually small advocacy NGO sector, a rare phenomenon for a country that claims to be a democracy. According to an international survey taken in the 1990s by the Johns Hopkins Comparative Non-Profit Research Center, "environment and advocacy" category NGOs accounted for a mere 0.6 per cent of total employment for the entire NPO sector. This compared with an average of 2.8 per cent in developed countries.[27] Since Japan's largest NGO, the Japan Wild Bird Society (120,000 members), is to be found in the environment category, the same as advocacy, one can reasonably assume that full-time workers in Japan among advocacy groups – such as might be expected to take issue with the government on the plight of "comfort women" – would number no more than a few dozen people at the very most. (In the German case, the environment/advocacy category accounts for 2.5 per cent of the nonprofit sector of employment, a ratio more than four times that for Japan.)

That the passage of the new NPO Law has failed to create a nurturing environment for Japanese civil society can be seen from statistics released by the Prime Minister's Office in 2000. Of some 26,000 *kōeki hōjin* registered in Japan as of that year, about 18,000 had fewer than ten employees; 4,500 were unable to afford a single full-time staff person. Referring to such figures, Robert Pekkanen has observed, "Political-institutional barriers are higher in Japan that in other advanced industrialized democracies, preventing the development of independent civil society organizations."[28]

A Gresham's law of zealotry

There is reason to believe that past and present legal and fiscal constraints on civil society organizations have combined to discourage ordinary citizens from participating in advocacy and created conditions favoring the rise of small contentious groups, ideologically rigid, staffed by a cadre of committed activists. Japanese advocacy NGOs have consistently acted as competitors to the state on historical issues. The expression "historical reconciliation" (*rekishi wakai*) is virtually unknown in the Japanese advocacy community, whose members generally prefer to use the term *rekishi mondai*, "the history question."

Not surprisingly, the domestic debate on historical issues is shrill, caustic, and unforgiving. One example should suffice. In December 2000, the advocacy NGO VAWW convened a "Women's International War Crimes Tribunal on Japan's Military Sexual Slavery." While the mock trial definitely qualified as transnational nonstate activity, the project cannot be described as being intended to achieve historical reconciliation. Describing the entirely predictable guilty verdicts the tribunal rendered on the defendants, among them the by then deceased Emperor Hirohito, VAWW's website states: "this Judgement bears the names of the survivors who took the stand to tell their stories, and thereby, for four days at least, put wrong on the scaffold and truth on the throne."[29] (Incidentally, at the VAWW mock trial no provisions were made for the accused to be represented by defense.)

By now it should be clear that nonstate and state actors concerned with the historical question in Japan – with particular reference to Japan–Korea relations – interact with each other very differently from the patterns described by Gardner Feldman. The government-supported nongovernmental history textbook commissions,[30] which made dialogues on historical issues between Germany and its former adversaries possible, find no genuine counterparts in East Asia. Although Gardner Feldman placed these commissions in the complements pattern of TNA activity, in the case of Japan–South Korea textbook dialogues one would have to define such TNAs as competitors to the government.[31] In June 2005, scholars appointed by the governments of South Korea and Japan announced that they had failed to reach agreement on major historical issues dividing the two countries. By way of contrast, two history textbook supplements, one published by a joint Japan–South Korea group of educators and another written by a Japan–ROK–PRC group, saw the light of day earlier the same year. Both intended to counter the nationalistic textbook of the so-called Tsukuru Kai (The Japan Society for History Textbook Reform) supported by right-wing members of the ruling Liberal Democratic Party.[32]

Some conclusions and proposals

Examining European examples of TNA activity is helpful in that we can see clearly that the kind of vibrant, mainstream civil society especially in the advocacy field evident in the US and Europe is virtually absent in Japan. We can also conclude that for various historical and structural reasons state–NGO relations – especially in the advocacy area – are so hostile in Japan that it is unrealistic to expect European-style government–TNA relations to develop quickly in Northeast Asia. Although the positive effects of government-sponsored reconciliation programs such as officially initiated cultural exchanges, the broadcasting of soap operas on television, joint hosting of sports events, and the promotion of "years of citizens' exchanges" ought not to be dismissed wholesale, such top-down campaigns fail to address historical issues.

An obvious question for concerned third parties is: if Japan lacks homegrown TNAs then should Europe and America make available the services of their own TNAs? The answer is yes. The first round of Franco-German textbook talks held in the early 1930s was underwritten by the Carnegie Corporation, which is still engaged in brokering peace throughout the world. Although the original Franco-German talks broke down in 1935, the recommendations made by participants at the final meeting before the Second World War were accepted in full when talks resumed in 1950. One outcome of Carnegie's prewar funding of textbook talks was the Georg Eckert Institute for Textbook Research at Braunschweig, a repository of more than half a century of German experience in textbook negotiations with former enemies and victims, which recently mediated between Israeli and Palestinian educators. A German political foundation might do well to consider extending invitations to Chinese, Korean, and Japanese delegations of educators to tour the facilities and perhaps stay long enough to spend time around a negotiating table.

Another area in which the European experience offers a positive example is in the setting up of foundations whose aim is to turn the sufferings of victims into opportunities for reflection and a renewal of a commitment not to repeat the mistakes of the past. As mentioned above, the agreement in 2001 to compensate victims of Nazi forced labor in former Eastern Bloc countries included the establishment of the German Future Fund. By way of contrast, the Asian Women's Fund is to be disbanded in 2007. What a shame that the process of remembering the sufferings of the *ianfu* cannot be utilized positively to overcome the past by, for example, setting up a joint government–industry fund in Japan to underwrite the study at Japanese universities by needy but gifted students from Asian countries. Such a project would serve as a permanent act of atonement as well as a commitment to future cooperation. The Chinese and Korean graduates of Japanese universities funded by such a program could act as bridges between Japan and China, as well as Japan and Korea, in future economic and cultural relations.

Youth exchanges are another set of activities where foreign foundations could cooperate with local organizations. An integral part of the reconciliation movement in Europe after the Second World War was the promotion of youth tourism. The Japanese government is at present in the middle of a campaign to promote inbound tourism, but the goal of the program is limited to improving the bottom line of the ailing domestic tourism industry. With a little extra effort – and outside encouragement – the Japanese government's "Visit Japan" campaign (Yōkoso Japan) could be turned into an opportunity to promote Japan–Korea and Japan–China dialogues in a friendly atmosphere at a very basic level.[33] Not all examples of tourism as a peace mechanism need to come from Europe. South Africa has been a pioneer in the establishment of transnational nature reserves. There has been talk of turning the Korean Demilitarized Zone into a peace park, and a smaller group has proposed a similar idea for parts of the disputed Southern Kuriles, islands occupied by the Soviet army in 1945 but claimed by Japan.

One of the most successful examples of TNAs working together to overcome racial hatred and forge an alliance that has stood the test of time is the work of US philanthropic organizations in the immediate postwar period in Japan. In three decades after the Second World War, a group of US foundations – Carnegie, Rockefeller, Ford, Mellon and the Asia Foundation – together spent in excess of $50 million to promote Japanese studies in the US and understanding of America by Japanese.[34] The health of the US–Japan relationship today is living testimony to the success of their efforts. For successful examples of reconciliation in Northeast Asia, Japanese leaders – and well intentioned third parties – can choose from a long menu of programs and projects undertaken by American foundations in Japan, including the founding of International House in Tokyo (largely by the Rockefellers), free distribution of books to colleges and libraries (the Asia Foundation), funding of area studies (Carnegie), and foreign language teaching (Ford Foundation).

Finally, it should be remembered that the Nobel Prize committee is one of the earliest examples of nonstate transnational work; it rewards those who promote peace and understanding. US and European foundations might wish to encourage Japanese, Korean, and Chinese philanthropists to join forces to create a common East Asian prize that highlights and rewards the activities of homegrown TNAs working toward historical reconciliation.

It may take generations before Japan's fiscal and administrative practices are liberalized sufficiently to permit the growth of more independent, mainstream NGOs that can fulfill roles as TNAs contributing to the process of historical reconciliation. In the meantime, however, already foreign TNAs have plenty of opportunities to apply in Japan and Northeast Asia expertise as funders and practitioners. Although Japan's polarized political and civil society environment has failed to attract large numbers of ordinary citizens as volunteers, the work of foreign TNAs could very well act as a magnet for participation by a so far silent, but moderate, majority in history-related fields.

Notes

1 Lily Gardner Feldman, "The role of non-state actors in Germany's foreign policy of reconciliation: catalysts, complements, conduits, or competitors?," unpublished paper, American Institute for Contemporary German Studies, Johns Hopkins University, June 2005 (quoted with permission of author).
2 Sven Saaler, *Politics, Memory and Public Opinion: The History Textbook Controversy and Japanese Society* (Munich: Judicium, 2005), p. 138. Quoting the results of a survey of Japanese public opinion about Japanese war responsibility carried out by NHK, Japan's public broadcasting network, in 2000, Saaler concludes, "The results suggest that a clear majority of Japanese believe that Japan still has continuing responsibility for the war [the Second World War], a belief that follows logically from the perception of the war as a war of aggression." In the survey referred to by Saaler, 51 per cent of respondents agreed with the statement "the Second World War was a war of aggression by Japan against its neighbors." Just 15 per cent of those surveyed disagreed with that question. Fifty per cent also agreed that "unresolved problems" required the attention of "later generations" (Saaler, p. 143).
3 For a detailed description of the programs and funding strategies in Japan and the US of the Carnegie Corporation, the Rockefeller Foundation, the Ford Foundation and the Asia Foundation in promoting intellectual and cultural exchanges in the immediate postwar and early Cold War periods, see the Japan Center for International Exchange's forthcoming publication, *The Role of Philanthropy in Postwar US–Japan Relations*.
4 Gardner Feldman, "The role of non-state actors," p. 3.

5 Wolfgang Hoepken, Director of the Georg Eckert Institute of International Textbook Research, writes, "An early goal of the [Georg Eckert] institute was to eliminate, through collaboration with international partners, the hostile images and negative stereotyping of other people and countries, which early textbooks had promoted, and thereby to come to a consensual narrative of past and contemporary history. Its basic intention was the 'decontamination' of textbooks and historic concepts that had been poisoned by nationalistic misuse of history." Andrew Horvat and Gebhard Hielscher, eds, *Sharing the Burden of the Past: Legacies of War in Europe, America and Asia* (Tokyo: The Asia Foundation/ Friedrich Ebert Stiftung, 2003), p. 3.

6 Gardner Feldman, "The role of non-state actors," p. 7.

7 On a personal note, my own interest in European models of reconciliation was greatly stimulated thanks to the work of Gebhard Hielscher, a former Tokyo representative of the Friedrich Ebert Stiftung with whom I cooperated in hosting a series of reconciliation-related symposiums. See http://www.ajr'azaidan. org/english/forums/13-11-2001/index.html as well as references in this chapter to Horvat and Hielscher, eds, *Sharing the Burden of the Past*.

8 In 2004 Korean and Japanese newspapers reported that a number of the Korean Buddhist paintings, stolen from a Buddhist temple in Akashi, in western Japan, had turned up in South Korea. The thieves, two South Koreans, stated at their trial that they felt no remorse because the paintings were originally Korean. These days, no one but a handful of scholars in South Korea and Japan recognize that these paintings represent a shared cultural legacy and that they predate the invasions of Korea by Hideyoshi in the late sixteenth century or Japan's colonial domination of Korea in the twentieth century, eras when Japan did in fact plunder Korea of its cultural artifacts.

9 The Washington-based National Endowment for Democracy attempted in 2000 to encourage the creation of a Japanese foundation devoted to the advocacy of democracy throughout Asia. As of the time of writing no Japanese political foundation with aims and programs similar to the German Stiftungs or with transnational capacity has been set up.

10 Peaceboat's ability to function as a TNA is closely related to the success of its business model. A disproportionately high percentage of the income of Japanese NGOs in the humanitarian and social development field, an area in which Peaceboat is also active, comes from "for profit" activities that are necessitated by the lack of other kinds of support from either government or private foundations. For a description of the utter poverty of Japanese nonprofits working in the advocacy and international relations areas see Kaori Kuroda, "Current issues facing the Japanese NGO sector," *Informed* 8 (May 2003), an Internet publication of the International NGO Training and Research Centre, at www.intrac.org. The need for "earned income" by Japanese NGOs of the kind that might act as TNAs in historical issues becomes clear on p. 29 of Kuroda's article where she states that as of February 25, 2003 "only 12 organizations out of 10,000 non-profit corporations incorporated under the [1999] NPO Law have been approved as qualified non-profit organizations" permitted to receive tax-deductible donations from private individuals and corporations. In other words, although the 1999 NPO law has provided civil society organizations with legal status it has not made it possible for them to grow into viable organizations capable of acting as TNAs in any of the various roles described by Gardner-Feldman.

11 Peaceboat is international in ways that many Japanese NGOs involved in international relations are not: a significant number of its paid staff are Japanese-speaking foreign nationals. Other than operating cruises, Peaceboat works together with the European Centre for Conflict Prevention to put on conferences and symposiums on peace-building.

12 Nicola Piper, "Transnational women's activism in Japan and Korea: the unresolved issue of military sexual slavery," *Global Networks* 1/2 (2001), 155–70, at 163. Piper makes reference to a suggestion that "many Korean feminist groups draw on a nationalist discourse of the comfort women as embodying foreign domination of Korea." This question has serious implications for future, broad-based transnational activity because the Japanese and South Korean NGOs focus on the comfort women issue for totally different reasons: for the officially approved South Korean women's groups the sufferings of the former comfort women are part of a narrative of national humiliation, a shared tragedy with symbolic meaning, the constant retelling of which is part of an exercise in patriotism; for the much smaller Japanese feminist NGOs the sufferings of the comfort women are part of a gender politics for which, at least for the time being, there is little broad-based support in Japan. In the context of a Europe–Asia comparison, this rift is highly significant: TNA activity in Europe represented a desire on the part of people of diverse nationalities to forge a shared vision of the past.

13 "[T]hose who stick to the pacifist constitution – mainly on the Left – will use, as a reason for their position, the fact that the Japanese cannot be trusted with military power. Look what happened in World War II. It was uniquely atrocious and horrible and should never happen again. The more they make those arguments, those who are interested in changing the constitution and want Japan to regain the sovereign right to wage war will have to minimize the historical facts with comments like 'every country has waged a war like that and besides it was an anti-colonial war'." Ian Buruma, "Commentary" in Horvat and Hielscher, eds, *Sharing the Burden of the Past*, p. 140.

14 "Robert Fish, a PhD candidate at the University of Hawaii, examined all major editions of Japanese high school history texts published by the three largest publishers in the postwar period. He found that Nanking is included by all three publishers, which account for roughly 75 per cent of the market." Charles Burress, "The American indictment: the Japan that can't say sorry," in Horvat and Hielscher, eds, *Sharing the Burden of the Past*, p. 127.

15 Bureaucrats did dip into the public purse to make payments to former comfort women by setting up a separate budget item for "medical needs." These funds, which were calculated depending on the costs of medical care in the women's home countries, varied from the equivalent of US$12,000 in the case of the Philippines to US$30,000 for Korean, Taiwanese, and Dutch women. The official funds, however, were not paid directly to the women but on their behalf to medical and other institutions in their home countries as part of an elaborate arrangement designed to placate hardliners who felt that any direct payments from government coffers would undermine Japan's official position that it owed no compensation to foreign individuals. (Personal interview with Ms Momoyo Ise, former director of AWF, October 8, 2005.) For a detailed description of the use of both private and government funds, see *"Ianfu" mondai to Ajia josei kikin* ("The 'comfort women' problem and the Asian Women's Fund"), AWF, September 2004.

16 For a comprehensive treatment of the Asian Women's Fund and its difficulties in providing compensation to *ianfu*, see: C. Sarah Soh, "Japan's National/Asian Women's Fund for "comfort women," *Pacific Affairs* 76/2 (2004), 209–33. Soh observes: "Despite the assumed good will of the advocates for the victims they represent, it is necessary for supporters and observers alike to be alert regarding the insidious workings of power relations found in most political movements, the leaders of which are apt to maneuver and disregard the voices of the subaltern (as in the case of dissenting South Korean survivors) even after they have spoken."

17 *Tsugunai jigyō wo oeta ima* (Final report on the conclusion of the atonement program), Program report, AWF, 2002, p. 5.
18 In the dispute over the AWF between the government and activist NGOs, it is not too difficult to perceive a political fault line. Apichai Shipper and Loren King write in "Associative activism and democratic transformation in Japan" (unpublished paper, MIT, February 18, 2002): "103 of 107 Japanese staff and volunteers of these groups had never voted for the ruling Liberal Democratic Party" (p. 20). Although Shipper and King studied NGOs involved in supporting illegal foreign workers and victims of trafficking, a number of the same organizations have taken anti-government positions on the former comfort women.
19 For accounts of events leading up to the creation of the German Future Fund, see Otto Graf Lambsdorff, "The long road toward the foundation Remembrance, Responsibility, and the Future," and J. D. Bindenagel, "US–German negotiations on and executive agreement concerning the foundation Remembrance, Responsibility, and the Future," in Horvat and Hielscher, eds, *Sharing the Burden of the Past*, pp. 152–60 and pp. 161–72, respectively.
20 The German Future Fund (official name, Fund for Remembrance, Responsibility and the Future) was set up in response to the launching of a number of lawsuits against German companies in the United States by survivors of Nazi forced labor. Chancellor Helmut Kohl, a conservative, had opposed any arrangements to pay former slave laborers. http://www.religioustolerance.org/fin_nazi.htm Jan 18 2002.
21 See Saaler, *Politics, Memory and Public Opinion*.
22 Takayoshi Amenomori, "Defining the nonprofit sector: Japan," in Lester M. Salamon and Helmut K. Anheier, eds, "Working Papers of the Johns Hopkins Comparative Nonprofit Sector Project," (1993), p. 8 accessed on the Internet at: www.jhu.edu/ccss/pubs/pdf/japan.pdf.
23 "Rekishi kyōkasho kenkyū: Kankoku teian wo Nihon kyohi" (Japan rejects South Korean invitation to engage in joint history textbook research), *Hokuriku Chūnichi Shimbun* evening edition (July 22, 1997), 1.
24 Nicola Anne Jones, "Institutional windows: assessing the scope for civil society–state engagement in democratizing South Korea," accessed at: http://politics.soc.ntu.edu.tw/news/3-2%20Nicola%20Anne%20Jones.pdf.
25 Gardner Feldman, "The role of non-state actors," p. 6.
26 It is worth mentioning that Tokyo and Seoul are at odds over the name "Sea of Japan." The South Korean government is waging an international campaign to convince publishers of maps around the world to remove "Sea of Japan" from maps and replace it with "East Sea" the direct translation of Tonghae, the Korean name of the body of water.
27 Naoto Yamauchi et al., "Japan," in Lester K. Salamon et al., *Global Civil Society: Dimensions of the Nonprofit Sector* (Baltimore, MD: The Johns Hopkins Comparative Nonprofit Sector Project), p. 250.
28 Robert Pekkanen, "Molding Japanese civil society: state structured incentives in the patterning of civil society," in Frank J. Schwartz and Susan Pharr, eds, *The State and Civil Society in Japan* (Cambridge, 2003), p. 129.
29 VAWW site: http://www1.jca.apc.org/vaww-net-japan/english/womenstribunal2000/whatstribunal.html.
30 Jean-Claude Allain, in Horvat and Hielscher, eds, *Sharing the Burden of the Past*, p. 23, writes: "The make-up of the [French German Textbook] Commission is an important aspect because it contributes to its smooth operation. . . . None [of the members] have an official mandate from national (or state) governments and they can express themselves on the basis of their personal analysis or conviction with total academic freedom."

31 There have been two attempts by two groups of Japanese and South Korean educators to emulate history textbook reconciliation along European models. The first, initiated in 1990, broke down in 1993. Fujisawa Hōei, a professor of education at Kanazawa University (at the time), recalled later the serious shortage of either private or public funding for the project. For information regarding the first Japan–South Korea textbook dialogues, see Fujisawa Hōei "Kōryū to kyōdō no kokoromi" (An attempt at exchange and cooperation), *Sekai* (October 1998), 81–6, and for a report on the second group's efforts, see "Nikkan no rekishi musunde" (Linking the histories of Japan and South Korea), *Asahi Shimbun* (August 18, 2001), 21.

32 Although the Japan–ROK–PRC group's textbook has become a bestseller, high sales figures should not be confused with widespread support. The initial high sales figures for the commercial version of the nationalistic Tsukuru Kai's 2001 textbook, *A New History of Japan*, also should not be confused with any swing to the right in public opinion.

33 "Political reconciliation went hand in hand with reconciliation among people. . . . Since the 1950s, every summer millions of students began touring Europe individually, favored by the various programs set up in all countries in order to promote youth tourism." Fernando Mezzetti, "Historical reconciliation in Italy," in Horvat and Hielscher, eds, *Sharing the Burden of the Past*, p. 50.

34 Kim Gould Ashizawa, "The evolution of foundation policies in Japan," in *The Role of Philanthropy in Postwar US–Japan Relations* (Tokyo: JCIE, 2006).

12 Economic integration and reconciliation in Northeast Asia

Possibilities and limitations

Wonhyuk Lim

In 2004, Fuji Xerox Chairman Yotaro Kobayashi did something very unusual for a Japanese businessman. He publicly criticized the prime minister for making visits to Yasukuni Shrine, where the Japanese war-dead, including Class-A war criminals, are honored. In making his statement, he was careful to base his criticism on economic, rather than moral, grounds. He argued that the prime minister's visits to Yasukuni Shrine would be bad for Japanese business, especially in China. Shortly after Kobayashi made his public comment, he was condemned as a traitor and was harassed with death threats from right-wing organizations in Japan. Two Molotov cocktails were found near the entrance to his residence, and a bullet was delivered in an envelope to his address.[1]

In a number of ways, this incident was symbolic of the possibilities and limitations of economic approaches to promoting reconciliation and cooperation in Northeast Asia. Regional economic integration, and the opportunities it created, led a businessman like Kobayashi to speak out against the forces of ultraconservative nationalism. Yet, at least on the surface, his public statement appeared to be motivated mainly by economics, not by a deep desire to promote mutual understanding between nations with historical animosity toward each other. Regarded as a business move,"a statement like Kobayashi's risked criticism not only from right-wing organizations in Japan, but also from people outside Japan expecting to see more genuine gestures for reconciliation. Whereas the former could accuse Kobayashi of betraying the nation, the latter could criticize him for being insincere. They both could claim he just did it for the money."Although increasing economic integration and deepening interdependence might enhance the prospects for coexistence between formerly hostile nations, there seems to be a limit to how much economic exchanges can promote mutual understanding and harmony. In David Crocker's terminology, economic integration might facilitate thin" reconciliation, but have only a limited effect on thick"reconciliation. [2]

This chapter looks at the possibilities and limitations of using economic integration to promote reconciliation and cooperation in Northeast Asia, a region that has witnessed a great deal of conflct and tension since the mid-nineteenth century. While the continuing economic growth of the region and expected increase in the relative significance of intraregional trade may facilitate economic integration, geopolitical considerations interacting with historical animosity might actually increase tension in the region. It would require conscious efforts on the part of political leaders and civil society organizations to come to terms with history and craft a shared vision for the future.

This chapter is organized as follows. The first section provides a brief theoretical discussion on reconciliation and cooperation, starting with Immanuel Kant's theory of perpetual peace. It looks at how structural variables such as democratization and globalization may interact with nationalism to affect reconciliation and cooperation. The second section looks at "the burden of history," focusing on factors that have traditionally shaped international relations in Northeast Asia. This section highlights the emergence of Western and Japanese challenges to the traditional Sinocentric order in the nineteenth century, and emphasizes that with the resurgence of China, this triangular interaction is likely to shape the region's future as well. The third section analyzes the evolving pattern of economic relations in East Asia in recent years. Although the problem of reconciliation mainly concerns countries in Northeast Asia, discussions on economic integration schemes usually include Southeast Asia as well, and it would be useful to look at East Asia as a whole. East Asia has become an economic bloc comparable in size to Western Europe or North America, and intraregional trade is likely to become increasingly significant.

The fourth section looks at the external economic strategies of major players in East Asia. Whereas China has been engaged in proactive economic diplomacy on all fronts, Japan has been somewhat reactive, responding to ambitious Chinese initiatives on economic integration. Preoccupied with the North Korea problem, South Korea has mainly focused on promoting cooperation in Northeast Asia. ASEAN (Association of Southeast Asian Nations) has sought to achieve tighter regional integration in Southeast Asia as well as with China, Japan, and South Korea, but the progress of its efforts has been hampered by the different levels of economic development among the member countries. The fifth section examines possible trajectories for regional integration in Northeast Asia. Because regional integration schemes have the potential to cause a significant shift in international relations, they may become a new source of tension both within the region – for example, between China and Japan – and with extraregional players such as the United States. The challenge for Northeast Asia is to find an alternative that is effective in promoting reconciliation and cooperation but is at the same time nonthreatening to extraregional countries.

Theoretical background

The idea that voluntary economic exchanges can contribute to peace has been around for a long time.[3] Close interaction between people from different nations allows exchanges of ideas and sentiments, making it easier to understand other people's views. When two sides can realize gains by trading with each other, they are likely to try to work out contentious issues between them and develop this mutually beneficial relationship further – unless the military balance is such that one side is tempted to risk war and take over the other side.

Immanuel Kant was one of the first thinkers to argue that economic exchanges among nations tend to contribute to peace as long as these exchanges take place on a fair and voluntary basis. However, trade among nations was only a small part of his theory of "perpetual peace." In fact, he analyzed structural conditions for peace at three different levels: domestic politics, international relations, and cosmopolitan system. He clearly understood the interrelated nature of the challenges.[4]

At the level of domestic politics, Kant argued that republicanism was a precondition for peace. He defined republicanism as being characterized by the separation of powers and by a representative system of government. Kant noted that in a republican system, citizens would have a voice in important national decisions, and compared with an absolutist monarch, they would tend to be much more hesitant to start a war. By contrast, an absolutist monarch would more likely go to war on a whim because he is largely shielded from the consequences of his decisions. At the international level, Kant advocated a federation of free states as a realistic option to secure peace. While the creation of an international state or a world republic might be an ideal way to end international anarchy, Kant believed it was unlikely that nation-states would agree to give up their sovereignty. Finally, looking at the relationship between the individual and the world, Kant argued that for there to be perpetual peace, every individual should be accepted as a citizen of "the universal state of mankind."

Many of Kant's ideas on peace appear to be relevant for promoting reconciliation and cooperation as well. A system of governance based on accountability and transparency is likely to allow greater introspection and public discussion. Under such a system, chauvinistic or jingoistic sentiments are likely to be subjected to closer scrutiny before they have a chance to lead the nation astray. Such a political system is also conducive to the development of civil society, which can promote mutual understanding among citizens of different nations. A federation of free states, agreeing to respect each other's sovereignty and build mutual trust through arms control and expanded interaction, is likely to reduce the possibility of renewed conflict. Such an international arrangement basically institutionalizes reconciliation and cooperation, for which trade is an important contributing factor. Finally, the idea of treating every individual as a citizen of the world allows people to transcend national boundaries and look at the problem of injustice from a universal perspective.

There are some important caveats in applying this framework, however. First, while a system of governance based on accountability and transparency is likely to be conducive to reconciliation, it is probably counterproductive for a nation to demand that another nation adopt such a system as a prerequisite for reconciliation. To the extent that interaction with the outside world facilitates change, making reconciliation conditional on the democratization of the other side is actually likely to impede such a political transition. Moreover, the key to reaching reconciliation is to move the hearts and minds of the peoples, rather than the leaders, of the nations involved. Certainly, West German leaders like Willy Brandt in the 1970s did not wait until Poland was democratized to issue their apologies to the people of Poland. In the Northeast Asian context, the democratization of China and North Korea should not be a precondition for reconciliation.[5] Second, to be effective, a federation of free states should come *after* reconciliation rather than before it. Before crafting a shared vision that transcends national boundaries, the nations that make up a federation should first come to terms with history. Because nationalism was instrumental to the outbreak of historical hostilities in Northeast Asia as well as other parts of the world, nationalism would have to inform the discussion on reconciliation. Advocacy of a regional or supranational identity would ring rather hollow before national wounds are healed. Finally, while the idea of accepting every individual as a citizen of the world allows people to look at the problem of injustice from a universal perspective, there should be consistency in applying this principle across time and national boundaries. It would seem rather disingenuous to criticize another country for its human rights abuses without coming to terms with one's own human rights abuses perpetuated against citizens of other countries in the past. For the nations in Northeast Asia to move to the future, they must first take a look back at history.[6]

The burden of history

For many centuries, China was a dominant force in Northeast Asia, if not the world. As late as 1820, according to Angus Maddison's estimate, its GDP accounted for over 25 per cent of the world's total output, and its place in the world seemed secure.[7] However, in the course of subsequent decades, the Sinocentric "world order" in the region unraveled under the attack of intruding Western powers and a rising Japan.

In particular, the emergence of Japan as a revisionist power in Northeast Asia was an important event because it fundamentally changed the dynamics of international relations in the region. Combining the Japanese ethos with Western technology, Japan rapidly modernized itself and adopted an increasingly proactive foreign policy.[8] Although some intellectuals in Korea and China hoped that Japan would lend a helping hand in the modernization of their countries, their hopes were dashed as Japan became an imperialistic power of its own.[9] China's defeat in the Sino–Japanese War of 1894–5 accelerated the demise of the Ching Dynasty, and the destruction of the Russian Fleet by the Japanese Navy in 1905 dealt a devastating blow to the

Russian empire. Japan's brutal colonial rule in Korea also left a bitter legacy.

Japan initially defined its role as a "junior partner" of global powers such as Britain and greatly expanded its influence in East Asia. Starting in the 1930s, however, Japan began to pursue an independent course of military adventurism. Seeking to dominate East Asia and to expel Western powers from the region, Japan called for the establishment of a "Greater East Asia Co-Prosperity Sphere," under the slogan of "Asia for Asiatics." Although Japan's defeat in the Second World War marked the end of this ambitious project, Japan's foreign policy before 1945 seems to have significant implications for regional cooperation in East Asia after the end of the Cold War.[10]

In this regard, it may be useful to draw lessons from Europe. A thought experiment by analogy may be particularly useful. In Europe, the initial impetus for regional cooperation came from the historical failure to cope with Germany as a revisionist power. Emerging victorious from the Second World War yet continuing to be concerned with Germany, France took the initiative to promote regional cooperation that included Germany, which, for its part, made efforts to become a trustworthy neighbor. The unification of Germany served as a major driving force for the creation of the European Union, as Germany and its neighbors agreed to make Germany an integral part of Europe rather than an unhinged revisionist power.

The origin of the European Union can be traced back to the Schuman Declaration of May 9, 1950. In proposing this plan, Robert Schuman and Jean Monnet sought to arrest the relative decline of Europe in the postwar US–Soviet bipolar system and to prevent the outbreak of war in Europe, especially between France and Germany. Acknowledging that a united Europe would *not* be made "all at once, or according to a single, general plan," Schuman expressed preference for a gradual approach, and, as "a first step in the federation of Europe," he called for the pooling of coal and steel production and sought to "change the destinies of those regions which [had] long been devoted to the manufacture of munitions of war."

Accordingly, when France, West Germany, Italy, and the Benelux countries established the European Coal and Steel Community (ECSC) in 1951, they not only sought to pursue common economic interests, but also intended to contribute to peace in Europe by jointly overseeing the production, distribution, and consumption of basic raw materials for the manufacture of heavy weapons – namely, coal and steel. In 1957, these six nations established the European Atomic Energy Community (EURATOM), and created the European Economic Community (EEC) by signing the Treaty of Rome. In 1967, the six member nations merged EEC, ECSC, and EURATOM institutions, creating *de facto* a single organization (the European Communities) even if, legally, the three Communities retained their own separate legal identity. To guarantee the free flow of labor as well as finished goods, the member nations coordinated their job training and social security policies, and established the European Social Fund for the retraining and re-employment of laid-off workers. Although the EC member nations had already agreed in 1969 to establish a single economic and monetary policy by 1980, the two oil shocks in the 1970s impeded their progress toward complete economic integration. With the adoption of the Delors Report in 1989, however, the member nations (by then twelve in number) reasserted their desire to create a single Europe, and by signing the Maastricht Treaty on European Union in December 1991, they substantially expanded the scope of European cooperation to push for common foreign and security policies and justice and domestic affairs policies as well as economic and monetary union. The unification of Germany in 1990 was a decisive factor in Europe's renewed push for integration.

Events took a rather different turn in Northeast Asia after the Second World War. The historical failure to cope with Japan as a revisionist power had been broadly similar to the European experience with Germany, but China did not have a chance to patch things up with Japan after the war, which instead established close relations with the United States as its "junior partner." No supranational body was created along the lines of the European Steel and Coal Community. Although many hoped that the end of the Second World War would open a new era of reconciliation and cooperation in Northeast Asia, the ensuing Cold War made it all but impossible for the countries in this region to work together toward a common future. Instead, the intense US–Soviet rivalry during the Cold War resulted in the partition of the region along ideological lines and greatly increased risks of conflict. Nowhere was this more evident than in Korea, as the nation was divided along the thirty-eighth parallel in 1945 and became a battleground for an internationalized civil war from 1950 to 1953, pitting South Korea and the United States against North Korea and China.

Although the collapse of the Soviet Union in the early 1990s removed most of the structural constraints that had impeded regional integration, genuine reconciliation and cooperation in Northeast Asia remain an elusive dream. There are basically two reasons for this slow progress. One has to do with Japan's failure to address its past wrongdoings in a credible and consistent manner. Although the Japanese government has issued a number of official apologies, the most significant of which might be Prime Minister Murayama's in 1995, these apologies have been often followed by "misstatements" from influential Japanese politicians who tend to beautify Japan's past colonial rule. These misstatements not only cast doubt on the sincerity of the official apologies, but also tend to overshadow the significant efforts that Japan's civil society has made in order to resolve historical problems through international cooperation. The other reason has to do with the generally negative attitude of the United States toward regional cooperation in Northeast Asia, for fear of being excluded from the region.[11]

These two elements are closely linked. As long as Japan subscribes to the logic of *datsua* ("escape from Asia") and regards the Japan–US alliance as one of overriding importance, Japan's willingness to work for reconciliation and cooperation in Northeast Asia would be greatly diminished. In this case, Japan would likely reinforce US concerns about regional cooperation in Northeast Asia and take advantage of the bilateral alliance in its quest to become a "normal" country, volunteering to assume a larger share of the burden in international affairs. An unrepentant Japan intent on expanding its military role under the US–Japan alliance would not be trusted by its neighbors, even if economic interaction in the region continues to increase. Such an outcome would not be conducive to the stability of the region.

To promote reconciliation and cooperation in Northeast Asia, political breakthroughs should be supplemented by increased economic and cultural exchanges. Consistent and credible actions should be taken to build trust. Also, potentially enormous benefits from the integration of Northeast Asia should be spelled out, for countries both inside and outside the region. The construction of energy, information, and transportation networks and the integration of national markets in Northeast Asia should offer tremendous business opportunities. In this regard, it is worth noting that unlike the Soviet Union during the Cold War, China has actively sought foreign direct investment (FDI), and heavy economic interaction on a firm level may serve as a check against geopolitical strategists who tend to take the nation-state as a unit of analysis. For Northeast Asia to secure peace and prosperity, it is essential that the region be open to the world's major corporations; in turn, to become an inviting place for these corporations, Northeast Asia should be a peaceful and prosperous region. Regional cooperation in Northeast Asia should be used as a building block for global economic integration. The creation of a "Fortress Northeast Asia" should not be the objective.

Evolving pattern of economic relations in East Asia

Geographically, Northeast Asia is a region that includes China, Japan, and South Korea as well as Mongolia and North Korea.[12] Together with ASEAN 10 (Brunei, Cambodia, Indonesia, Laos, Malaysia, Myanmar, Philippines, Singapore, Thailand, and Vietnam), they constitute East Asia. The ten member-nations of ASEAN and the three large economies in Northeast Asia comprise what is commonly known as ASEAN plus 3. Although there is a continuing debate on whether East Asia constitutes a "natural" grouping, economic interaction within this fast-growing region has intensified over the past few decades, particularly among the ASEAN plus 3 countries. The region is now a large and growing market in its own right, and intraregional trade and investment flows have become more important over time. The transformation of East Asia from an export production base for the rest of the world to an increasingly integrated market has significantly enhanced prospects for regional cooperation.[13]

In 1960, the combined GDP of ASEAN plus 3 was only two-fifths of US GDP, with Japan contributing 81 per cent of the total, followed by China

Table 12.1 Regional comparison of GDP and population (2003)

Region	GDP (US$ billion)	Population (million)
ASEAN plus 3	7,028	2,001
ASEAN 10	686	537
China	1,410	1,288
Japan	4,326	127
South Korea	605	48
NAFTA	12,342	425
US	10,882	291
EU 15	10,750	392

Source: World Development Indicators and ASEAN Statistical Yearbook 2004.

with 8 per cent.[14] As Table 12.1 shows, by 2003, the combined GDP of ASEAN plus 3 had become approximately 70 per cent of the GDP of the US or European Union.

As Table 12.2 shows, the total GDP of Asia as a whole is expected to surpass that of the US in 2025, while the combined GDP of ASEAN plus 3 is forecast to be slightly less than that of the US. Within East Asia, there will be an important change as well. China's GDP, which was only about one-third of Japan's GDP in 2003, is expected to surpass Japan's in 2025.

These prospects have far-reaching implications for international relations in East Asia. Will China begin to throw its weight around and challenge US supremacy in the region, much like Japan did before 1945? Will it act like the US when it was beginning to emerge as a global power and establish a Monroe Doctrine of its own in East Asia and seek an "open door" policy in other continents? Will Japan idly stand by when China is almost certain to overtake Japan as an economic powerhouse? Will it choose to cooperate with China or try to form a united front with the US against China? As these questions suggest, changes in the relative size of the economies are likely to have a significant effect on the external strategies of these countries.

Another factor that will have a significant effect is change in the relative importance of intraregional trade. The relative importance of intraregional economic interaction in East Asia has undergone a dramatic change over the past century. If dependence on intraregional trade is used as a measure of regional cooperation, East Asia had a much higher level of regional cooperation in the prewar period. The gravity coefficient for the East Asian trading bloc showed a secular decline between the mid-1930s and the mid-1980s, when it began to rise again. The gravity coefficient in the mid-1930s was more than twice the level in the mid-1980s.[15] There is little evidence that the relative decline in intraregional trade adversely affected the economic performance of East Asian countries, which took advantage of increased opportunities for interregional trade in the postwar period. In fact, the relative decline in intraregional trade coincided with the remarkable growth

Table 12.2 Long-term forecast for GDP in major regions

	Nominal GDP growth (annual)					Nominal GDP (US$ trillion) (World share, % in parentheses)		
	2001–5	2006–10	2011–15	2016–20	2021–5	2003	2015	2025
World	7.7	6.3	5.6	5.5	5.3	36.44 (100)	81.49 (100)	137.72 (100)
US	4.8	5.3	5.8	5.7	5.7	11.00 (30.2)	21.32 (26.2)	37.19 (27.0)
EU	12.3	4.7	3.5	3.6	3.5	10.52 (28.9)	21.17 (26.0)	30.04 (21.8)
Japan	1.5	6.1	4.5	2.9	2.1	4.29 (11.8)	8.57 (10.5)	10.94 (7.9)
BRICs	–	–	–	–	–	2.87 (7.9)	11.47 (14.1)	25.89 (18.8)
China	11.9	15.0	10.6	9.4	8.6	1.41 (3.9)	6.30 (7.7)	14.93 (10.8)
India	9.6	9.8	9.1	9.2	9.0	0.54 (1.5)	1.81 (2.2)	4.33 (3.1)
Brazil	2.9	6.5	7.0	6.7	6.4	0.49 (1.4)	1.33 (1.6)	2.51 (1.8)
Russia	23.4	11.2	10.1	9.5	5.1	0.43 (1.2)	2.04 (2.5)	4.12 (3.0)
Asia	4.8	8.8	7.1	6.3	6.1	8.17 (22.4)	21.72 (26.7)	39.60 (28.8)

Source: Global Insight, World Economic Outlook, January 2005.

of outward-oriented industrializing economies in East Asia, which exported the bulk of their final goods to high-income countries in North America and Europe. The heavy dependence on extraregional demand, however, seemed to rule out tighter regional integration in East Asia, because much of intra-regional trade was derived from the outside. After analyzing trade patterns based on 1999 data, a Japanese researcher even warned against making too much out of economic interdependence in East Asia.[16]

Demand from North America and Europe is likely to remain important for the foreseeable future, but there are signs that intraregional demand has become more important in recent years. In particular, if China's impressive economic growth is sustained, its role as a market for final demand will become increasingly important.[17] Currently, China is serving as "the world's factory," but rising affluence in its coastal areas and ambitious investment projects in underdeveloped regions in the west and northeast are creating a great deal of final demand. China's rapid economic growth offers great opportunities for East Asia to increase intraregional trade. According to an estimate based on a computable general equilibrium (CGE) model, China is projected to become the largest Asian importer by 2005. Contrary to the view that China's exports will stifle growth among its neighbors, China's expansion, particularly when accelerated by its World Trade Organization (WTO) initiative, is projected to open unprecedented market opportunities for Asian exporters.[18] Spearheaded by China's rapid growth, continuing economic expansion and increasing intraregional interaction in East Asia is enhancing the prospects for tighter integration.

External strategies of major players in East Asia

Faced with significant political and economic changes in East Asia, major players in the region are formulating external strategies to advance their national interests. Building on the strength of its rapid economic growth, China is engaging in proactive economic diplomacy on all fronts. At the same time, China is trying to keep a low profile and avoid creating the impression that it is out to challenge the status quo in international relations.[19] China's regional initiatives have put Japan on the defensive. Although Japan initially wanted to be quite selective in signing preferential trade agreements, dealing first with advanced industrial economies such as Singapore and South Korea, it increasingly finds itself having to respond to China's regional agenda, especially in Southeast Asia. South Korea, for its part, is mainly concerned with promoting cooperation in Northeast Asia as a way of addressing the North Korea problem. ASEAN is actively engaged in trade negotiations with countries in East Asia as well as from the outside, but the lack of a unified internal market has weakened its bargaining position.

The slogan of "peaceful rise" sums up China's current external strategy. China is trying to maintain its rapid economic growth and establish strong economic relations on all fronts while presenting itself as a benign, nonhegemonic power. Through such a strategy, China is in effect minimizing the possibility of containment by Japan and the United States. China is forging close economic relations with other countries by offering access to its huge market, especially in the wake of its accession to the WTO in 2001. Although foreign businesses are aware of the risks of "boomerang effects" when they transfer technology to their Chinese counterparts, the competitive nature of the market entry game places serious limitations on their choices. China is also reaching out to resource-abundant countries around the globe in order to secure raw materials to sustain its economic growth. A good example is the establishment of the Shanghai Cooperation Organization in 2001 linking China with Kazakhstan, Kyrgystan, Tajikistan, Uzbekistan, and Russia. This organization helps China to improve its energy security and increase its influence in the oil- and gas-rich countries in Central Asia.[20]

The rapid expansion of its domestic market is leading China to play an increasingly prominent role in regional cooperation in East Asia. For political as well as economic reasons, China has been making serious efforts to sign a free trade agreement with ASEAN countries, which, in turn, see preferential access to the Chinese market as a possible solution to their present difficulties. In particular, ASEAN countries hope that a free trade agreement with China would enable them to reap an "early harvest" of China's WTO accession commitments, although they are also concerned about the possibility of Chinese goods flooding their markets. In 2002, China committed itself to creating a free trade area with ASEAN by 2010. In 2004, as a gesture of goodwill, China reduced tariffs on goods imported from ASEAN 6 (Brunei, Indonesia, Malaysia, the Philippines, Singapore, and Thailand) and unilaterally eliminated tariffs on goods imported from the four latecomers in ASEAN (Cambodia, Laos, Myanmar, and Vietnam). China has been active in Northeast Asia as well. In 2002, it proposed an FTA with Japan and South Korea, and a year later, the three parties agreed on fourteen priority areas for trilateral cooperation. Although the quality of institutions in China is not up to par with advanced industrial countries, China has used its sheer size and potential to advance major initiatives in regional cooperation. China enjoys a very strong bargaining position because it can offer its external partners huge benefits from market liberalization in the wake of its WTO accession if they in turn agree to provide China with needed capital, technology, or geopolitical gains.

Although Japan's departure from multilateral principles predated China's regional initiatives,[21] Japan has yet to formulate a comprehensive external economic strategy. At a fundamental level, Japan is still struggling with the same problem of identity it has faced since the second half of the nineteenth century: is Japan inside or outside Asia? Japan's "escape from Asia" and domination of Asia defined the two phases of Japanese foreign policy before the Second World War II. The question is whether Japan can now craft a new role as a benevolent neighbor and respected leader in East Asia instead of becoming a "junior partner" of a global power or a military adventurist on its own.

So far, Japan's approach has been piecemeal and reactive. In response to the weakening of multilateralism since the late 1980s, Japan has taken a more positive view toward preferential trade agreements, but its inefficient agricultural sector has limited its options. Japan signed an economic partnership agreement with Singapore in 2002 and with Mexico in 2004, but these agreements were defensive and exploratory in nature. Far more significant would be an economic partnership agreement between Japan and South Korea. As the only two OECD members in East Asia, Japan and Korea are in the position to advocate deep regional integration based on a high level of institutional quality, going beyond WTO consistency.[22] The strategic significance of this economic partnership would go beyond trade and investment areas, however. It would mark a new era for the two traditional rivals and give China something to think about. Unless Japan and South Korea make it clear to China that their economic partnership agreement is open to further membership, there is even a chance that China might interpret this agreement as a potential building block of containment against China as both Japan and South Korea have a military alliance with the United States. Just as China's initiative toward ASEAN has led to a competitive response from Japan, the proposed economic partnership agreement between Japan and South Korea has prompted China to push for a trilateral agreement involving all three countries right from the start.

As a divided land-bridge in Northeast Asia, South Korea's external strategy in recent years has focused on addressing the North Korea problem. Korea is not a small country, with the combined population of North and South Korea exceeding that of Britain, France, or Italy, but the presence of two regional powers, China and Japan, is likely to limit South Korea's role in East Asia – especially when North Korea's economic problems and military threats demand attention.[23] In particular, North Korea's nuclear challenge is a source of tension that should be addressed as soon as possible.

The outline of a solution to the nuclear problem is reasonably clear.[24] The US should end what North Korea regards as the "hostile policy" toward it, and North Korea should freeze and then dismantle its nuclear program under inspection. Through various programs to assist North Korea's economic development, the international community should convince North Korea that a nonnuclear future will be better for it than a nuclear one. To resolve North Korea's nuclear problem and to promote peace and security in Northeast Asia, South Korea is pushing for the construction of energy and transportation networks in the region, facilitating economic development not only in North Korea but also in China's northeastern provinces and the Russian Far East. Such investment projects will also create business opportunities for firms from this region as well as from the outside, and allow them to share in the benefits of increased regional integration.

As for preferential trade agreements, South Korea's approach has been largely defensive and exploratory, much like Japan's. In 2004, South Korea signed a free trade agreement with Chile and Singapore, both of which present few problems for South Korea's protected agricultural sector. Beyond the two agreements, however, it is not clear what steps South Korea will take even as it continues to participate actively in regional dialogue such as the ASEAN plus 3 meetings. Negotiations for a free trade agreement with Japan have been going on in the past few years, but progress has been slow due to resistance from some manufacturing sectors as well as concern at China's negative reaction to the bilateral agreement. Also, although some have recently advocated a bilateral free trade agreement with the United States for the sake of high politics more than economics, they have yet to make it clear what they plan to do with agricultural liberalization under GATT/WTO Article 24. Those who champion a bilateral free trade agreement with China face the same problem.

Although ASEAN has been a promoter of regional cooperation since its establishment in 1967, its success has been rather uneven. Initially formed as an anticommunist bloc against the expansion of China and the Soviet Union, ASEAN was slow to integrate economically. In fact, it was not until 1992 that ASEAN established the ASEAN Free Trade Area (AFTA) with a plan to eliminate tariffs among the member countries. It was hoped that AFTA would serve as an economic glue holding ASEAN together after the end of the Cold War. However, ASEAN has made only slow progress in economic integration, primarily due to the 1997 economic crisis and the expansion of ASEAN to incorporate Cambodia, Laos, Myanmar, and Vietnam. Although the enlargement achieved the political objective of uniting all of Southeast Asia, it widened the differences in the level of development among member countries, making ASEAN less cohesive. ASEAN leaders reaffirmed the ASEAN Vision 2020 at the 2003 Summit and agreed to establish the ASEAN Community by 2020, but they decided to adopt a pragmatic "2 + X formula" reflecting that not all ten member states are willing and able to move at the same pace. This "variable geometry" allows Singapore and Thailand to take the lead and other countries to join later in regional integration efforts. When extended to negotiations with non-ASEAN countries, however, such a nonunified approach may generate "spaghetti bowl" effects.

As far as negotiations between non-ASEAN countries and ASEAN as a group are concerned, ASEAN has taken a rather eclectic approach. ASEAN is conducting free trade negotiations with major economies such as China, India, Japan, South Korea, and the United States, among others. At the same time, ASEAN is making efforts to integrate more tightly with China, Japan, and South Korea as a group in the ASEAN plus 3 framework. As these bilateral or plurilateral negotiations are being conducted ahead of the realization of the single ASEAN market, however, a unified ASEAN negotiating position is not easy to achieve.

Possible trajectories for the future

During the Cold War, most countries in East Asia belonged to one of the two competing hub-and-spoke alliances headed by the United States and the Soviet Union. Primarily for historical reasons, including military conflicts in the twentieth century, there was very little multinational cooperation in East Asia at the governmental level. Yet economic linkages were extensive, at least in the nonsocialist part of the region. Japan provided the lion's share of intermediate goods to outward-oriented industrializing economies, which exported final goods to the American and European markets. The 1985 Plaza Accord accentuated this trend, as the appreciating yen led Japan to increase its investment in Southeast Asia. Although there was no preferential trade agreement in East Asia, extensive international production networks were established in the region to reap the benefits of global trade.[25] At least until the end of the 1980s, East Asia took advantage of globalization without giving preference to regional integration. For the most part, export-oriented countries in this region adhered to multilateral principles.

A number of developments since then, however, have led East Asia to take a more favorable view of regional integration. The end of the Cold War and economic reform in transition countries such as China and Vietnam greatly enhanced the prospects for tighter integration in East Asia. Also, the signing of the North American Free Trade Agreement (NAFTA) and the formation of the European Union spurred exploratory discussions on "defensive" responses from East Asia. The 1997 economic crisis highlighted the need to create transnational institutions such as an Asian Monetary Fund to protect the collective interests of the countries in the region.[26] Finally, the rapid rise, or more accurately, resurgence of China prompted a search for an international arrangement designed to minimize the risks associated with a shifting balance of power. Sea changes in international relations triggered by the end of the Cold War and the rise of China are increasingly forcing countries in East Asia to look at preferential trade agreements with geopolitical and economic significance.

For instance, China and Japan are competing to strengthen ties with Southeast Asia by signing a free trade agreement with ASEAN. Japan and South Korea are negotiating a free trade agreement, raising concern on the part of China. The United States is also keeping an eye on developments in East Asia, for fear of being excluded from any significant regional agreement. Combined with the very real possibility of major shifts in international relations, historical rivalry among major players is making any ambitious regional initiative by one country a potential source of tension in East Asia. At the same time, the region already has in ASEAN plus 3 a forum where various concerns can be addressed in a constructive manner.

Against this background, it may be useful to consider possible trajectories for regional integration in East Asia. The region has four major players: ASEAN, China, Japan, and South Korea. The pattern of regional integration in East Asia will largely be determined by their interaction. By offering an asymmetrical liberalization schedule, China has made much more progress in its negotiations with ASEAN than have Japan and South Korea. Unlike Japan or South Korea, China is not hampered by an inefficient agricultural sector. While there is some concern about the possibility of Chinese imports flooding the market, ASEAN countries can expect an "early harvest" if they sign a bilateral agreement with China ahead of other countries. The competitiveness gap between ASEAN and China is likely to widen in China's favor as China increasingly attracts more FDI than does ASEAN.[27] Delaying a free trade agreement with China will only reduce net benefits to ASEAN.[28] Consequently, the best strategy for ASEAN countries is to push for an early agreement with China while securing concessions from China to reduce adjustment costs in their domestic markets.

Japan and South Korea can move toward a free trade agreement of their own to facilitate industrial restructuring and promote investment. Although some Chinese scholars have expressed reservations about this agreement, a trilateral free trade agreement is not realistic at this point, not least because of GATT/WTO Article 24 and the vulnerability of the agricultural sector in Japan and South Korea. It will be more realistic to seek first at least partial solutions to agricultural problems during the course of multilateral trade negotiations, which offer greater room for compensatory mechanism. As in the case of NAFTA, which was expanded from a bilateral agreement between Canada and the US to incorporate Mexico, a bilateral agreement can develop into a trilateral agreement when the shock from liberalized trade can be contained at a manageable level. However, the enthusiasm for or urgency of a bilateral agreement between Japan and South Korea may not be as high as is the case regarding the one between ASEAN and China. In particular, the competitiveness gap between Japan and South Korea may not widen even if the signing of the agreement is delayed. While the bilateral agreement may create dynamic benefits by facilitating industrial restructuring in both countries and promoting investment flows from Japan to South Korea, short-run gains from trade liberalization are likely to be unevenly distributed in Japan's favor because Japan's current average tariff rate is lower than South Korea's. These issues must be addressed before the bilateral agreement can be successfully concluded.

The two sets of bilateral agreements can then serve as the building blocks for more extensive regional cooperation in East Asia and beyond. If and when Japan and South Korea are ready to address agricultural liberalization issues, China and ASEAN on the one side and Japan and South Korea on the other can join forces, either individually or as a duo. It is also at this juncture that a free trade agreement with the United States can be discussed in a substantive manner. The risks associated with a shifting balance of power in East Asia should be minimized through such cooperation. For the foreseeable future, the ASEAN plus 3 framework is likely to provide a forum for constructive discussions on promoting reconciliation and cooperation.

Conclusion

Although economic integration seems to offer tantalizing possibilities for formerly hostile nations in Northeast Asia, it would require more than trade and investment ties for these nations to come to terms with history and craft a common vision for the region. Not only are there inherent limitations in using economic exchanges to promote mutual understanding, but also geopolitical considerations interacting with historical animosity may trump commercial interests favoring regional cooperation. As Yotaro Kobayashi's case shows, entrepreneurs doing business in foreign countries have a good incentive to guard against the forces of ultraconservative nationalism because, after all, they have to be attentive to local sentiments if their business is to prosper; however, business leaders are vulnerable to criticism because, no matter what they do, they are seen to put money before anything else. A strictly commercial rationale for reconciliation and cooperation is not likely to be very effective in promoting genuine understanding between formerly hostile nations. Also, geopolitical considerations may override commercial interests and influence the pattern of economic exchanges in a way that is likely to raise, rather than reduce, tension between historical rivals. Although China has managed to attract a great deal of FDI from former foes as well as friends, there is no guarantee that economic interaction will continue to expand as Japan and the US increasingly speculate about China's ultimate objective.[29]

It would require conscious efforts on the part of civil society and political leaders to overcome the limitations of purely economic approaches. A political breakthrough in an effort to come to terms with history should be supplemented by increased economic and cultural exchanges to broaden mutual interests and understanding. Consistent and credible actions on the part of political leaders are important so that there will be neither "apology fatigue" nor "misstatement fatigue." Once significant progress has been made with regard to historical problems, civil society and political leaders should make efforts to construct and institutionalize a shared identity and a future vision that transcend national borders. To minimize the risk of conflict, proponents of these regional integration schemes should make it clear that they are to be the building blocks of larger integration. With ASEAN and South Korea effectively playing the role of mediators between China and Japan, coordination and consultation within the ASEAN plus 3 framework would be desirable. Also, potentially enormous benefits from economic integration should be spelled out, for countries both inside and outside the region. The construction of energy, information, and transportation networks and the integration of national markets should offer tremendous business opportunities. It is essential that Northeast Asia be open to the world's major corporations so that they would have a stake in engaging with, rather than containing, nations in the region and in arguing effectively against geopolitical strategists who tend to see more potential for conflict than cooperation.

Notes

For their helpful comments, the author would like to thank the participants at the conference Rethinking Historical Injustice in Northeast Asia: The Korean Experience in Regional Perspective, held at the Asia-Pacific Research Center, Stanford University, on May 27–28, 2004.

1 See "Editorial: firebomb threat," *Asahi Shimbun* (January 14, 2005), and Norimitsu Onishi, "The Japan–China stew: sweet and sour," *New York Times* (January 19, 2005). Onishi notes that "China is considered partner by Japanese business interests and rival, if not outright adversary, by political class."
2 See David Crocker, "Reckoning with past wrongs: a normative framework," *Ethics and International Affairs* 13 (1999), 43–64.
3 On the intellectual history of peace, see Istvan Kende, "The history of peace: concept and organization from the late middle ages to the 1870s," *Journal of Peace Research* 26 (1989), 233–47.
4 See Immanuel Kant, *Kant's Political Writings*, ed. Hans Reiss (Cambridge: Cambridge University Press, 1970). The author would like to thank Young-Joon Park for his helpful comments on this section.
5 In recent years, some American academics and policymakers have been floating the idea of forming a "value alliance" with nations that share the core values of democracy and market economy against "the irredeemable forces of darkness" in the post-9/11 world. See, for instance, Victor D. Cha and David C. Kang, *Nuclear North Korea* (New York: Columbia University Press, 2003). The risk inherent in such a confrontational and Manichean approach is that it may actually reduce the prospects for reform in countries targeted by the alliance and greatly increase the possibility of conflict.
6 Asking the German people to accept the past and seek reconciliation with other nations, former German President Richard von Weizscker once said: "Seeking to forget makes exile all the longer; the secret of redemption lies in remembrance."
7 For historical perspectives on China's economic performance, see Angus Maddison, *Monitoring the World Economy, 1820–1992* (Paris: OECD, 1995), p. 30, and Angus Maddison, *Chinese Economic Performance in the Long Run* (Paris: OECD, 1998).
8 See Michio Morishima, *Why Has Japan Succeeded? Western Technology and the Japanese Ethos* (Cambridge: Cambridge University Press, 1982). For a comparative study of China and Japan in the nineteenth century, see George M. Beckman, *The Modernization of China and Japan* (New York: Harper & Row, 1962).
9 See Kazuyoshi Uehara et al., *A Modern History of East Asia*, trans. from Japanese to Korean by Kyu-Soo Lee et al. (Seoul: Yet Oneul, 1994).
10 On the evolution of Japan's foreign policy before 1945, see Sang-Jung Kang, *Toward a Northeast Asian Common House*, trans. from Japanese to Korean by Kyung-Duk Lee (Seoul: Puriwa Ipari Publishing Co., 2002).
11 See Sunhyuk Kim and Yong Wook Lee, "New Asian regionalism and the United States: constructing regional identity and interest in the politics of inclusion and exclusion," *Pacific Focus* (October 2004).
12 The Russian Far East is sometimes included in this grouping.
13 See Francis Ng and Alexander Yeats, "Major trade trends in East Asia: what are their implications for regional cooperation and growth?", World Bank Policy Research Working Paper 3084, 2003.
14 See Lawrence Lau, "Asian regional economy in a multilateral setting," paper presented at the Symposium on Asian Network of Economic Policy Research (ANEPR) 2003–2004: Asia in Search of a New Order, organized by the Research Institute of Economy, Trade, and Industry (RIETI), Tokyo, January 16–17, 2004.

15 For a historical analysis of changes in the gravity coefficient in East Asia, see Peter Petri, "The East Asian trading bloc: an analytical history," in Jeffrey A. Frankel and Miles Kahler, ed., *Regionalism and Rivalry: Japan and the US in Pacific Asia* (Chicago, IL: University of Chicago Press, 1994), pp. 21–52. See also Eisuke Sakakibara and Sharon Yamakawa, *Regional Integration in East Asia: Challenges and Opportunities, World Bank East Asia Project* (Tokyo: Global Security Research Center, Keio University, 2003).

16 See K. Sugiura, "The fantasy of Asia's inter-dependence," FRI Research Report No. 79 (Tokyo: Fujitsu Economic Research Institute, 2000). In 1999, Japan's exports to the US amounted to $130.0 billion, while its imports from the US were only $57.5 billion. AXJ9 (Asia Excluding Japan: China, Hong Kong, Indonesia, Malaysia, the Philippines, Singapore, South Korea, Taiwan, and Thailand) exported $234.6 billion to the US but imported only $107.3 billion. By contrast, AXJ 9's exports to Japan were $118.4 billion, while its imports from Japan amounted to $151.9 billion.

17 On the impact of China's economic growth, see Fred Hu et al., "The five great myths about China and the world," (New York: Goldman Sachs, 2002). The five great myths are: (a) China is going to take over the world; (b) "New Industrial China" is hollowing out manufacturing and stifling growth in the rest of the world; (c) low wages, high productivity growth and a grossly undervalued currency are relentlessly raising China's competitiveness; (d) structural imbalances are driving deflation at home and abroad; (e) Japan, ASEAN and the rest of Asia are fighting for their lives against the rising mainland economy.

18 See David Roland-Holst, "An overview of PRC's emergence and East Asian trade patterns to 2020," ADB Institute Research Paper 44 (Tokyo: ADB Institute, 2002).

19 Given China's efforts to present itself as a benign and nonhegemonic power, the way it handled the Koguryo controversy was something of a surprise. With its territory extending from the northern half of the Korean peninsula to Manchuria, the ancient kingdom of Koguryo had the potential to develop into a contentious issue between Korea and China for some time. A major controversy erupted in 2004 when the Chinese Foreign Ministry decided to remove Koguryo from the ancient history of Korea in its Internet-based country profile section on Korea. When South Korea protested, China responded by deleting the entire pre-1948 history of Korea. The only consolation to Koreans was that China was at least fair enough to do the same to Japan. With North Korea being as dependent as it is on China, some Koreans interpreted the Chinese action as an attempt to do the historical groundwork to expand its influence into the Korean peninsula. The Chinese could have said that Koguryo was a multiethnic ancient kingdom whose rulers were Korean but whose cultural heritage was shared by China and Korea, but for some unknown reason, the Chinese Foreign Ministry decided to go well beyond that. The Koguryo controversy led many Koreans to take a second look at China.

20 See Howard W. French, "China moves toward another west: Central Asia," *New York Times* (March 28, 2004).

21 See Naoko Munakata, "Evolution of Japan's policy toward economic integration," mimeo, Center for Northeast Asian Policy Studies (CNAPS), Brookings Institution, 2001.

22 On the precedent-setting effect of the economic partnership agreement between Japan and South Korea, see Fukagawa, "Japan's view on Northeast Asian community: institutional approach from economic partnership agreement (EPA)," mimeo, University of Tokyo, 2003.

23 For a discussion on South Korea's role in promoting regional cooperation, see Chang-Jae Lee, "East Asian economic regionalism and the role of South Korea,"

paper presented at the conference Korea as a 21st Century Power, held at the University of Cambridge, April 3–6, 2002.

24 On the contours of a solution to North Korea's nuclear problem, see Wonhyuk Lim, "North Korea's economic futures: internal and external dimensions," in Jonathan D. Pollack, ed., *Korea: The East Asian Pivot* (Newport, RI: Naval War College Press, 2004), pp. 71–195.

25 On Japanese investment in Southeast Asia, see Seiichi Masuyama, "The role of Japan's direct investment in restoring East Asia's dynamism: focus on ASEAN," in Seiichi Masuyama, Donna Vandebrink, and Chia Siow Yue, eds, *Restoring East Asia's Dynamism* (Tokyo: Nomura Research Institute, 2000), pp. 213–96.

26 On evolving views toward regional integration in East Asia, see C. Fred Bergsten, "The world economy after the Cold War," *Foreign Affairs* 69/3 (1990), 96–112 and T. J. Pempel, "Regional ups, regional downs," in T. J. Pempel, ed., *The Politics of the Asian Economic Crisis* (Ithaca, NY: Cornell University Press, 1999), pp. 62–78.

27 In 1990, a year after the Tiananmen demonstrations, the net FDI inflow for China was $3.5 billion; the net FDI inflow for ASEAN 10 was $12.8 billion. By 1993, however, China had overtaken ASEAN 10, and the gap continued to widen in subsequent years. In 2003, the net FDI inflow for China was $53.3 billion; the comparable figure for ASEAN 10 was $19.1 billion. For Indonesia, Malaysia, the Philippines, and Thailand, the net FDI inflow in 2003 was actually less than what these countries had attracted in 1990, respectively.

28 On this point, see Mohd Haflah Piei, "The East Asia Free Trade Agreement: an ASEAN perspective," paper presented at the conference Prospects for an East Asian Free Trade Agreement, organized by the Korea Institute for International Economic Policy (KIEP), Seoul, September 27, 2002.

29 See, for instance, Zbigniew Brzezinski and John J. Mearsheimer, "Clash of the titans," *Foreign Policy* (January/February 2005), 46–50.

Epilogue

Lessons and future agenda for reconciliation in Northeast Asia

Soon-Won Park, Daqing Yang, and Gi-Wook Shin

As Yoichi Funabashi notes in a volume on the Asia-Pacific reconciliation, there is no uniform universal formula for reconciliation; it is a multifaceted process requiring varied inputs and action at many levels.[1] It is an approach that we have embraced here too. As such, it is worthwhile to review each of the modes of reconciliation – apology politics, litigation, common history, and intersocietal communication – to assess their achievements and short-comings, draw some lessons from them, and suggest future tasks.

Lessons of reconciliation

Apology diplomacy has been a major tactic in the reconciliation process. Since 1984, there have been nine official apologies in the course of the Japan–Korea summits: by Emperor Hirohito during President Chun's visit in 1984; by Emperor Akihito during President Roh's visit in 1990; by Prime Minister Miyazawa (focusing on the comfort women issue) in his visit to Seoul in 1992; by Emperor Akihito during President Kim Young Sam's visit in 1994; by Prime Minister Murayama Tomohiro in 1995 (in commemoration of the fiftieth anniversary of the end of the war); by Prime Minister Obuchi Keizo during President Kim Dae Jung's visit in 1998; by Prime Minister Koizumi Junichiro during his Seoul visit in 2001; at the Jakarta Asian–African summit meeting in May 2005; and a speech given in the commemorative ceremony of the sixtieth anniversary of the end of the Second World War in August 2005. In retrospect, the years of the mid-1990s – centered as they were on Prime Minister Murayama's leadership – were a high point in apology diplomacy. At that point, the two countries seemed very close to the peaceful reconciliation phase. Murayama created the Asia Women Fund through the unofficial channel, for the purpose of compensating comfort women, showing his administration's commitment to the cause (although the Korean government rejected the proposal in the end). In June 1996, every one of the seven new middle-school history textbooks selected by the Education Ministry that year included a one-line description of the comfort women. It was a significant gesture of repentance from the Japanese political leadership to clear up the comfort women controversy.

Yet the apology tactic was very much exhausted at the interstate level, even to the extent of "apology fatigue," according to the conservative Japanese press like *Sankei Shimbun*. It also provoked reaction from nationalist Japanese: in December 1996, the Society for Creating New Textbooks (*atarashii kyokasho o tsukurukai*), a symbol of rightist neo-nationalism in Japan from the mid-1990s, for instance, was organized in response to this mood of repentance and reconciliation.[2] The most significant lesson of this apology tactic was that it revealed weakness in the Japanese political elites' commitment to the cause. Throughout the 1990s, Japanese political elites showed almost schizophrenic ambivalence – to borrow *Asahi Shimbun*'s Wakamiya Yoshibumi's term – between formal apology and frequent misstatements that glorified their colonial rule.[3] The Japanese prime ministers' deliberate visits to the Yasukuni Shrine provided another revealing example of the confusing message they send to their Asian neighbors. In the end, lack of courage prevented them from admitting past wrongs and moving forward. The Korean side has slowly but gradually realized that the formal ritual of apology is but one element in the complexities of the politics of remembrance between the two countries.[4]

In helping to reach a settlement between the victims and those responsible for crimes against them, *litigation*, instead of interstate compensation, has been adopted as a major tactic in addressing historical injustice. Unlike in the West, however, its efficacy has proven to be very limited. Almost all lawsuits filed by Asian victims in Japanese courts were either thrown out or unresolved, although the court did recognize the fact of their suffering. The Bush administration's negative attitude toward US ex-POWs' legal battles against the Japanese government and private corporations is another example. The victims' unsuccessful litigation struggle using the Hayden Bill of California between 1999 and 2004 further proved the limits of litigation tactic.

Realizing its limits, Korean legal activists have made some adjustments in their use of the litigation tactic. Instead of just focusing on the compensation issue, they have pressed political leaders to admit moral responsibility and resolve problems politically, as a package deal. More human rights-oriented demands for the dead, such as the establishment of historical archives, memorial projects, removing the enshrining of Korean victims from the Yasukuni Shrine, and clearing up family registers are all projects that await political resolution at the intergovernmental level. All of these hint at a possible East Asian model for conflict resolution, borne out by deep-seated awareness of the differences between Asian moral culture and the Western legal culture.

The continued *tension over history textbooks*, in 1982, 2002, and 2005, attests to the central importance of a shared view of history in regional reconciliation. The frequent clashes over history between Northeast Asia's close neighbors can be attributed to the lack of a reconciled view of the past. Realizing the importance of a shared history, Korea and Japan have begun a new approach to regional history. In October 2001, Prime Minister Koizumi visited Korea in the course of a seven-and-a-half-hour schedule, during which he and President Kim Dae-Jung agreed to establish a Forum for China–Japan–Korea Joint Historical Studies. The agreement was realized in February 2002, when the two governments appointed twelve advisory committees from each nation. It was a gesture of political commitment toward the state-sponsored effort for understanding mutual histories and resituating them in a new regional history framework. No outcome has yet been realized.

Still, throughout the history textbook controversies, a kind of public history education took place in a manner that classroom education could never have achieved. Through media coverage and public discussion of history textbook issues, many learned and thought about the Nanjing Massacre, the comfort women system, wartime forced labor and ex-POWs, and the 731 Unit vivisection as part of regional wartime experience, and re-examined them with new sensitivity, in light of universal human rights. Both elites and the public in Korea and Japan have widened their scope of understanding of the Asian regional history problems that cross their own national borders. In addition, by admitting serious mutual ignorance, both societies have learned more about each other's problems.

Koreans, for instance, have learned about the divided memories of the past among Japanese political elites and members of civil society, and particularly about the lack of political courage among Japan's conservative political elites. Although the view is not yet mainstream, a critical minority in Korea now understands that this ironic ambivalence of victim/aggressor identity in the conservative Japanese elites (unlike their German counterparts) has been the core obstacle to Japan's reconciliation with its Asian neighbors. Korea addressed various issues of internal injustice (mainly those of pro-Japanese collaborators, civilian massacres during the Korean War, and human rights violations by the Park and Chun military dictatorships) in the public realm through magazine stories, TV dramas, films, Internet sites, exhibitions, conferences, and lawsuits.[5] Self-reflective debates on the problems of Korean national historiography, Koreans' own double standards, and the ambivalence of their victim/aggressor identity continue today.[6]

Another important achievement is *intersocietal communication and bonding* developed in the process of historical redress. Increasing numbers of civic activist groups in Japan and Korea worked together in history redress movements, including data and testimony collection, documentary film making, and public history propaganda work. Bilateral, state-oriented approaches to this history issue have now expanded to multifaceted, transnational activism in which government, civil society, academics, and the media all became involved.

For instance, scholars of Korea and Japan have worked together to move toward a mutual understanding of regional history. In November 2004, they formed Hanil yŏndae 21 (Korea–Japan Solidarity 21) to promote self-criticism and reflection and to build regional solidarity between the two nations for the twenty-first century. Also, after several years of collaborative work, a

regional NGO consisting of historians from China, Japan, and Korea produced the first-ever East Asian common history guidebook, *A History that
Opens to the Future: The Contemporary and Modern History of Three East
Asian Countries* (*Mirai o hiraku rekishi* or *Miraerŭl Yŏnŭn Yŏksa*) in early
2005. It is hoped that this landmark work will help to achieve one of the
most challenging, long-term goals of regional reconciliation: to teach the
reconciled past to young people in Japan, Korea, and China.

Growing cultural interactions are encouraging as well. The 1998 official
cultural opening of the two societies, co-hosting of the 2002 World Cup
games, and the pop culture industry boom, which even coined the term
"*hallyu* (the Korean wave)" in Asia, have all softened deep-seated antagonism,
mistrust, and fear. Many young Japanese are aware of the recent Korean
cultural renaissance in TV drama and filmmaking, and the Japanese media
are increasingly buying these Korean cultural products. High school history
teachers and students of both countries are holding joint summer camps
every year to learn more about Japanese and Korean history. These kinds of
multilevel cultural interactions across the borders will be useful resources
in achieving the ultimate grace of forgiveness, the liberation from the old
victim/aggressor identity, and the development of a new regional identity
based on the vision of peaceful coexistence.

Agenda for the future

Despite some success, Northeast Asian nations still have many issues to
resolve before achieving thick reconciliation. In particular, the experiences
of the 1990s prove the liability of the politics of nationalism: an obsession
with national history based on a single historical memory, like the history
textbook, has been a key cause of Asia's history problem. Thus, how we
train diverse young Asians, instilling in them the need for critical and
independent thinking about their respective pasts, and how we cultivate a
mutually acceptable, new national history of each country, resituated in
a shared regional identity, will be a major challenge for the future. Nationalism, regionalism, and internationalism will always coexist, but they need
not contradict one another. In this critical time of change and desire
to cultivate a shared view, we need to redefine these mutually reinforcing
ideologies beyond a narrow, exclusive sense of nation.

In this regard, it is worth updating the history problem between South
Korea and China to understand its multilateral, political components.
Although the military forces of the PRC and ROK fought bitterly for three
years in the Korean War, there now seems to be little open animosity
between the two countries. Instead, considerable goodwill exists in Korea
toward its giant neighbor. Things changed somewhat in the summer
of 2004, when a controversy over the ancient Koguryŏ history surfaced
between South Korea and China. Specifically, both countries co-registered,
with the UNESCO World Cultural Heritage, the historical relics of the

Koguryŏ Kingdom (37 BC to 668 AD), which had stretched over today's Manchurian and North Korean territories. In the process, the Chinese government claimed that the kingdom was a peripheral local state that had belonged to ancient China. This claim had less to do with ancient history *per se* than with current Chinese minority policies, which are based upon a multiethnically unified, "one China" concept. Besides, the heart of this issue lies in China's rising state-oriented nationalism on the one hand, and some Koreans' lingering ethnic nationalism (in the concept of "irredentism") on the other. Many Koreans believe that the Chinese government is consolidating control over the three Manchurian provinces because it is concerned about the political role that approximately two million Yanbian ethnic Koreans might play in Korea's eventual reunification. It is doubtful that the Yanbian Koreans (as with the roughly 700,000 resident Koreans in Japan) feel that they belong entirely to North or South Korea. Nevertheless, the incident provided a timely wake-up call for South Korea, and there was an outburst of protest among the Korean public. Although the two governments had effectively contained the issue by late 2004, the controversy may erupt again in the future.

A few months later, the tension over history resurfaced, this time between Japan and Korea. On March 1, 2005, in his speech commemorating the March First Independence Movement of 1919, President Roh strongly warned that Korean leaders' relative restraint on history issues should not be taken to mean they had all been resolved. As if to prove his prediction, the Korean government and public reacted vehemently to the passage of an ordinance in the Shimane Prefecture in Japan designating a "Takeshima Day." This Japanese claim was not new and the dispute over the Dokto/Takeshima island was also much about fishing rights, but its passage by overwhelming majority (33 versus one abstention) reflected rising nationalist sentiments among Japan's politicians. Koreans interpreted the island's 1905 incorporation by Japan as inseparable from Japan's encroachment on Korea; Japan's renewed claim meant that it has not completely disavowed the old colonialist mentality. Added to this was the news that the new version of Japan's history textbook, submitted for approval, again contained distortions. Accordingly, a new outburst of anti-Japanese sentiments spurred Korea to put a number of exchange programs with Japan on hold and the government adopted a new doctrine highlighting the history issues with Japan. In a strongly worded speech to the nation, President Roh pledged to continue the fight against Japanese ultranationalists. On March 26, the "Joint Historical Research Committee," established between Korea and Japan in March 2002, ended its three-year operation, unable to reach agreement on a number of issues.

The renewal of the history issue between Japan and Korea, the recent emergence of history problems between Korea and China, and deteriorating sociopolitical psychology between Japan and China clearly illustrate that memories and reconciliation in the Northeast Asian region are rooted not only in the colonial and Pacific War injustices, but also in much deeper, more complex, historical and cultural relations. All East Asian nations share some sense of victimization and tend to blame others, rather than take responsibility. The legacy of victim psychology and conflict-ridden history has not been favorable for Asian regional integration. It is time for these nations to come to terms with the past and move forward with a shared vision for the future of the region. Increased interaction among these nations in trade and cultural exchange in recent years gives some hope for Asian regional cooperation, but until they come to terms with the past, we believe, there will be clear limits to how far they can go.

In the past, some scholars and leaders of East Asia invoked "Asian values" (primarily Confucian heritage) as a common ground for East Asian community. Yet, in our view, this approach is backward-looking and does not offer a viable vision for the future. We also believe that unless East Asian nations move beyond their own exclusive nationalism toward a shared vision, one cannot expect successful cooperation. China, Japan, and Korea often argue over history, but it is nonetheless true that elements in their shared past may also contribute to a regional identity. Coping with Western influence since the nineteenth century is but one area of common ground. There was indeed an era during which intellectual exchanges took place among these countries: for example, the three now share many new terms across their respective languages, as well as their experience with building modern nation-states and economies. It is true that integration in Europe has moved much further than in Northeast Asia. At the same time, it must be remembered that, compared to Europe, the geopolitical and economic environment in East Asia has only recently become conducive to regional integration.

East Asian nations need to promote "thick" reconciliation that will foster a shared understanding of the past and a vision for the region that transcends victimhood and narrow, exclusive notions of national identity. However tempting, politically convenient, and even psychologically satisfying it may be to blame others, such an approach will neither heal past wounds nor provide a foundation for the future. Cultivating a redefined, shared view of the region rests on the shoulders of visionary political leaders and members of civil society. Thick reconciliation must be based on democratic values and respect for human rights, and both state and society will have to be actively involved. It requires educating younger generations to look at the past in a new way, and to reach beyond national borders. There is more hope for Japan–Korea reconciliation because both are democratic but a vastly improved Japan–Korea relationship will almost certainly prompt China to reconsider its own frosty political relations with Japan.

It is a critical time for a new Northeast Asia. Regional relationships are at stake, as are Japan's, Korea's, and China's connections to the United States, which is preoccupied elsewhere. These relationships are evolving as China continues to rise and extend its influence. At the same time, growing tensions between Japan and its Asian neighbors over history issues, especially the China–Japan rivalry, gives some concerns to American policy-makers. In the final analysis, however, international society must understand that the complex layers of Northeast Asian history must be faced and accepted before they can be laid to rest. Overcoming the historical injustice that has divided the countries of Northeast Asia is not only a sensible basis for true reconciliation; it is a prerequisite for building a new regional community and identity.

Notes

1 Yoichi Funabashi, *Reconciliation in the Asia-Pacific* (Washington, DC: USIP Press, 2003).
2 See *Han'guk Ilbo* (October 16, 2001).
3 For more on the Japanese conservatives' view of Asia, see Wakamiya Yoshibumi, *Sengo hoshu no Ajia kan* (Tokyo: Asahi Shimbunsha, 1997).
4 Victor Cha argues that the issue of apology is necessary, but not sufficient, for reconciliation to begin. See Victor Cha, "Hypothesis on history and hate in Asia: Japan and the Korean peninsula," in Yoichi Funabashi, ed., *Reconciliation in the Asia-Pacific* (Washington, DC: USIP Press, 2003), pp. 37–59.
5 The two most successful blockbuster films of 2004, the "Silmido" (Silmi Island) and the "T'aegukki hwinallimyŏ" (Dashing with the T'aegukki Flag), featured covered-up stories of domestic historical injustices, during the Park military government period and the Korean War time, respectively.
6 There has been increasing criticism of teaching middle and high school students with just one official history textbook written by the government's National History Compilation Committee. Likewise, there are increasing comments on the problem of memorization-oriented history classroom teaching, which many now view as detrimental to critical thinking and the development of broad perspectives among students. Many believe that the nationalist way of thinking is at odds with the creative evaluation of the past and South Korea's move to a democratic civil society. Accordingly, there has been a call for new, unofficial history textbooks in Korea. See *Han'guk Ilbo* (April 17, 2001, and August 15 and 21, 2001). Korea's own revision of its history textbooks – which includes recovering of hidden materials, more personal accounts of the domestic historical injustice, and promotion of unofficial counter-narratives – is on the list of the seventeenth National Assembly session between 2003 and 2007.

Index

Abe, Shinzo 159, 160
Akçam, T. 179
Albright, Madeleine 162
An, Pyong-Jik 57
Anderson, B. 133, 149
apology diplomacy 254–5
Appadurai, A. 193–4
Arendt, H. 125
Armenian massacres 174, 175–6; denial by state 179–81, 187–8; and emotional nationalism 183; as genocide/holocaust 176–8, 180–81
Aron, R. 79
ASEAN: evolving economic pattern 241–4; external strategies 244–7; future possibilities 248–9
Asia Tribunal on Women's Human Rights 37, 42–6; and feminism in Japan 46; global feminist scope 45–6; testimony of comfort women 43–5; themes 42–3
Asian Women's Fund (AWF) 182, 221–3; contrast with German Future Fund 222–3; and historical controversy 221–2
Aylwin, Patricio 102

Bae Yong-joon 200
Baker, Howard 162
Bar Association of Japan 39–40
Befu, H. 148
Berktay, H. 175–6, 181, 187
Brandt, Willy 238
Brown, Cornel 97
Buddhist culture 105
Buruma, I. 183
Burress, C. 179, 182
Bush, George W. 162, 164, 167, 169–70

Cameron, J. 83, 88
Ch'ae, Myŏng-Shin 120–21
Chalk, F. 77
Chang, I. 63–4, 176
Chang, Wan-Ick 67
Chile, Third Wave transition 102, 108–9
China: as economic power 238, 241; external economic strategy 244–5; history problem with Korea 257–8
Ch'oi, T.-J. 116
Chong, Chae-Won 65
chŏngsindae see women volunteer laborers
Chun, Doo-Hwan 59, 103
Chuter, D. 17–18
Cohen, S. 178–9, 180
colonial modernity 18–19
comfort women: and *chŏngsindae see* women volunteer laborers; and colonial modernity 18–19; compensation 182; critical anthropological approach 17–20, 31; as gendered structural violence 18, 27–8; global feminist focus 50–51; historical background 20–21; Japanese response to history 37–9, 181–2, 184; and licensed prostitution 19; litigation movements (1990s) 60–61; as military sex slaves 17–18, 21–2, 41–2; NGO trials 37; and patriarchal culture 30; person-centered approach 18–19; and power differentials 29–30; recruitment 27–8; and relations with Japan 22; representations 21–2; resignification 36–7, 50–51; response to litigation 36; 'settling the past' 20–21; and sex tourism 22; and sexual culture

Koyang massacre 84
Kwangju Compensation Law 9

Lee Ch'ang-dong 198
Lee, Sun Gŭn 86
legal activism *see* litigation
licensed prostitution 19
litigation 255; European model for 64,
  65; movements, 1990s 60–61, 71–2;
  movements, 2000s 67; trends, post
  2001 61–3; victimhood redefined
  66–8

MacArthur, Douglas 87
McDonald, G. K. 49
Maddison, A. 238
Maier, C. 1, 181
mass killings 77–8, 83–5, *see also* Jeju
  April Third Incidents; Vietnam War,
  South Korean participation
Matsui, I. 182
Mayor, F. 195
memorial museums *see* war memorial
  museums
mercenary question 120–22
Ministry of Patriots and Veterans
  Affairs (MPVA) 103–4
Miyata, T. 57
Muccio, John J. 85, 86
Murayama, Tomiichi 154, 182, 222

Naimark, N. 180
Nakamura, T. 57
Nam, Sang Whi 86
Namibia 173, 174–5
Nanjing Massacre 174, 176; and
  emotional nationalism 183; as
  genocide/holocaust 176–8; Japanese
  denial 182–3
National Guidance League 80–90;
  executions of 82–3, 90; Japanese
  origins 80; and political prisoners
  80–81
national human rights 67
nationalism 7–8
NGA *see* Korean Council for Women
  Drafted for Military Sexual Slavery
Nichols, D. 82
Nichols, Donald 88
Nihonjintsuma 157
Nishihara, M. 161
North Korea: abductions and
  reconciliation 158, 159–62; as
  guerilla/partisan state 154; as

Japan/US policy axis 167–8,
  169–70; Japanese fears of 156–7;
  normalization with Japan 155–7; as
  nuclear power 165–7; as problem
  state 155–6, 164–5, 170; and
  P'yŏngyang Declaration 157–9;
  second visit to P'yŏngyang 162–4;
  and sense of grievance 154–7
Novick, P. 183, 209
Nuremberg Tribunals, Charter 98

Obuchi, Keizo 10, 196
Oguma, E. 148
Osborne, J. 75

Park, Chung-Hee 59, 124–5
Park, Kyong-Shik 57
Park, Won-Sun 84
Peaceboat 219
Peach, Major 83
politicization of war 77–8
pop culture diplomacy 192–5, 211–13;
  audience reception 209–11;
  contextualization 195–201; critical
  interventions 209–11; ethnicity
  over friendship 203–4; *Friends*
  201–2; *hallyu* 200–201, 209, 211,
  257; intersocietal cultural exchange
  200–201; Korean wave 199–200;
  love bridging cultural distance
  202–3; media effects 209–11; mixed
  motivations/messages 208; mutual
  understanding and shared values
  204–7; societal agency 198–200;
  state-led initiatives 196–8; television
  drama and film, critique 201–8; *2009
  Lost Memories* 201–2; World Cup
  (2002) 197–8
Presidential Commission on Suspicious
  Deaths 9
P'yŏngyang Declaration 157–9

reconciliation 2–4; and economic
  integration, theoretical basis
  236–8; external injustice 2–3; forces
  affecting 4–8; future agenda 257–9;
  geopolitical calculations 3; and
  globalization 5–6, 7–8; internal
  injustice 3–4; Korea-Japan 10, 21,
  68; lessons 254–7; and nationalism
  7–8; regional integration 6–7; thick-
  thin 2, 259, *see also* democratization
regional integration *see under* forced
  laborers, Second world War

Yuki, Fujime 49
Yun, Chŏng-ok 24–5
Yushukan 142–9; and ethnic
  nationalism 147–9, 150–51;
  extension to Shrine 143, 144–5;
  historical context 143–4; and

national identity 144; and pan-
  Asianism 147; popularity 149–51;
  and spirit of the samurai 146, *see
  also* Japan

Zalaquett, J. 100

WITHDRAWN